The Political Economy
of Regionalism

NEW DIRECTIONS IN WORLD POLITICS
JOHN G. RUGGIE,
GENERAL EDITOR

The Political Economy
of Regionalism

Edited by Edward D. Mansfield
and Helen V. Milner

COLUMBIA UNIVERSITY PRESS

NEW YORK

Columbia University Press
Publishers Since 1893
New York   Chichester, West Sussex

Copyright © 1997 Columbia University Press
All rights reserved

Library of Congress Cataloging-in-Publication Data
The political economy of regionalism / edited by Edward D. Mansfield
and Helen V. Milner.
      p.   cm. — (New directions in world politics)
   Includes bibliographical references and index.
   ISBN 0-231-10662-9 (cl). — ISBN 0-231-10663-7 (pa)
   1. Trade blocs. 2. Regionalism—Economic aspects.
3. Regionalism. I. Mansfield, Edward D., 1962–   . II. Milner,
Helen V., 1958–   . III. Series.
   HF1418.7.P65   1997
   337—dc21   96-54832
                                                        CIP

⊗

Casebound editions of Columbia University Press books are printed
on permanent and durable acid-free paper.
Printed in the United States of America
c 10 9 8 7 6 5 4 3 2 1
p 10 9 8 7 6 5 4 3 2 1

NEW DIRECTIONS IN WORLD POLITICS
JOHN G. RUGGIE,
GENERAL EDITOR

Jock A. Finlayson and Mark W. Zacher, *Managing International Markets: Developing Countries and the Commodity Trade Regime* 1988

Peter M. Haas, *Saving the Mediterranean: The Politics of International Environmental Cooperation* 1990

Stephen C. Neff, *Friends But No Allies: Economic Liberalism and the Law of Nations* 1990

Emanuel Adler and Beverly Crawford, *Progress in Postwar International Relations* 1991

J. Ann Tickner, *Gender in International Relations: Feminist Perspectives on Achieving Global Security* 1992

John Gerard Ruggie, editor, *Multilateralism Matters: The Theory and Praxis of an Institutional Form* 1993

Barry Buzan, Charles Jones, and Richard Little, *The Logic of Anarchy: Neorealism to Structural Realism* 1993

Ronnie D. Lipschutz and Ken Conca, editors, *The State and Social Power in Global Environmental Politics* 1993

David A. Baldwin, editor, *Neorealism and Neoliberalism: The Contemporary Debate* 1993

Karen Litfin, Ozone Discourses: Science and Politics in Global Environmental Cooperation 1994

Ronnie D. Lipschutz, editor, *On Security* 1995

Contents

Acknowledgments

The chapters in this book were initially presented at a conference at Columbia University in March 1995. Generous funding for this conference was provided by Columbia University's Center for International Business Education, Center for the Social Sciences, and School of International and Public Affairs; and by Princeton University's Center for International Studies.

At this conference, Joanne Gowa, Miles Kahler, and John McLaren served as discussants for these chapters. We are indebted to them and the anonymous reviewers for Columbia University Press for their helpful comments. We also acknowledge the administrative support provided by Columbia University's Institute of War and Peace Studies and the secretarial assistance provided by Jana Harrison.

Contributors

Rachel Bronson is a Ph.D. candidate in the Department of Political Science at Columbia University.

Benjamin J. Cohen is Louis G. Lancaster Professor of International Political Economy at the University of California, Santa Barbara.

Joseph M. Grieco is Professor of Political Science at Duke University.

Stephan Haggard is a Professor in the Graduate School of International Relations and Pacific Studies at the University of California, San Diego.

Charles A. Kupchan is Associate Professor of International Relations at Georgetown University and Senior Fellow for Europe at the Council on Foreign Relations.

Edward D. Mansfield is Associate Professor of Political Science at Ohio State University.

Helen V. Milner is Professor of Political Science at Columbia University.

Pier Carlo Padoan is Professor of Economics at the University of Rome.

Beth V. Yarbrough is Professor of Economics at Amherst College.

Robert M. Yarbrough is Adjunct Associate Professor of Economics at Amherst College.

The Political Economy
of Regionalism

ONE

The Political Economy
of Regionalism: An Overview

Edward D. Mansfield
and Helen V. Milner

During the past decade, a resurgence of interest in regionalism has occurred on the part of policy makers, business executives, and scholars. The advent of the North American Free Trade Agreement (NAFTA), the ongoing process of economic integration in Europe, the formation of Mercosur, and the possibility of an Asia-Pacific economic bloc have led to lively and widespread debates concerning the causes and effects of regionalism. Many of these debates center on the economic implications of regionalism, a topic on which a large and rich literature exists. Others revolve around the effects of political factors on regional blocs and the influence of these blocs on the tenor of international and domestic politics. Yet very little recent research has been conducted on the political economy of regionalism. The purpose of this volume is to address this important topic. The following chapters address a wide variety of issues pertaining to the political economy of regionalism, but two are dealt with at length.

First, how can we explain the contemporary proliferation of regional arrangements?

The late 1950s and early 1960s were characterized by the formation of various regional arrangements, which sparked much theoretical work on their causes and effects. But many of these arrangements were stillborn; and most failed to accomplish their stated purposes. These developments contributed to the pattern of global, multilateral economic organization that prevailed throughout much of the post-World War II era. Of late, however, the pace of multilateralism has slowed, and a resurgence of regional organizations has occurred. It is important to analyze the sources of this resurgence.

Second, why are regional organizations characterized by such diversity of institutional forms?

Why, for instance, does the European Union (EU) have such a different institutional structure than NAFTA, which in turn differs so much from the organization for Asia-Pacific Economic Cooperation (APEC)? Why are groups of states choosing particular institutional forms to organize their regional interactions? Moreover, do the particular institutional forms chosen influence the durability of these arrangements and their effects on relations among members?

The chapters in this book therefore take up issues concerning why regional arrangements are formed, the conditions under which these arrangements "deepen," and why various regional arrangements take on different institutional forms. Moreover, whereas existing studies of regionalism typically focus on a single issue-area, the contributors to this volume explore trade, financial, and security relations. This broad focus brings into clearer relief the differences, similarities, and interrelations among these issue-areas. But common to all of these chapters is the view that the interaction between political and economic factors is crucial to explaining regionalism.

Not only does this book contribute to a fuller understanding of regionalism, it also bears on a number of recent theoretical debates in the fields of international relations and political economy. For example, various chapters address current controversies about the merits of neorealist and institutional explanations of international relations. Others use new trade theories to understand the sources of regionalism and its expansion. Still others rely on propositions from the "new institutionalism" to explore the current wave of regional arrangements. Finally, some attempt is made to apply constructivist approaches to the study of regionalism. In addition, the chapters in this volume also bear on longstanding debates in the field of international relations concerning the relative importance of domestic and international factors in explaining international outcomes.

In the remainder of this chapter, we discuss the themes that frame this book and the debates to which they contribute. At the outset, however, we seek to clarify what is meant by a region and, hence, by regionalism.

Defining Regions and Regionalism

Despite the interest that regionalism has attracted, the definition of a region remains in dispute. This issue is hardly new. In his seminal study of customs unions, written almost half a century ago, Jacob Viner (1950:123) observed that "Economists have claimed to find use in the concept of an 'economic region,' but it cannot be said that they have succeeded in finding a definition of it which would be of much aid . . . in deciding whether two or more territories were in the same economic region."

Rather than attempt to resolve this dispute, the authors in this volume use different definitions of a region—and hence regionalism.[1] One central difference among these definitions hinges on whether a region connotes geographic proximity. A number of authors consider a region to be a geographically specified area. Based on this definition, regionalism refers to the disproportionate concentration of economic flows or the coordination of foreign economic policies among a group of countries in close geographic proximity to one another. It also refers to the concentration of political-military relations among geographically proximate states.

But existing studies differ over the sources of the geographic concentration of economic and political-military relations. For example, some studies argue that regionalism emanates from the "natural forces of proximity, income and policy convergence, and greater intra-firm trade; in this view, regionalism may owe little to policy-induced discrimination" (Fishlow and Haggard 1992:12). Other studies consider regionalism to be the product of policy choices by national decision makers. Based on this definition, regionalism is an outgrowth of government policies (like the formation of the European Community [EC] and the EU) intended to increase the flow of economic or political activity among a group of states in close geographic proximity.

Following the existing literature on this topic, most of the chapters in this volume define a region in terms of geographic proximity. But they differ as to whether "natural forces" or government policies are the central source of regionalism.

In contrast, other authors define regionalism in nongeographic terms. For example, Benjamin Cohen posits that a group of countries collectively relying on one member's currency constitutes a currency region, although these countries need not be located in close proximity. Further, countries that share common cultures, languages, religions, or ethnic backgrounds—

but not geographic proximity—could be considered regional partners. This notion of regionalism flows from the idea that various nongovernmental factors can induce increased levels of economic and political activity among countries, whether they are located nearby or not. In a similar vein, Charles Kupchan adopts a social constructivist perspective and argues that a region is comprised of states with a shared sense of communal identity.[2] The sources of this communal identity vary among different regions. But in his view, it is a precondition for identifying a group of states as sharing a region, regardless of their geographic locations.

Further, many extant analyses of regionalism focus on the wide variety of preferential economic arrangements negotiated by states, which may or may not (e.g., the U.S.–Israeli Free Trade Area) involve geographically proximate partners. Edward Mansfield and Rachel Bronson adopt such a focus in their analysis of the effects of preferential trading arrangements (PTAs) on trade flows. These nongeographic definitions of regionalism contrast with the more typical definitions, which emphasize geographical proximity. However, both of these definitions have guided research on regionalism and both are used by the authors of the following chapters.

SOURCES OF REGIONALISM

One central purpose of this book is to examine the sources of regionalism. Existing studies often point to potential improvements in the welfare of members to explain why regional groupings form. For example, the seminal work of Viner (1950), James Meade (1955), and Richard Lipsey (1960) suggests that PTAs can enhance members' welfare if these arrangements create more trade among members than they divert from efficient producers outside PTAs. Further, Murray Kemp and Henry Wan (1976) have demonstrated that any group of states can form a PTA that neither degrades the welfare of any member nor adversely affects states outside the union. They also argued that incentives exist for such a PTA to expand until it includes all states (i.e., until free trade exists on a global basis). Still others have argued that regional economic arrangements can improve the welfare of members because these unions are likely to be vested with considerably more market power than their constituent members, thereby enhancing the ability of members to use an optimal tariff to improve their terms of trade vis-à-vis third parties (Krugman 1991, 1993a).

Analyses of regionalism's welfare implications have been extremely influential and are addressed in some of the following chapters, including Cohen's study of currency regions and Pier Carlo Padoan's study of the EC and EU. However, this book's primary focus is on the *political* factors that influence regional arrangements.

A wide variety of research was conducted on this issue during the 1960s and early 1970s, on the heels of the formation of various regional arrangements (e.g., Haas 1958; Nye 1971; Russett 1967). Some of the arguments made in the following chapters are similar to those made in this earlier literature. Since this earlier wave of research on regionalism, however, new theoretical developments have occurred in both international economics and international politics. This book makes extensive use of these developments to explain the recent resurgence of regionalism. For example, important contributions made to realist theory since the late 1970s (Gowa 1994; Grieco 1988; Waltz 1979) are reflected in Joseph Grieco's and Mansfield and Bronson's chapters. Propositions from the "new institutionalism" inform the chapters of Padoan and Beth Yarbrough and Robert Yarbrough. In addition, strategic trade theory, developed in the 1980s, provides the basis for some of Helen Milner's and Padoan's respective arguments.

INTERNATIONAL EXPLANATIONS OF REGIONALISM

Certain chapters in this book locate the source of regionalism at the level of the international system. These chapters, however, reflect longstanding cleavages among scholars of international relations regarding which systemic factors account for patterns of global outcomes. One primary cleavage is between those scholars who emphasize power relations and those who highlight international institutions (Baldwin 1993). By comparing these approaches, this book provides additional empirical evidence with which to evaluate the competing claims made by advocates of each. In the remainder of this section, we summarize the controversy between institutional and power-oriented explanations and discuss how the following chapters contribute to debates over their merits.

Institutional Explanations of Regionalism

Much of the early work conducted by political scientists on regionalism focused on economic and political integration. Among the most influential approaches to the study of integration were functionalism and neofunctionalism. Exponents of these approaches posit that governments tend to forge international institutions in order to meet various functional needs. They often argue that the expansion of economic activity creates incentives for states to further liberalize and standardize economic exchange because doing so enhances the economic welfare of participants (e.g., Deutsch et al. 1957; Haas 1958, 1964; Mitrany 1943). Nonstate actors can play a central role in this process. For example, Ernst Haas (1958) focuses in part on interest groups and political parties to explain the EC's origins. By fostering economic growth and managing international economic problems, regional institutions generate the support of groups within states and demands by these groups for further integration.[3] This "spillover" process leads to ongoing integration, which promotes the development of regional institutions. In the opinion of functionalists and neo-functionalists, this process also promotes political cooperation among participating countries.

Recently, these older functionalist perspectives on regionalism have been combined with developments from "new institutionalist" studies (Moe 1984; Shepsle 1982; Williamson 1985). Contemporary work in this area often highlights the ability of international institutions to help ameliorate international market failures (e.g., Axelrod and Keohane 1986; Keohane 1984; Lipson 1984; Oye 1986; Stein 1984). International institutions create incentives for states to cooperate by reducing collective action problems; by lengthening the "shadow of the future," thereby enhancing the prospects for states to engage in strategies of reciprocity; and by increasing the ability to link various issues, thereby increasing the costs for states of failing to comply with established rules and norms. Functional and institutional perspectives are analyzed in the chapters by Yarbrough and Yarbrough, Kupchan, Grieco, Padoan, and Stephan Haggard.

Central to the performance of international institutions is the selection of mechanisms for adjudicating disputes among members. Yarbrough and Yarbrough address this issue. They point out that the selection of effective mechanisms for resolving commercial disputes is fundamental to generating compliance with these mechanisms by parties to PTAs. Yarbrough and Yarbrough analyze four prototypical dispute-settlement mechanisms, which vary depending on the ability of a third-party adjudicator to enforce judgments against a state violating institutional rules. Consistent with the functional and institutional explanations discussed above, they argue that the incentives for agreement on dispute-settlement mechanisms are considerable among states that engage in large amounts of trade, as well as states that conduct trade in politically sensitive sectors and states for which trade creates the need to adjust frequently to unforeseen contingencies.

In many cases, however, states have divergent preferences regarding the dispute-settlement mechanism that should be used. Much of Yarbrough and Yarbrough's chapter centers on identifying the factors that will influence the mechanism that is selected. They argue that this choice will depend on the degree to which preferences converge among members and the costs to states of failing to successfully coordinate the selection of a mechanism. Yarbrough and Yarbrough conclude that the likelihood of selecting mechanisms that involve greater third-party authority increases as the preferences of states become more harmonious and the costs of failing to coordinate on the selection of a mechanism rise.

Kupchan also examines the functional role played by regional institutions in his analysis of European security affairs. Many analysts have argued that, in the wake of the cold war, European security can be best guaranteed by expanding the North Atlantic Treaty Organization (NATO). Kupchan maintains that this argument is flawed. Instead, he advocates an innovative solution to this problem, which is predicated on the creation of three new regional subgroupings that will provide collective security guarantees to members. Security cooperation would occur on a pan-European basis; however, three distinct defense organizations would be established, covering East Europe, Central Europe, and West Europe. These subregional organizations would be woven together by creating two "pivot" states, Germany and Ukraine, that each would be a member of two of these organizations. Kupchan argues that, unlike NATO expansion, which defies the logic of power balancing, the creation of regional security bodies is likely to consolidate a stable balance of power on the European continent since it relies on institutional commitments consistent with the more proximate strategic interests of Europe's major powers.

This aspect of Kupchan's argument is at odds with functional approaches. He sees little functional need for the states that would be included in his proposed Central European organization to develop a new regional institution. Instead, Kupchan offers a constructivist view of regionalism, in which regions are the ideational products of states sharing a sense of communal identity. For Kupchan, ideational changes precede changes in behavior, including the formation of cooperative regional security groupings.

Grieco analyzes whether functional approaches can help to explain the degree to which a formal regional institution has been established in

Western Europe, East Asia, and the Americas. He maintains that functional arguments imply that institutions within a given region are more likely to form when economic interactions within the region increase. Grieco finds limited support for this position. He concludes that the usefulness of functional explanations of regionalism varies considerably depending on the region being studied. The increased institutionalization of the EU during the past twenty years and the formation of NAFTA can be explained with reference to functional arguments, whereas developments in East Asia and Latin America cannot.

Does the Number of Actors Influence Regionalism?

As noted above, scholars of international institutions often argue that institutions help resolve collective action problems. It is widely recognized that such problems tend to become more severe as the number of actors attempting to coordinate a given activity increases (Olson 1965). Thus, one rationale for the establishment of regional institutions is that they help overcome collective action problems among large numbers of states located in a given region. This, in turn, suggests that the ability of regional institutions to meet their objectives might depend on the number of members.

This issue is taken up by both Haggard and Padoan. However, they address different aspects of the relationship between the number of parties to regional institutions and the ability of these institutions to meet their objectives. They also arrive at different conclusions.

Haggard analyzes why new regional agreements have recently arisen in the Asia–Pacific region and the Western Hemisphere and the source of variations in the strength of these institutions. He argues that the number of parties to a regional agreement does not explain why these agreements have been concluded. From a theoretical standpoint, Haggard maintains that a group's size need not be related to its ability to provide collective goods and that the magnitude of the transaction costs faced by members need not depend on their number (while acknowledging that enforcement and distributional problems will be heightened as the number of members increases). Rather, the number of parties to a regional agreement is likely to influence its success because as this number increases, so too does the likelihood that the preferences of members diverge. Haggard views the extent to which the preferences of members converge or diverge as central to determining a regional agreement's effectiveness. He argues that the convergence of preferences among the United States, Canada, and Mexico with respect to intraregional liberalization helps to explain NAFTA's origins. The absence of such a convergence among the East Asian states helps to explain the institutional weakness of arrangements such as the Association of Southeast Asian Nations (ASEAN) and APEC.

Conversely, Padoan views the number of members as fundamental to the prospects for a regional agreement's success. But, unlike Haggard, the central purpose of Padoan's chapter is to explain the optimal number of participants in regional economic arrangements. And unlike Haggard, Padoan's primary empirical referent is the EU. Padoan points out that regional institutions must determine which states will be included and excluded. He develops a model in which the formation of such an institution depends in part on the number of states willing to participate. Further, the costs of maintaining and managing the institution once it has been formed are directly related to the size of its membership. Padoan maintains that integration tends to occur in discontinuous waves and that expansion tends to occur when the macroeconomic conditions of members improve, economic integration among them deepens, the level of international conflict increases (thereby enhancing the political benefits of membership), or the institution's strength increases. He also concludes that the optimal number of members in a regional club may depend on whether it is designed to coordinate commercial or monetary relations. The fact that the EU seems committed to both trade and monetary union is likely to enhance the difficulty of arriving at an optimal number of members.

Power Relations and Regionalism

Standing in contrast to functional and institutional explanations of regionalism are those that emphasize power relations. Chief among them are neorealist theories of international politics, which highlight the anarchic nature of the international system and the pressure that this places on states to attend to their security (Waltz 1979). These theories view nation-states as the primary actors in the international system. As such, they attach little importance to domestic groups and the transnational actors that functionalists highlight. Further, neorealists argue that the demands placed on states to enhance their security and the importance of political-military power in this regard render the distribution of power among states the central influence on international outcomes.

Recent research by realists has emphasized three factors that are likely to bear on the political economy of regionalism. First, realists have stressed that concerns over the asymmetric distribution of gains from exchange among states are likely to inhibit international cooperation (e.g., Grieco 1988). States benefiting less from cooperative arrangements run the risk that their political-military security will be undermined relative to those benefiting more, which may impede the formation of regional agreements designed to promote economic exchange. Second, a number of studies have argued that alliance politics shape patterns of international trade (Gowa 1994; Gowa and Mansfield 1993), and that states are more likely to liberalize commerce with political-military allies than with actual or potential adversaries. This argument suggests that the ability of regional trade arrangements to promote commerce may depend on the political-military relations among their members.

Third, much recent research by realists has highlighted the influence of hegemony (Gilpin 1975, 1987; Krasner 1976). A hegemonic system is one dominated by a single state that possesses both the capacity and the willingness to order international relations. A number of studies have concluded that the erosion of hegemony tends to give rise to (among other things) the evolution of protectionist economic blocs (Gilpin 1975, 1987; Krasner 1976), although the available evidence bearing on this issue is ambiguous (Mansfield 1993; McKeown 1991; Milner 1991; Oye 1992). All three of these new developments in realist theory have potential implications for the study of regionalism that are addressed by Grieco, Cohen, and Mansfield and Bronson.

Grieco addresses both the issues of hegemony and relative gains. His primary focus is on the relationship between the distribution of power in a region and the degree to which formal economic institutions are developed within it. From his analysis of Western Europe, East Asia, and North America, Grieco concludes that a regional hegemon is neither necessary nor sufficient for the development of regional economic institutions.

Hegemony, however, is only one aspect of power relations. Grieco also develops what he refers to as the "relative disparity shift" hypothesis, which pertains to the effects of changes in the capabilities of states within a region and the expectations of states regarding future changes of this sort. Grieco posits that when the relative disparity in capabilities within a region is shifting over time, disadvantaged states will oppose the development of formal regional institutions. This suggests that the relative stability of capabilities, which depends in part on the relative gains from regional cooperation and the expectation that such stability will persist, contributes to the establishment and deepening of formal regional institutions. In contrast, instability of capabilities limits the likelihood that a regional institution will form. Grieco's results provide some support for this hypothesis.

Cohen also analyzes the effects of power relations on regional economic relations. In his study of currency regions, Cohen argues that international monetary relations both shape and are shaped by the international distribution of power. On the one hand, as the political space over which a given country's currency performs the function of money (i.e., its authoritative domain) widens, so too does this country's influence over those other states that rely on it. Moreover, during periods characterized by a monetary hegemon, international financial relations tend to be relatively stable and weaker states come to depend on the dominant power to provide financial stability. On the other hand, a hegemonic power is limited in the monetary policies it can pursue by the need to ensure that foreigners retain confidence in its currency, since sudden or substantial devaluations or conversions of its currency could have devastating effects on its economy.

Like Cohen, Mansfield and Bronson analyze the effects of power relations on economic flows. But unlike Cohen, they focus on explaining trade flows. Their analysis centers on comparing the effects of political-military alliances and PTAs on bilateral trade flows involving the major powers. Based on a statistical analysis of the period from 1960 to 1990, they find that alliances have had a considerable influence on commerce. Mansfield and Bronson also find that PTAs promote trade among members; however, their effects are weaker and quantitatively smaller than those of alliances.

Mansfield and Bronson argue that the effects of alliances on trade reflect the fact that trade flows generate efficiency gains that can be used to enhance the political-military capacity of states. As such, trade relations can influence power relations among states. Since major powers are likely to possess sufficient market power to influence their terms of trade, they have little incentive to liberalize trade with actual or potential adversaries. Imposing an optimal tariff redistributes the gains from trade—and the attendant gains in potential political-military power—from a major power's adversary to the major power, thereby enhancing its security.

However, major powers do have an incentive to liberalize trade with their allies. In contrast to trade relations with adversaries, states derive political benefits from the commercial gains of allies. The efficiency gains generated by free trade bolster the potential power of the trade partners, thereby strengthening the alliance as a whole. As a result, alliances help to internalize the security externalities associated with trade and thus promote trade among members.

Domestic Explanations of Regionalism

Besides international factors, some analyses of regionalism emphasize the effects of domestic political and economic factors. There exists a large and rich literature on the political economy of foreign economic policy, much of which highlights interest-group politics and societal pressures. The abundant literature on endogenous trade policy exemplifies this type of approach (e.g., Baldwin 1985; Caves 1976; Pincus 1977). Scholars working in this tradition emphasize the distributive consequences of economic policies for domestic groups. Those groups suffering losses due to a particular policy or changes in a policy will oppose it, while those benefiting from the policy will support it. Various domestic groups thus will demand different policies, and a government's economic policy choices often will reflect the underlying preferences of the strongest and best-organized interests within society (e.g., Frieden 1988; Milner 1988; Rogowski 1989).

Another strand of this literature emphasizes the national decision makers who formulate policy and the domestic political institutions that regulate the interaction between societal and state actors. Some of these studies argue that decision makers formulate economic policy for the purpose of advancing the national interest (e.g., Krasner 1978), whereas others (e.g., Grossman and Helpman 1994; Magee, Brock, and Young 1989) maintain that public officials do so in order to advance their own interests (for example, retaining political power or accruing economic resources for their personal use). Further, the influence of domestic political institutions on foreign economic policy has been extensively studied, and it is now widely recognized that the structure of these institutions contributes to (among other things) the ability of societal interests to place pressure on public officials who formulate policy (e.g., Katzenstein 1978; Gourevitch 1986; Mansfield and Busch 1995; Nelson 1988).

Despite the richness of this literature, it has produced few attempts to explain patterns of regionalism.[4] A number of chapters in this volume seek to redress this gap in the literature.

Milner argues that the form regional arrangements take reflects political leaders' rational responses to their domestic situation. Because of pressures exerted by firms with an interest in such arrangements, political leaders will sometimes view regionalism as appealing. The literature on strategic trade policy provides a basis for this argument (e.g., Krugman 1986). Within sectors of an economy that are imperfectly competitive and characterized by increasing returns to scale, firms have incentives to expand the size of the markets they serve. Under certain conditions, this, in turn, leads them to press for liberalization on a regional basis, especially if the size of their home market is modest.

Public officials, in the context of Milner's model, attempt to promote their re-election prospects by maximizing the consumer surplus generated by trade. These officials also are compelled to accommodate special interests, including firms, in order to retain political office, since firms provide campaign contributions and other support that influences a candidate's likelihood of election. Thus, leaders will selectively agree to liberalization of certain sectors, while excluding others. The shape of the regional agreement will be a rational response to political leaders' domestic political situation.

Milner's analysis suggests that regional agreements should yield greater intra-regional liberalization for the goods of firms in industries characterized by increasing returns to scale than the goods of firms in other industries. Based on statistical tests of industries included in NAFTA, she finds support for this position. Milner also finds, however, that the extent to which imports have penetrated an economy influences the relationship between scale economies and liberalization.

Haggard's analysis of regionalism also addresses the effects of domestic politics. He argues that the bargaining agenda leading to the formation of regional groupings is largely shaped by the major power(s) in the region. Haggard further maintains that the U.S. has been the dominant power in both the Asia-Pacific region and the Americas. The United States has used access to its market to generate leverage in both regions. In addition, domestic politics, especially domestic distributional conflicts stemming from the effects of trade policy, has had a central influence on U.S. policy preferences with respect to regional economic arrangements. Like Milner, Haggard argues that the discriminatory effects of regionalism can in part account for its popularity among certain domestic groups. He points out that the formation of a regional grouping can become the locus of new, regional protectionist forces as well as a means for focusing the interests of liberalizing ones.

In addition to the interests of major powers, Haggard argues that the interests of weaker parties to regional agreements also affect the nature of bargaining among regional partners. He links patterns of regional institutionalization to domestic economic conditions in members. Haggard posits that one reason why economic arrangements in the Americas are characterized by greater institutionalization than those in the Asia-Pacific region is that, in contrast to most East Asian countries, many countries in Latin America have undergone severe domestic economic crises in recent years. This has led them to prefer "deeper" economic integration, which, in turn, requires greater institutionalization. This increasing convergence of preferences among countries in the Americas has made regional agreements easier to construct than in Asia.

Like Haggard, Cohen also highlights the effects of domestic distributional issues on regional arrangements. He places particular stress on conflicts of interest between state and societal actors and within the private sector. Cohen argues that governments have an incentive to retain as much control as possible over domestic monetary policy. The formation of a currency region reduces their ability to finance public spending via inflation. Societal actors are likely to switch their investments from those denominated in the local currency to those denominated in foreign currencies rather than allow their wealth to be degraded. However, Cohen points out that certain segments of society will face greater difficulty making these changes than others. He analyzes how currency regions differentially influence the fortunes of various societal groups, as well as the overall impact of these regions on state-society relations.

VARIATIONS IN REGIONAL FORMS: CAUSES AND EFFECTS

One striking feature of contemporary regional arrangements is the institutional variation among them. The EU, for example, is highly institutionalized, whereas NAFTA is far less so, and less so still is APEC. Despite the potential importance of these differences, little attention has been devoted to their implications for patterns of international economic and security relations. One purpose of this volume is to examine the sources of these institutional variations and whether they contribute to the ability of regional agreements to meet their objectives.

Sources of Institutional Variations

Grieco and Haggard each attempt to explain variations in the extent to which a formal institutional structure exists across regional arrangements. As noted earlier, Grieco attributes differences in the degree to which regional economic arrangements are formally expressed to what he refers to as the "relative disparity shift." He maintains that highly institutionalized regional arrangements are most likely to exist when: (1) the distribution of capabilities among members is relatively stable, and (2) members expect no sudden change in this distribution. Grieco argues that, under these circumstances, weaker members are more likely to engage in arrangements that, by liberalizing economic exchange, seemingly will increase their vulnerability to more powerful members. If, on the other hand, states view capabilities as likely to shift unexpectedly, weaker members may fear that liberalizing international economic relations will further undermine their political power with respect to stronger members.

Haggard argues that the degree of institutionalization within a region depends on the preferences and bargaining power of members. The formation of NAFTA, which is moderately institutionalized, was possible because of the unusual extent to which Canada and Mexico depend on the United States for their economic (and political) well-being. In addition, changes within all members—especially Mexico—led to a convergence of their preferences for economic liberalization. In contrast, East Asian countries have a much more diverse set of economic preferences than countries in North America and, particularly in the case of Japan, they oppose U.S. efforts toward deeper formal integration.

Milner examines why various regional trade agreements vary in the degree to which they liberalize trade across different sectors. Her answer to this question centers on the market structure of various sectors and the demands placed by interest groups on domestic leaders. Firms in sectors characterized by increasing returns to scale are expected to demand and receive greater intraregional liberalization than other firms. At least among democracies, variations in industry structure may go a long way toward accounting for sectoral variations in the content of regional trade agreements.

Yarbrough and Yarbrough analyze the factors influencing the institutional mechanism that is chosen to settle disputes among parties to PTAs. They argue that the extent to which members' preferences converge and the costs borne by states if they fail to coordinate contribute to this choice.

The Depth of Regional Integration

Besides the degree of institutionalization, other aspects of variation across regional institutions also are addressed in this volume. Central to much of the literature on regionalism has been the degree to which integration deepens over time among parties to a regional arrangement. As discussed above,

Padoan argues that the number of parties to a regional agreement is likely to influence the depth of commercial and monetary integration among members, whereas Haggard disagrees with this assessment. Instead, Haggard argues that the deeper and more extensive institutionalization of economic relations in the Americas than in East Asia is due primarily to the nature of distributive conflicts among members of these regions. In Haggard's view, deeper cooperation has been possible in the Western Hemisphere because those states that were affected most adversely by economic integration within this region were located elsewhere. Any tendency for these regional arrangements to replace goods produced more efficiently outside the region with those produced less efficiently within it therefore constituted a benefit for members.

In a different vein, Mansfield and Bronson suggest that the depth of regional integration may depend on the nature of political-military relations among states in a region. By promoting the flow of trade among members, deepening commercial integration generates security externalities. Because these externalities are internalized by alliances, commercial integration is likely to be deeper among allies than among other states.

Kupchan focuses on political-military relations among states, as well. But he maintains that the depth of regional integration depends on the extent to which states identify themselves as being part of the region. As these regional identifications deepen, so does the degree to which regional security cooperation becomes possible. Further, Kupchan views the depth of regional security integration as depending on the type of institution that is used to promote members' security. Collective defense institutions generate the greatest depth, followed by collective security institutions, and cooperative security institutions. Kupchan argues in favor of the regionalization of European security and the use of collective security arrangements for this purpose.

Yarbrough and Yarbrough's analysis also bears on the depth of regional integration. On the one hand, they argue that as the depth of commercial integration among states increases, so too do the benefits to them of coordinating on the establishment of dispute-settlement mechanisms. On the other hand, the establishment of more costly dispute-settlement mechanisms (i.e., those in which third parties are vested with more authority) will deepen commercial integration among parties to the arrangement.

Finally, on this issue, Cohen suggests that the depth of integration in a currency region will depend on the authoritative domain of the most widely used currency. This domain is, in turn, determined by market forces, state interests and power, and the relative influence of state and societal actors in formulating a country's monetary policy.

Among economists and political scientists, interest in regionalism has been longstanding. A surge of interest in this topic accompanied the wave of attempts to form regional institutions in the 1950s and 1960s. But many efforts to design effective regional arrangements failed, and scholarly research on regionalism subsequently diminished. Recent events have led to a resurgence of interest in this topic in both academic and policy circles. The end of the cold war has generated increased calls on the part of some states for regional security arrangements. Further, a variety of regional economic arrangements have been formed during the past decade and it seems likely that others soon will follow.

Much current work on this issue focuses on the economic determinants and implications of regionalism. A distinctive feature of this book is the authors' focus on the interaction between political and economic factors in explaining regionalism.

The chapters that follow not only contribute to a better understanding of regionalism, they also contribute to a number of important debates in the field of international relations. One central debate hinges on the relative merits of international institutional and (neo)realist explanations of international relations. The former emphasizes how the expansion of economic activity generates pressures for enhanced regional or international coordination by enabling such organizations to fulfill functions that states can no longer perform. The chapters by Cohen, Haggard, Milner, Padoan, and Yarbrough and Yarbrough provide support for institutional and (neo)functional explanations. Another strand of scholarship pertaining to international institutions highlights the tendency for states' identities to be socially constructed and for the international system's structure to be affected by policy choices made by states. Although Kupchan's chapter departs in certain ways from these perspectives, his analysis lends some support to them.

In contrast, (neo)realists emphasize the anarchic nature of the international system and power relations among states. In their view, countries' concerns about threats to their security help to explain patterns of regionalism. The chapters by Grieco and Mansfield and Bronson provide some support for (neo)realist explanations.

Another prominent debate in the field of international relations centers on the relative importance of international and domestic factors in explaining international outcomes. This book addresses both international and domestic sources of regionalism. Whereas many of the following chapters emphasize international factors, Cohen, Haggard, Milner, and Padoan point to the importance of factors internal to states in shaping patterns of regionalism and find that it is not only international pressures that drive states to form regional economic groupings.

Clearly, we cannot resolve either of these longstanding debates in this volume. The following chapters do, however, provide new lenses through which to evaluate them.

This book also examines the sources of variations among regional institutions. In sum, the following chapters suggest two central forces that shape these variations: (1) the nature of states' preferences and the degree of divergence among them, and (2) the distribution of capabilities among members of regional institutions. In addition to analyzing differences in institutional forms across regions, the following chapters examine differences in regionalism across issue-areas. Unlike many studies, this book explores a number of issue-areas, including trade, finance, and security relations. This broad focus brings into clearer relief the variations, similarities, and interrelations among these issue-areas. For example, Haggard, Milner, and Padoan emphasize the close relations between trade and financial flows; and Mansfield and Bronson highlight the connections between security and trade relations.

Finally, this volume integrates new theoretical developments from international politics and political economy into the analysis of regionalism. Following recent trends in (neo)realism, Grieco, Mansfield and Bronson, and Cohen explore how hegemony, concerns about relative gains, and alliances affect regionalism. Drawing on recent developments in international trade theory, Milner and Padoan advance arguments about how different industrial structures affect the prospects for regionalism. Using the tools of the new institutionalism, Haggard and Yarbrough and Yarbrough emphasize the importance of international institutions, showing that variations in form influence an institution's functions. Further, Kupchan maintains that insights from constructivist approaches can be used to analyze regional security arrangements. This volume, then, represents an advance over previous studies of regionalism because it explicitly brings to bear recent theoretical work on this topic.

The importance of understanding regionalism should not be understated. It has been argued that the hostilities borne of the regional, discriminatory economic arrangements during the interwar period produced

tensions contributing to the onset of World War II. Though less cata-
clysmic, many observers fear that the current wave of regionalism will
undermine the liberal economic system that has guided international relations for the past half century. This could have disastrous consequences,
leading once again to political conflict among economic blocs. Others,
however, are more sanguine. They view regionalism as a potentially liberalizing force, arguing that the promotion of economic openness within
each region is a stepping stone to greater openness throughout the world.

The contributors to this volume are not of a single mind concerning
either the causes or effects of regionalism. In combination, however, they
offer a variety of important and new insights into the political economy of
this phenomenon.

*Acknowledgment: We are grateful to Benjamin Cohen, Stephan Haggard, Charles
Kupchan, Walter Mattli, Beth Yarbrough, and two anonymous reviewers for comments
on this chapter.*

NOTES

1. For other definitions of a region, see Thompson (1973) and Lake (1997).

2. For a discussion of constructivist approaches, see Wendt (1992).

3. It should be noted that the nonstate actors on which functionalists and neofunctionalists
focus are not limited to domestic groups. For example, Sandholtz and Zysman (1989) have
emphasized the role of the EC Commission and transnational corporations in the development
of the Single Market in Europe.

4. For some exceptions, see Busch and Milner (1994) and Grossman and Helpman (1995).

TWO

The Political Economy of Regionalism in Asia and the Americas

Stephan Haggard

Recent writing on regionalism[1] has been preoccupied with its economic and political consequences. At one pole are those who argue that regionalism threatens to fragment the multilateral trading system into rival blocs (Krugman 1991; Garten 1992). At the other pole is the more benign view that regional arrangements are compatible with the multilateral order and may constitute a path toward deeper integration (Aho and Ostry 1990; Fishlow and Haggard 1992; Lawrence 1996; Oye 1992: ch. 7; Schott 1991). This controversy has obscured the question of why new regional arrangements have arisen at this historical juncture, most notably in the Asia-Pacific and Western Hemisphere, and why they have taken the form they have. Why have these agreements not degenerated into closed blocs? What accounts for their substantive agendas and levels of institutionalization? In particular, why did the North American Free Trade Agreement (NAFTA) take a very comprehensive and highly institutionalized form, the Free Trade Area of the Americas the shape of a less comprehensive but nonetheless formal set of commitments to negotiate, while the Asia Pacific Economic Cooperation remains weakly institutionalized?

I begin with an evaluation of the argument that regionalism can be explained as a response to large number problems, transactions costs, and diseconomies of scale at the multilateral level. Frustration with the multilateral process did contribute to regional initiatives in Asia and the Americas. I argue, however, that these theoretical arguments are flawed in ways that are symptomatic of larger weaknesses in the neoliberal institutionalist research program. A theory of regional cooperation—and of cooperation more generally—cannot be built around models of collective action and transactions costs alone; it must address the more fundamental question of the policy preferences and capabilities of the relevant actors.

To construct such a political economy approach to regional cooperation, I focus on the distributive conflicts that are at the core of any regional arrangement. These take two forms, the first of which centers on discrimination: the conflict between the insiders and outsiders to a given agreement. In theory, regional agreements can become the locus for protectionist log-rolls. However, the extent of discrimination in the construction of regional arrangements can also be checked in three important ways: the embeddedness of the regional arrangement in an overarching multilateral structure (the GATT/WTO); the threat of retaliatory responses; and a nondiscriminatory policy stance on the part of individual country members. These factors, each of which has deeper domestic roots in the process of internationalization (Milner, this volume), help explain why regionalism in the 1980s and 1990s has not taken the mercantilist form that was characteristic of regionalism in the 1930s.

The second set of distributive issues that arise in the formation of regional groupings are those among the potential members. In contrast to analyses that model trade bargaining as a prisoners' dilemma (Keohane 1984), I explore several more traditional models that portray trade bargaining as a distributive game between large and small players. These models call our attention to issue-linkage, influence attempts and the efforts by smaller countries to establish credibility. They also capture the fact that the United States has increasingly used access to its market to leverage reforms abroad.

Although regional initiatives do reflect the American trade policy agenda, it is not sufficient to examine the United States alone; attention must also be given to the interests and capabilities of potential followers (Lake 1988). To some extent, the new regionalism reflects a process of convergence based on unilateral reform efforts; nonetheless, asymmetries in power and preferences remain crucial. In North America, the United States enjoys unusual bargaining advantages that come from the high dependency of Canada and Mexico on the United States and particularly severe crisis conditions in Mexico. South American countries also experienced crises that stimulated economic reform and generated an interest in reaching agreements with the United States. Trade dependence on the United States was substantially less than Mexico's, however, and thus the gains from hemispheric cooperation less compelling. In East Asia, U.S. influence was yet weaker as a result of the presence of two major powers, the region's economic success, and the rapid growth of intraregional trade. I show how these structural differences across the three regions have affected the nature of the major cooperative agreements: the NAFTA, the FTAA and the APEC.[2]

THE QUESTION OF NUMBER

Trade theory tells us that on pure welfare grounds, the larger the number of participants in a trade agreement, the better. The economics literature on customs unions thus emphasizes that they are a second-best solution driven by "noneconomic" factors, such as an (irrational) preference for regional over extraregional production and rent-seeking (Gunter 1989; Krauss 1972). Under these premises, regional agreements should be unstable. Given that there are welfare gains from a larger union, there is always an incentive to expand a given arrangement until an equilibrium of global free trade has been reached.

Political economists working in a new institutionalist vein have offered two reasons why this happy outcome has not been reached (Aggarwal 1985; Keohane 1984; Oye 1986; Yarbrough and Yarbrough 1992).[3] First, international cooperation over trade is modeled as an n-person prisoners' dilemma game, in which there are strong incentives to defect; second, reaching agreements is hindered by transactions costs. The literature on cooperation has focused on two solutions to these problems which permitted multilateral free trade to flourish in the postwar period: hegemony and the existence of international institutions. Regionalism is portrayed as a third solution to these collective action and transactions costs problems, but one that has emerged only as hegemony has declined and multilateralism faltered.

The reason why declining hegemony would give rise to regionalism depends on the variant of the theory employed. For those who saw the benefits of U.S. dominance primarily in the solution of collective action problems, regionalism is interpreted as a response to the declining provision of public goods (Yarbrough and Yarbrough 1992:89). The effort to launch the European Monetary System in the wake of the collapse of Bretton Woods provides a particularly clear example. A second explanation of regionalism centers on the shortcomings of multilateral institutions (Schott 1989:19–22; Aho and Ostry 1990; Wonnacott and Lutz 1989:62). International regimes foster cooperation by providing institutional solutions to the problem of large numbers (Oye 1986). As the effective number of countries in the GATT grew, however, diseconomies of scale became manifest. The organization fell victim to the criticism that it was too slow, that negotiations were too complex, and that rules were inadequate and poorly enforced.

Bilateralism and regionalism constituted both an alternative to multilateralism and a strategic signal to negotiating partners within the GATT, particularly the Europeans, that the default option of no agreement was acceptable. Four important regional initiatives—the U.S.–Canada FTA, the NAFTA, APEC and the East Asian Economic Grouping—emerged either during the protracted GATT "pre-negotiations" (from the 1982 Ministerial Declaration to the Punta del Este Declaration in 1986) or during the course of the Uruguay Round negotiations themselves.

On closer inspection, most of the arguments for the benefits of small size are highly questionable and typically rest on the underlying structure of preferences, rather than number, as the root cause of cooperation. I will consider three arguments about number: those focused on privileged or k groups; those about the transactions costs associated with *reaching* agreements; and those about the transactions costs associated with *monitoring and enforcing* agreements.

Russell Hardin (1982) has shown that the arguments about size in Mancur Olson's (1965) *Logic of Collective Action* are fundamentally confused. Olson offers a formal definition of privileged and latent groups which rests on whether the net return to the group from the payments for public good are positive: if they are, the group is privileged, if not, it is latent. He also offers a looser typology of groups as "small," "intermediate" and "large" which is based purely on number. On the basis of this second approach he makes the observation that as numbers go up, the share of the benefit from the collective good goes down and individuals have a greater incentive to shirk. As Hardin (1982:42) concludes, "it is easy to see that the division into privileged and latent groups does not imply any logical connection between group size and these two categories. One can easily define conditions under which the smallest of all possible groups (a two-member group) can be latent." Conversely, "large" groups can be privileged if they are net gainers from the provision of the public good. Cooperation ultimately depends not on number, but on the distribution of preferences with respect to the provision of the public good.

It could still be possible that higher numbers result in increasing difficulties in reaching agreements, including over the allocation of the costs for the provision of the public good; this is where the costs of both organization and transacting become relevant. But transaction costs associated with reaching agreements will depend on the nature of the decision-making procedures, not on number. Consensus decision making makes it harder to reach decisions, because any party exercises a veto. But reducing the number to two under consensus decision making will not lead to agreement if the two parties have divergent preferences. The most difficult problem in finalizing the Uruguay Round did not center on a large numbers problem but on disagreements between the United States and Europe on agriculture and services.

The move to majoritarian decision making may alleviate these problems, but any majoritarian voting procedure—even among three parties—is subject to cycling unless the preferences of all actors are single-peaked. Recent literature suggests how delegation provides solutions to these problems of collective action and social choice, and offers an unexplored theoretical avenue for understanding agenda control and centralization in international organizations. The principle supplier rule in GATT negotiations constitutes an example of such delegation; because of the effective power of the United States, Japan, and the EC to set the agenda within the GATT, the "effective" number of members in that institution is actually *lower* than in APEC, where decision is by consensus. The formation of informal negotiating groups or caucuses, particularly the G-9 and G-10, played a similar function in negotiating the Punta del Este Declaration. Again, it is not number per se but procedural rules, and behind those procedural rules the preferences of the main actors over those rules, that determines transactions costs.

What about the costs of monitoring and enforcement? In her ambivalent defense of hegemonic stability theory, Joanne Gowa (1989) notes that enforcement is a public good subject to collective action problems. Hegemons are well-suited to manage these problems. Oye (1986:19) argues similarly that "as the number of players increases, the feasibility of sanctioning defectors diminishes." It is far from clear why this is the case. First, the model assumes that there are no economies of scale in monitoring, even though it is precisely information which regimes are supposed to supply. But more importantly, this view misunderstands how trade agreements are monitored. It is not primarily international organizations nor even governments that monitor the trade policies of foreign governments, but interested firms. With such a decentralized system of monitoring, it is not clear that there are disadvantages in larger numbers; indeed, the opposite may be the case.

Nor is it clear why enforcement will be undersupplied as numbers increase. Whether the system is hegemonic or multipolar, effective sanctioning is carried out by large powers; this is true even under a system of third party enforcement. The calculation of large states about whether to sanction will hinge on a variety of political, economic and strategic calculations, but can be reduced to the expected net return from doing so. It may be possible that an increase in numbers will produce more "small" free riders, against which the cost of sanctioning outweighs the benefit; it is highly unlikely, however, that "large" free riders will be allowed to persist undetected or unpunished.

Recent history confirms that this is the case. As the advanced developing countries have become more significant players in the international trading system, they have come under strong pressure to abandon their claim to "special and differential" treatment and to assume their full obligations within the multilateral system (Haggard 1995:ch. 2). Indeed, there are more complaints about the surplus of enforcement, particularly through such mechanisms as 301, than about its deficit!

The point is not to argue that number is insignificant. Rather, it is to underline *why* number is likely to be important: when the numbers of parties to an agreement increases, there is an increased probability that members' preferences will diverge, the core will shrink, and the probability of striking a bargain will fall. To understand the prospects for cooperation, therefore, it is important to understand the trade policy preferences of the potential members of a regional agreement and the distributive bargains that are required for cooperation to occur.

THE POLITICAL ECONOMY OF DISCRIMINATION

In contemplating the construction of a regional arrangement, potential members must assess two distributional questions. The first is the effect of their actions on third parties; the second is the distribution of gains among the members. The analysis of the welfare effects of customs unions on non-members has become more complex since Viner's (1950) original treatment.[4] There are also important differences in the political economy of customs unions—Viner's preoccupation—free-trade areas (Krueger 1995), and the deeper regulatory coordination which is at the heart of recent regional integration (Lawrence 1996). Nonetheless Viner's basic insight on trade creation and diversion is still a useful starting point for understanding the political economy of discrimination. Trade creation occurs as the removal of the tariff on intra-union trade shifts members' demand from domestic production to lower-cost output from a union partner; diversion takes place when the tariff preference for union members shifts demand from a nonunion source to a higher-cost union supplier. The establishment of a customs union will improve world welfare if trade creation dominates trade diversion, even though distributional effects between insiders and outsiders may remain.

Viner's formulation was fundamentally indeterminant with respect to the question of whether such agreements will be discriminatory, or even welfare enhancing. In an important paper, Kemp and Wan (1976) demonstrate that it is always possible to form a regional integration agreement in such a way that the members are better off without making any nonmembers worse off.[5] There are, however, two political economy reasons why this may not occur: the ability to exploit the market power that results from the formation of a regional arrangement; and the political bargains required to reach the regional agreement in the first place.

Krugman (1991) provides an example of the former approach in his model of "bad bilateralism" (see also Froot and Yoffie 1993). Since a customs union is larger than its constituent parts and therefore enjoys greater market power, it may be able to impose an optimal external tariff. Krugman's approach does not appear empirically plausible; there is no evidence that any current regional arrangement has sought to exploit its market power to set optimal tariffs vis-a-vis the rest of the world. However, the formation of a regional arrangement, or the threat of its formation, could be used to extract other concessions from nonmembers. This might occur either by forming a coalition within a multilateral institution, such as the GATT, or simply by improving the reserve position of its members in bilateral bargaining. Such motives have been a factor in recent regional initiatives. The founding of APEC in 1989 following an Australian initiative had as one of its objectives to create a consultative body, or caucus, in the GATT negotiations (Higgot, Cooper and Bonnor 1990:839; Funabashi 1995:107–8). Prime Minister Mahatir's language in proposing the formation of the East Asian Economic Grouping in 1991 made similar references to the GATT, but explicitly mentioned the need to counter emerging blocs in North America and Europe (Low 1991:375; Funabashi 1995:686–69, 205–11). Perhaps the most revealing comment comes from testimony given by Clayton Yeutter, the

U.S. Trade Representative, at the time of the negotiation of the U.S.– Canada FTA:

> There is a bit of leverage here, in that it indicates to the rest of the world that we, the United States, can make progress in opening up borders and confronting trade barriers either bilaterally or multilaterally. Our preference is the multilateral route . . . but if the multilateral route should prove fruitless for any one of a variety of reasons, this certainly indicates that we can achieve success bilaterally and that we are prepared to pursue these basic objectives on a bilateral basis should that become essential.
>
> (Yeutter 1988:98)

However it is interesting to note that in all three cases the stated purpose of the threat did not point in the direction of Krugman's "bad bilateralism." Rather, disaffected parties sought to speed the *multilateral* liberalization process; I return to the relationship multilateralism and regionalism below.

The second reason that the Kemp-Wan results might not pertain has to do with protectionist interests in the member countries which see the regional agreement as an opportunity to counter competitive pressures from outside while providing more assured markets within it. In a typically sage essay, Albert Hirschman points out how politics inverts economic logic:

> The larger the trade creating effects, that is, the greater the need to reallocate resources in the wake of tariff abolition, the greater will be the resistance to the union among various highly concentrated and vocal producer interests of the member countries. . . . Thus trade creation is a political liability. Trade diversion implies, on the contrary, that concentrated producer groups of the member countries will be able to capture business away from their present competitors in nonmember countries.
>
> (Hirschman 1981:271)

Such political processes did operate in the negotiation of the NAFTA. Given that the NAFTA is an FTA not a customs union, the source of regional rent-seeking was not the common external tariff but the formulation of rules of origin (Simpson 1994; Krueger 1995). Two industries provide examples. In the automobile industry, the main objective of the American Big Three was to open the Mexican market while guaranteeing that Mexico did not become an export platform for Japanese or Korean producers (Hufbauer and Schott 1993:37–43; Molot 1993). Canadian producers had concerns that overly restrictive rules of origin would limit assembly operations by curtailing imports from East Asia. American actions gave grounds for such fears. In a well-publicized case, U.S. officials claimed that Honda Civics exported from Canada to the United States failed to meet local content requirements. For its part, the Mexican government hoped to engineer the liberalization to provide some protection to the local parts industry.

NAFTA calls for tariffs on passenger vehicles to be eliminated over a period of ten years. Even more important are the phasing out of a variety of other Mexican restrictions—trade-balancing requirements, domestic content requirements, quotas on certain products—that had been at the heart of the country's industrial policy toward the industry. A regional content requirement of 62.5 percent—higher than the 50 percent of the U.S.–Canadian FTA—will be phased in over eight years, with a stricter net-cost method of measuring regional content than operated in the U.S.–Canada FTA. Nonmember firms supplying the U.S. market from Canada or Mexico would face only a 2.5 percent tariff in the United States should they fail to comply with the rules of origin (tariffs in Canada and Mexico are substantially higher) but this does constitute a disadvantage in a highly competitive industry. Moreover, the design of the phase-in tends to favor firms with investments in place, forces new entrants, such as the Koreans, to establish a regional presence, and will regionalize the transplant process.

The line-up in the textile industry was subtly different. Protectionist sentiment was stronger in the American industry, which was ultimately divided over the agreement even in the restrictive form it finally took. Canadian producers depended on the American market, but also on offshore sourcing of inputs. The Mexican industry, by contrast, stood to gain substantially, but at the expense of Caribbean and East and Southeast Asian producers. Since Mexico accounts for only 3 percent of U.S. imports of textiles and clothing, it was not fear of the inroads Mexico could make into the U.S. market that explains U.S. insistence on input sourcing restrictions; rather, it was the scope for third country investment in Mexico (Bannister and Low 1992). Though tariffs and quotas will be eliminated within North America over six to ten years, rules of origin in the textile sector are the most discriminatory of any of the NAFTA provisions. To qualify for preferences, textile and apparel must pass the triple transformation or "yarn-forward" test: in essence, finished products must be made from fabric spun from North American fibers, and must be both cut and sewn in the region. The strict rules of origin reduce, but do not fully offset, the incentives to investment diversion to Mexico. They do, however, create the potential for substantial trade diversion, particularly from the Caribbean Basin countries and East and Southeast Asian suppliers (Lande and Crigler 1993; Kim and Weston 1993).

These cases suggest that the negotiations over the formation of a regional grouping can become the locus of new, regional protectionist forces as well as a means for focusing the interests of liberalizing ones, as Oye (1992:ch. 7) has argued. As the cases also suggest, the politics is not simply one of gaining trade preferences and suppressing external trade; the opportunity to reap exclusive benefits from a regionally integrated production strategy is also key.

These possibilities for regional protection motivate the critique of regionalism. It is equally important, however, to underscore that there are three powerful constraints on regional rent-seeking. The first is the fact that regional institutions are nested within a broader multilateral structure that limits governments' freedom of maneuver. GATT discipline over regional trading agreements (Art. XXIV) is notoriously lax. But the most important constraint of the multilateral system is in binding those tariffs that do exist (thus increasing the costs of pursuing the "bad bilateralism" strategy outlined by Krugman [1991]) and providing the forum for negotiating reductions in preferential margins over time. In both regions, membership in, and commitment to, the WTO has spread.

The second constraint on an inward-looking bloc has to do with the response of those facing discrimination. Excluded parties may be induced to seek membership, but they can also retaliate. The difference in the bargaining power of the NAFTA countries and their East Asian counterparts is marked in this regard, and helps explain the failure of efforts to develop an exclusive East Asian club. The NAFTA was negotiated without consultation with any Asian partners and was presented to them as a fait accompli; Japan and other Asian countries finally came around to accepting the NAFTA but only because they recognized that its defeat would have had even more adverse implications for U.S. trade policy.

By contrast, the United States acted to deter even the most tentative move toward the formation of an exclusive East Asian regional arrangement. Prime Minister Mahatir of Malaysia made his proposal for an East Asian Economic Grouping (EAEG) in late 1990 and it gained force in the aftermath of the failure of the Brussels Ministerial meeting of the Uruguay Round talks in December 1990 (Low 1991; Funabashi 1995: 205–7; Higgot and Stubbs 1995). He called for the creation of an "economic bloc" that would include ASEAN, Burma, Hong Kong, China, Taiwan, South Korea, and Japan; Australia, New Zealand, Canada, and the United States were explicitly excluded. American Ambassador to Japan Michael Armacost signaled quickly that the grouping could "encourage economic rivalry" between Japan and the United States (*Far Eastern Economic Review*, April 18, 1991, p. 70). Japan was correspondingly cautious (Funabashi 1995:68–69, 205–11), as were Indonesia and Korea. Singapore was willing to consider the proposal, but emphasized that the EAEG be consistent with the GATT, that it "parallel" the interests of the APEC and have support from excluded members, and that it not be viewed as a substitute for ASEAN. By October the idea was dropped in favor of a looser consultative body, the East Asian Economic Caucus. Yet the United States pressed on with respect to the EAEC as well, in part because of increased sympathy to the idea in portions of the Japanese bureaucracy; Secretary of State James Baker pressed both Japan and Korea at the APEC meetings in November not even to participate in this consultative body (*Far Eastern Economic Review*, November 28, 1991, p. 26). Though the EAEC continues to live, its ambitions have been substantially checked. Such checks are also likely to operate on any discriminatory tendencies that appear among the major subregional groupings in Asia and the Americas, such as the ASEAN Free Trade Area, the Andean Pact, and the Mercosur.

The final check on the discriminatory nature of regional agreements has to do with the domestic political economy of trade policy. The standard assumption is that regional arrangements will be subject to the same protectionist biases visible in domestic trade policy, such as those arising out of the concentrated nature of the beneficiaries of protection and the diffused nature of the gainers from liberalization. However, this assumes an economy of a very particular type. As the new work on free trade lobbying by Destler, Odell, and Elliott (1987) and Milner (1988; this volume) has shown, the idea that free traders face unique collective problems is misguided. Imagine, in contrast to the typical image, that regional arrangements are being negotiated by governments which already pursue relatively free trade policies on a multilateral basis, and in which free trade interests are strong. In such a setting, the dynamic with outsiders changes significantly: the source of discrimination is not so much the wedge between internal free trade and tariffs toward third parties—since that wedge would be small—but the advantages that accrue to the community from other forms of policy coordination. It is to the nature of these internal bargains that I now turn.

NEGOTIATING REGIONS

Strategic behavior vis-à-vis international negotiations played some role in the initiation of new regional agreements and distributive conflicts between insiders and outsiders shaped their content to some degree. Nonetheless, the content of these agreements is primarily defined by bargaining among prospective members. How should these negotiations be modeled? The characterization of international trade politics as a prisoners' dilemma (PD) has been a popular strategy (Keohane 1984; Oye 1986; Yarbrough and Yarbrough 1992). But PD fails to capture the distributive element of trade bargaining, as well as the asymmetric character of North–South negotiations. If we assume a setting in which one of the parties to the agreement is a big, advanced and relatively open one (the United States) and the other is a smaller, less developed and relatively closed one, it is possible that the small country's preferences might yield a PD structure. If dominated by a protectionist coalition, the small country might favor mutual openness to the risk of a real trade war but would prefer access to the larger country's market while staying closed itself as first best. However, it is not clear that the large open country will necessarily see an advantage in defecting; rather, it may have a dominant strategy to cooperate (i.e., CC>CD>DC>DD) if the dominant political coalition favors free trade. This preference ordering would allow the small country to free ride.

This game is an asymmetric one which Lisa Martin (1993:104) calls "suasion" (figure 2.1). Suasion games have equilibrium outcomes that leave one actor unhappy. One option is to threaten to act irrationally by defecting if the small country does; the second solution is issue linkage. By linking issues, the larger party can either decrease the small party's benefit from defecting through threats or it can increase the returns from cooperation through side payments. These threats and sidepayments transform the payoff structure into a distributive game. Of course, it may be possible that no threat or inducement is adequate to budge the small player; influence attempts do not necessarily succeed. However much trade bargaining takes place precisely over the size (and credibility) of the

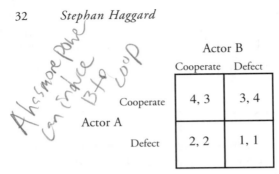

FIGURE 2.1. A Suasion Game.

inducement or punishment required to get cooperation (McMillan 1990).

A final possibility to be noted is that there is simply a convergence of preferences. Developing country followers may choose to liberalize on their own for a variety of reasons, ranging from international shocks to the triumph of liberal forces in the polity. As I will show, such convergence was an important factor undergirding cooperative agreements in both East Asia and Latin America. This purely domestic explanation for cooperative behavior nonetheless raises an important question: why would unilateral free traders still seek regional cooperation through formal agreements?

One set of reasons has to do with problems of credibility and commitment (Rodrik 1989; Calvo 1989). In undertaking reforms, governments in countries with a volatile policy history face an important political dilemma. For the program to hold, it is crucial that investment respond aggressively to new incentives. However most reforms are reversible and the government thus faces the problem of establishing credibility. Among the mechanisms available to do this are the delegation of authority to independent agencies, such as central banks, and the signing of international agreements, particularly those that provide means for oversight and enforcement. Regional agreements might be favored as one component of a domestic commitment technology.

In analyzing these strategic interactions—whether the suasion game, a distributive bargain, or the signaling game—it is important to underline that the relevant unit is not the *country*, but the *government*. We want to know what the costs and benefits of different forms of agreement are to the politicians who are engaged in efforts to build and maintain coalitions of support and stave off competitors. As I will show, this permits us to link such distributive bargaining at the international level to distributive politics at the domestic level.

The empirical question can now be restated. Why has the United States succeeded in signing a wide-ranging regional integration agreement with Mexico and Canada? Why did this agreement initially exert such a powerful influence on the discussion of regionwide initiatives in the Western Hemisphere and why has that influence declined? Why does the parallel movement toward regional cooperation in Asia appear both shallower and less formal in its institutional design?

I begin by showing in the next section that the trade policy agenda in both the Western Hemisphere and the Asia Pacific has, in fact, been shaped in important ways by the changing trade policy preferences of the United States. U.S. policy has gradually moved beyond commercial policy narrowly conceived to a range of investment-related and regulatory issues.

But American influence has been uneven. The United States enjoys a particularly strong position vis-à-vis Canada and Mexico. Because of their unusual dependence on the U.S. market, changing U.S. trade policy actions provided a powerful incentive for these countries to stabilize market access through a regional agreement. Severe crisis conditions in Mexico produced profound unilateral policy changes, but also placed a premium on reaching an agreement that would signal the leadership's commitment to the reform process.

The other major developing countries of Latin America—Brazil, Argentina, Peru, Colombia, Venezuela, and Chile—are also emerging from profound economic crisis, in the wake of which all launched wide-ranging economic reforms. These reforms stimulated an interest in reaching agreements with the United States and demonstrating the credibility of policy changes. South America is not well integrated with itself; thus the "default option" of intra-regional trade or cooperation that excludes the United States is less plausible. The very existence of the NAFTA also raised concerns of exclusion and trade diversion and thus created pressures to "bandwagon" on the agreement (Baldwin 1994). However South America's trade dependence on the United States is substantially less than Mexico's, and as crisis conditions eased the willingness to make adjustments to American demands declined.

In East Asia, there has also been interest in securing access to the U.S. market. Some smaller, open countries, such as Singapore, have shown a willingness to conclude bilateral free trade agreements or even to join the NAFTA. Yet a number of factors reduce American influence in Asia. In seeking to develop broader regional institutions, the United States must contend with two major powers—Japan and China—neither of which shares the U.S. interest in formal FTAs nor much of the deep integration agenda. The developing countries in the region have undertaken incremental reforms for over a decade, and have demonstrated their capacity to penetrate world markets; they need neither the trade stimulus nor the credibility enhancement that formal regional agreements might bring. Moreover, while the region is still dependent on the United States, it has also developed a dynamic set of trade and investment relations with itself that have succeeded in the absence of any formal organization. This regional political and economic structure has not precluded U.S. efforts to pursue its interests bilaterally; but it restricts the American ability to do so on a regional basis.

U.S. Interests in the New Regionalism

The objective of U.S. protection in the 1970s was straightforward: to shield American industries from low price competitors through the imposition of quotas, voluntary export restraints (VERs), orderly marketing agreements (OMAs), and sectoral accords (Yoffie 1983). In the mid-1980s, the United States began to employ contingent protection: measures designed to deter "unfair" practices. U.S. attention initially focused on subsidies and dumping, but the agenda expanded dramatically in the early years of the second Reagan administration as the executive sought to pre-empt congressional protection by mobilizing anti-protectionist groups (Destler, Odell, and Elliott 1987; Milner 1988): firms whose foreign operations and trade ties give them a particular interest in open trade policies both at home and abroad.[6]

The day following the Plaza accord, President Reagan announced a new trade policy package that emphasized bilateral actions to eliminate unfair trade practices abroad. In addition to aggressive pursuit of dumping and subsidy cases, the administration initiated three unfair trade investigations.[7] This proactive stance increased the influence of business on trade policy. Multinationals operating in particular countries had long complained about restrictions on their operations; the Reagan initiative provided the opportunity to weave these complaints together under the rubric of "trade-related investment measures." An emerging network of interested service industries, rooted particularly in financial services and telecommunications, constituted an important component of the new market-opening bloc (Aggarwal 1992). The chemical and pharmaceutical had long complained about inadequate intellectual property (IP) protection in the developing world, but in the 1980s, the entertainment industry and firms in the information and biotechnology fields also pressed for tougher protection. IP became a high priority of U.S. trade negotiators.

The culmination of this new approach came with the passage of the Trade and Competitiveness Act of 1988, and particularly its amendments to section 301 of the Trade Act of 1974 (Bhagwati and Patrick 1990).[8] The expectation that the developing countries would become primary targets of these new trade policy instruments was confirmed on June 16, 1989, when the USTR identified its first Super 301 cases. Of six barriers to be prosecuted under Super 301, three concerned Japan, but the other three were aimed at Brazil and India, not coincidentally, the two countries which had been most active in championing a third worldist position in the Uruguay Round negotiations.[9]

After 1989, the United States announced no new Super 301 priority countries, though it renamed India in 1990. This did not mean that the bilateral strategy had been abandoned; rather, the high profile approach designed to deter Congress gave way to bilateral negotiations and efforts to secure developing country concessions in the Uruguay Round. Table 2.1 collates information from the National Trade Estimate reports from 1989 through 1994 on developing country barriers in five areas: standards, government procurement, intellectual property, services, and investment rules. The number of countries cited expands steadily in the early 1990s; indeed, the only major developing economy to avoid citation on at least one of these five issues was Hong Kong. Not surprisingly, the middle-income developing countries of East Asia and Latin American figure prominently.

These trade policy initiatives implied that the United States would move on two tracks. While pressing for negotiations through the GATT, the United States would also proceed regionally and bilaterally on issues where there were either no multilateral rules, such as services, or existing conventions were deemed inadequate; intellectual property fell into this second category.

TABLE 2.1

*USTR Designation of Developing Country Trade Barriers:
Number of Countries Cited by Barrier, 1989-1994*

	1989	1990	1991	1992	1993	1994
Standards	6	6	6	6	6	9
Government procurement	6	9	9	10	10	13
Intellectual property	17	17	17	22	22	25
Service barriers	13	12	12	16	16	16
Total	57	58	59	70	79	80

SOURCE: Calculated from USTR, *National Trade Estimate: Report on Foreign Trade Barriers*, 1989–1994 Reports
NOTE: The total is of developing country citations. A number of developing countries are cited in more than one category, and four—Korea, Taiwan, Indonesia, and the Gulf Corporation council—were cited for trade barriers in each of the fine categories in 1994.

The key question is why some countries acquiesced to this new U.S. agenda by entering regional agreements.

The NAFTA: Canada and Mexico

One factor behind the strong Canadian and Mexican interest in seeking a regional agreement is their high level of dependence on the United States. However, this dependence has been a constant for both countries over the entire postwar period; some other conditions must have changed for pressure to arise for a regional agreement. One thing that had changed was the expansion of protectionist actions and the abuse of the administrative trade policy machinery in the United States. When Prime Minister Mulroney went to the House of Commons on September 25, 1985, to formally announce his intention to negotiate the agreement, a major justification was the need to reduce the risk to Canadian trade by establishing a dispute settlement procedure (Winham 1988:45). The United States confirmed Canadian concerns about the centrality of dispute resolution during the course of the negotiations by taking a number of administrative trade actions against Canada that were of questionable legality.[10] The creation of a quasi-judicial bilateral dispute settlement mechanism was thus a major objective of the Canadians; the cost, however, was the acceptance of an

American negotiating agenda that covered a wide array of investment-related issues.

Similar motives operated in Mexico's case. An analysis by Erzan and Yeats (1992:136) shows that of all the Latin American countries, Mexico had the largest amount of total trade adversely affected by American tariffs (those over 5 percent) and nontariff barriers. The negotiation of the NAFTA had already been preceded by a series of accords designed to minimize the uncertainties surrounding access to the American market. In mid-1985 the two countries signed a bilateral understanding on subsidies and countervailing duties that guaranteed Mexico the material injury test. In 1987 a bilateral framework agreement generated accords in two sectors that had faced U.S. quotas—steel and textiles.

However, it is important to underline that the ability to reach these agreements rested on fundamental coalitional shifts in the two countries that had already moved economic policy in a new direction. In Canada, the quest for a bilateral agreement was part of a larger reassessment of domestic policy by the Macdonald Royal Commission that questioned high tariffs and restrictions on foreign direct investment. The conservative Mulroney government embraced the Macdonald Commission's call for a bilateral FTA with the United States because it was in line with its own political and ideological objectives (Winham 1988:44).

In Mexico, the move toward freer trade unfolded in the wake of the debt crisis, and had gone a substantial distance prior to the NAFTA negotiations (Kaufman, Bazdresch, and Herredia 1994; Pastor and Wise 1994). The de la Madrid administration initially held the view that stabilization should precede structural adjustment and trade reform was therefore limited primarily to reversing the controls imposed during the crisis. The initial stabilization efforts did not hold, however, and by 1985 the views of technocrats within the administration about the relationship between stabilization and structural reform began to shift. Subsequent stabilization efforts were accompanied by the initiation of trade reform and by the time the Salinas administration took office in 1989, the trade reform had largely been completed (Lustig 1992:114–20). The reforms were not limited to trade. Changes in the investment regime began very soon after the debt crisis, but were pushed further in 1989. Intellectual property reforms began in 1987. Between 1989 and 1990, the government launched a series of deregulation initiatives: in finance, road transport, petrochemicals, telecommunications, sugar, mining and fishing.

Though foreign investment increased after 1987, it did not respond as hoped. Salinas was reported to have been particularly discouraged by a trip to Europe that revealed a preoccupation with developments in Central Europe and a lack of interest in, or knowledge about, the depth of the Mexican reforms (Pastor 1992). The turn to the NAFTA, and Mexico's willingness to accept the wide-ranging agenda of the Canada-U.S. agreement, thus constituted not only a change of policy but an *institutional* change that increased the cost of policy reversal and thus signaled Mexico's intent to investors.

Toward a Free Trade Area of the Americas

Two factors have pulled the Latin American countries toward deeper regional integration (Haggard 1996). One is the same crisis-driven reform process that operated in Mexico, resulting in a regionwide convergence around freer trade and investment. Chile was the first to initiate successful and sustained trade reforms in the region, beginning in the second half of the 1970s under Pinochet. These reforms were sustained following the transition to democratic rule in 1990, and Chile was the first Latin American country to signal its interest in joining NAFTA. Bolivia was also an "early adjuster" (World Bank 1993a:6); it initiated a wide-ranging trade liberalization program in 1985–86.

In the late 1980s and early 1990s, the pace of trade liberalization accelerated in Latin America, though not before macroeconomic mismanagement had contributed to a new round of balance of payments problems, accelerating inflation, and a reversal of earlier liberalization efforts in a number of countries.[11] Argentina began reducing tariffs in 1988, but it was not until the failed Alfonsin government left office in July 1989 and stabilization was initiated by his successor, Saul Menem, that trade reform came onto the agenda in a serious way. A similar pattern is visible in Peru: entering office during extreme crisis, the Fujimori government dramatically reduced tariffs and virtually eliminated QR's. In Venezuela, the 1983 debt crisis initially led to an even more complex and restrictive set of controls than had existed in the past.[12] Trade liberalization began in earnest with a change of government that brought an unlikely reformer to office, Carlos Andres Perez.

Brazil has had one of the most protectionist trade regimes in the region as well as an aggressive industrial policy. It is also by far the largest economy in the region and has as a result been less open than other smaller economies, despite its aggressive promotion of exports in the 1970s. Brazil has moved more cautiously in liberalizing trade than the other major Latin American countries and had substantial conflict with the United States over its trade policy. In 1988, Brazil was one of three countries targeted by the United States for Super 301 action on the basis of quantitative restrictions and a highly restrictive licensing regime. Following the eruption of hyperinflation in 1989 and the subsequent election of Fernando Collor de Melo in December of that year, Brazilian policy changed dramatically. By mid-1990, the new government had undertaken a radical trade reform that included a virtual elimination of quantitative restrictions, with the controversial exception of the informatics industry, and a four-year duty reduction plan.

The regionwide reform movement was not limited to trade policy. It extended to a liberalization of the rules governing foreign investment and an opening of the capital account, as well as a variety of domestic reform measures that had important implications for foreign investors, including changes in intellectual property rights and privatization (USITC 1992a; World Bank 1993a).

The unilateral shift to freer trade did not necessarily imply a commitment to regional organization. That process was heavily conditioned by the policy initiatives of the United States. The Enterprise for the Americas Initiative and the NAFTA established a baseline of expectations about the shape that hemispheric cooperation would take. The Enterprise for the Americas Initiative (EAI) announced on June 27, 1990, stated that the United States was willing to enter into free trade agreements with Latin American and the Caribbean countries, including through negotiations with subregional agreements (Weintraub 1991). Given that such a step was likely to be too dramatic for some countries to consider, Bush also offered the negotiation of bilateral "framework" agreements that would permit more incremental negotiations covering particular issues of relevance. Though the EAI and the NAFTA were not in any way linked at their inception, the completion of the NAFTA against the backdrop of the regionwide move toward liberalization established a strong expectation that NAFTA norms and standards would provide the foundation for hemispheric integration.

Nonetheless, there were multiple routes to the objective of hemispheric integration; prior to the Miami summit in December 1994, three contending visions circulated. One option was for the United States to negotiate bilateral FTAs, building on the framework agreements negotiated in the wake of the EAI. For the Latin American countries, this approach to regional integration had a number of disadvantages. The political process in the United States of securing the fast track authority necessary to conduct meaningful negotiations would necessarily open the door to an expansion of the trade policy agenda, as it did in the NAFTA. Moreover, since agreements would be negotiated bilaterally, they would not necessarily imply closer political integration *among* the Latin American countries themselves. It was precisely fear of such a hub-spoke outcome that led Canada to opt for full inclusion in the free trade negotiations with Mexico and which undoubtedly influenced Latin American countries to accept the FTAA.[13]

A second model saw a gradual incorporation of more countries into the NAFTA. This model would initially limit the range of participants, since only a few countries were likely to accept the intrusiveness of the NAFTA's provisions with respect to investment, the environment and labor. Nonetheless, a surprising number of countries, including Chile, Colombia and Argentina, signalled their willingness to consider NAFTA accession. Through the summer of 1994, this option was still considered the most likely route to a hemispheric pact. Even after the Miami summit, this option was kept alive by the invitation to Chile to negotiate NAFTA accession.

The third organizational option, and the most steeply discounted, was to move directly to a regionwide agreement. The Clinton administration's postponement of the quest for fast-track authority in September 1994 and early American statements downplaying the economic component of the agenda severely dampened hopes of any meaningful trade agreement. Nonetheless, the Plan of Action ratified by the summit opted strongly for the hemispheric option by establishing a timetable for the negotiation of a Free Trade Area of the Americas (FTAA) by no later than 2005. Rather than creating a new institution, administrative support for the ministerial meetings was placed in the hands of the Special Committee on Trade of the Organization of American States. Subsequent ministerial meetings in Denver (June 1995) and Cartagena (March 1996) established formal functional working groups preparatory to negotiations on a range of issues of interest to the United States, from standards to intellectual property.

Despite the apparent breakthrough of the Miami summit, it quickly became apparent that crucial issues of both organizational design and substance remained unsolved (Haggard 1996). In contrast to Mexico, the interests of the other major South American countries in reaching a regional agreement with the United States were more ambiguous. All have significant trade with the United States, but none is anywhere nearly as dependent as Mexico. Nor have they been affected to the same extent by tariffs and NTBs as Mexico. Many already enjoy relatively free access to the American market for their products, either because tariffs are already low, as is true for most raw materials, or because they enjoy preferences under the Generalized System of Preferences.

Because of the relatively diversified geographic structure of South America's trade, the increasing interest in hemispheric cooperation has been accompanied by a dramatic growth of subregional integration initiatives and bilateral FTAs among the Latin American countries themselves (Saborio 1992; Bouzas and Ros 1994; Haggard 1996). These "spoke-spoke" negotiations took a variety of forms. Some initiatives were directly linked to the North American complex. Before the negotiation of the NAFTA was even complete, Mexico had embarked on negotiations for free trade agreements with Chile and the Central American countries. In April 1991, Mexico announced that it would seek to establish a free trade zone with Venezuela and Colombia; the agreement between the so-called G-3 was signed in 1994. Mexico's bilateral agreements increasingly came to mimic the NAFTA structure.

A second variant of the "spoke-spoke" pattern involved cooperation among subgroups of South American countries, motivated in part by the promise of negotiations with the United States. The Southern Cone Common Market (Mercosur) between Argentina, Brazil, Uruguay and Paraguay was by far the most important of these. Signed in March 1991, in the wake of the EAI (Dandeker 1992), it quickly became clear that the Mercosur was not simply a vehicle for bargaining with the United States and in fact represented an agreement based on quite different principles than the NAFTA (O'Keefe 1995). Moreover, the Mercosur's large market and somewhat looser conception of integration acted as a magnet for other states, particularly as the American commitment to expanding the NAFTA faded. Chile, for example, began exploring a relationship with Mercosur in 1994, but its interest heightened in 1995 after the Clinton administration failed to secure fast-track authority for the Chilean NAFTA accession negotiations. In 1996 Chile entered the Mercosur.

The ultimate governance structure that might evolve out of this network of agreements was far from clear, but the ability of the United States to extend the NAFTA to the rest of the hemisphere was highly unlikely. At the core of the resistance to this idea was Brazil. Beginning in early 1994, Brazil began to lead an effort to construct a regionwide agreement "from below." In March 1994, Brazil called for the formation of a South American free trade agreement (SAFTA) and at a meeting in Cartagena Colombia in June 1994, the leaders of nineteen Latin American countries launched initial discussions on how the emerging patchwork of agreements might be merged into a single, unified structure. The Miami summit and the declining prospects for NAFTA expansion temporarily weakened the impetus to a separate South American agreement. But U.S. efforts to push the deep integration agenda at ministerial meetings in Denver in mid-1995 met Latin American resistance. As American trade policy became the victim of the budget wrangle and election year politics in 1995–96. the prospects of securing fast track disappeared. Discussions with Chile ground to a halt. Mercosur expansion gained momentum through agreements with Chile and Bolivia, and the once fanciful idea of a SAFTA appeared increasingly plausible. These various initiatives from below can be interpreted as reflecting both an attempt to increase Latin American, and particularly Southern Cone, bargaining power in any forthcoming negotiation with the United States (the power dimension) as well as the continuing ambivalence of the Latin American countries about the deeper forms of integration implied either by an extension of the NAFTA or the negotiation of bilateral FTAs (the preference dimension).

Predicting the course of hemispheric integration is treacherous, but there are a number of signs that hemispheric cooperation is likely to evolve toward deeper integration. The FTAA process involves a series of working groups considering a range of deep integration issues, with the expectation that their work will ultimately evolve toward concrete negotiations. Seeking an agreement among the diverse countries of the hemisphere will undoubtedly weaken it when compared to NAFTA; nonetheless, NAFTA standards constitute an important focal point in the region, one that is altogether lacking in Asia. However, it is also the case that the very diversity of interests and the existence of countries with divergent trade policies preferences, particularly Brazil, means that the ability of the United States to use the NAFTA as the template for these negotiations is limited.

PATTERNS OF COOPERATION IN ASIA: APEC

If trade patterns do not appear to provide the basis for the emergence of an exclusive Latin American or Asian bloc (Frankel 1992; Frankel, Stein, and Wei 1995), they do appear more propitious for the establishment of a Pan-Pacific organization that includes both Asian countries and the United States, Canada, Australia, New Zealand, and even other countries in the Western hemisphere. Not only does the American market remain important for Japan, the NICs, and ASEAN, but U.S. trade is increasingly concentrated in Asia as well. The Western hemisphere and Pacific Asia now account for over 70 percent of Pacific Asian exports. Despite the attention given to the role of Japanese foreign direct investment in creating a de facto Japan-centered region (Doner 1993; Lincoln 1993:ch. 5), American and Japanese investment have also played an important role in trans-Pacific trade as well. If there is evidence of "regional" deepening, it is along the lines of a larger Pacific bloc.

A number of transnational organizations and forums with an inclusive, trans-Pacific conception of membership have emerged in the region in the last two decades. Most of these organizations have played a role as a locus for the formation of transnational networks, but they have not graduated to the status of policy-making institutions let alone a forum for consideration of the deep integration agenda. The dominant intergovernmental institution in the region is the Asia-Pacific Economic Cooperation (APEC), initiated by Australia in 1988 (Higgot 1994; Funabashi 1995; Higgot and Stubbs 1995; Ravenhill 1995).

The 1993 meeting in Seattle, coming on the heels of President Clinton's victory in securing passage of the NAFTA, was a breakthrough for the organization and showed incipient signs of movement toward a more operational form. The summit adopted a Trade and Investment Framework and created a permanent committee to replace the Informal Group on Trade Liberalization; this alone marked an expansion of the organization's substantive ambitions. The 1994 APEC summit in Jakarta marked a great leap forward with the adoption of a proposal to free trade within the region by 2020.[14] With the political success of the 1993 and 1994 summits, it became increasingly clear that APEC was the central forum around which further regionwide institutional development was most likely to occur.

The substantive agenda of the APEC is an ambitious one, and parallels in some respects the range of issues addressed in the NAFTA and the FTAA working groups. The first report of the Eminent Persons Group (EPG) to the APEC Ministers set the goal not only of a free trade in the Asia-Pacific region, but an Asian Pacific Investment Code, cooperation on a range of deep integration questions, including competition policy, product standards, testing and monitoring procedures, and environmental protection, and the establishment of an APEC dispute settlement procedure (APEC 1993). The idea of creating a free trade area ran into substantial resistance at the Seattle summit; however the second report of the EPG (APEC 1994), completed in July 1994, contained a variety of ambitious proposals, including a nondiscriminatory free trade area, consideration of an investment code, discussion of environmental and competition policy and the establishment of a dispute settlement mechanism, on which progress was made in Jakarta. The Osaka summit of 1995 reiterated this agenda in substantial detail, and set out a range of issues on which action was to be taken by individual APEC members, by APEC fora, and by APEC in the context of multilateral fora (APEC 1995).

A number of features of the organizational structure of APEC differentiate it sharply from developments in the Western Hemisphere, however. First, Asian APEC members have been at great pains to stress the "open" nature of Pacific regionalism, by which is meant two things: a commitment to nondiscrimination and willingness to consider new members.[15] Even were the APEC to consider deeper cooperation that went beyond existing WTO commitments, either through sectoral liberalization, the negotiation of a regionwide investment code, or other functional agreements, the Asian countries in the region are generally committed to the principle that such cooperation would be extended on an MFN basis (Yamazawa 1992). Such agreements might prove subtly discriminatory to the extent that the agenda of cooperation is shaped by the interests of members. However, this extremely loose form of cooperation stands in sharp contrast to the NAFTA and the objectives of the FTAA, which include the negotiation of a traditional free trade agreement.

With respect to membership, open regionalism implies an open accession clause and the ability of new like-minded members to join; again, the basic form of the organization is extremely fluid. China, Taiwan and Hong Kong joined in 1992. Mexico and Papua and New Guinea were added in 1993, and a commitment was made to add Chile at the 1994 summit. Recently, the membership issue has been complicated by fears of congestion, and it was agreed prior to the 1993 summit to postpone the question of further members for three years. However, it is quite plausible that APEC will in the future come to encompass more members from the Western Hemisphere. By contrast, the prospects for NAFTA accession had wilted by early 1996 and the FTAA structure is highly unlikely to absorb extraregional members.

The most substantial difference between the APEC and its Western Hemisphere counterpart has to do with fundamental political processes and commitments. Not only are the *means* for achieving cooperation unclear, but the very nature of the commitments to be made are both equivocal and contested.

In its most minimalist form, "open regionalism" would consist of multiple tracks of liberalization and reform that would be dictated both by the diversity of the region and the political difficulty of tackling "sensitive" sectors (Yamazawa 1992). Negotiation would take place only among the "like-minded," and not in all sectors, with the result that the organization would tolerate very different speeds of liberalization and reform. The United States, by contrast, has opposed such an approach and argued that the APEC must be built on "comprehensive action" across all sectors. At the extreme, there would appear to be little need for negotiating concessions on a reciprocal basis at all; decisions would be left to national governments about how far and fast they are willing to go on the assumption that their national interest and peer pressure would gradually push them in the direction of multilateral liberalization. The United States has accepted the importance of unilateral actions, but has balked at the overly loose conception of "concerted unilateral action," and argued strongly for consultations that would guarantee the comparability of members' actions (Funabashi 1995: 101–2). Through the Osaka summit, these fundamental issues of institutional design had been finessed, but it appeared highly unlikely that the countries of the region would commit to a formal FTA any time soon.

The relative weakness of institutions in the Pacific has long been a subject of debate (Aggarwal 1994; Drysdale and Garnaut 1993; Higgot, Leaver, and Ravenhill 1993; Kahler 1994), but several important contrasts with North America and the Western Hemisphere provide insight into the issue. Despite—and arguably because of—the extremely rapid growth of trade and investment, there has not been strong demand within Asia for greater policy coordination. There is little evidence for the theory that higher levels of interdependence generate the demand for deeper integration, nor for the theory that trade generates PD situations which can only be resolved through hegemony or institutions. The openness of the U.S. market, natural economic forces of proximity, and the general complementarity of national policies have produced greater economic interdependence without substantial coordination at the regional level. Nor have the developing countries in the region experienced profound crises that would make tighter regional organization a desirable commitment mechanism.

The political as well as economic heterogeneity of the region also constitutes a barrier on reaching agreements. At the political level, broader Pacific organization has faced vexing problems of membership. Some of these have been linked with Cold War divisions, particularly how to accommodate China, Taiwan, and Hong Kong within one organization; this has now been solved. A second set of problems centers on ASEAN's fear that their integration effort would be diluted by inclusion in a wider organization, or that a larger organization would simply become a vehicle for the exercise of influence by Japan and the United States; this remains one of the most important barriers to deeper integration.

Economic policy diversity is also high. The profound shocks of the 1980s pushed Latin American countries in the direction of certain common policy responses. Despite the well-known and general pursuit of outward-oriented policies in the region—policies that would appear conducive to formal organization—the policy regimes of the countries in East Asia remain highly disparate. Singapore and Hong Kong are free ports. In Korea and Taiwan, the early export-oriented NICs, initial trade and exchange rate reforms date to the early 1960s but industrial policies were an integral part of their growth strategies (Haggard 1990). The ASEAN countries are now traversing a similar trajectory, though with different mixes of trade and industrial policies than the East Asian NICs (MacIntyre 1994). Vietnam and China are reforming socialist economies in which a substantial array of discretionary controls remain in place. With such widely divergent substantive interests, it is not clear what the core of formal cooperation would be; resistance to deeper integration from the more protected economies has underlined this fact.

A final political problem has to do with differences among the three major powers in the region, and goes to the central structural differences between the Pacific and Latin American regions. The United States has some interest in pushing toward deeper integration—or at least that portion of the deep integration agenda which is in America's interest—but Japan and China are more cautious; as a result, the region has a tripolar political structure. One reason for this caution, emphasized by Cowhey

(1994), is the American penchant for universal rules and the ability of the Japanese to achieve their objectives without them. Similar arguments can be made about China, whose rapidly expanding market and large size provide it numerous opportunities to conduct its foreign economic policy on a bilateral basis. An equally compelling reason for Japanese and Chinese skepticism is the fear that calls for deeper integration will be little more than a weapon trained on them; this concern is also shared by a number of other Asian countries.

ASEAN's concerns, its central importance for the success of APEC, and its ability to align with China on certain issues have also given it substantial leverage over APEC's policy agenda. In the Western Hemisphere, Latin American countries have been confronted with an agenda driven largely by U.S. interests. As APEC has evolved, by contrast, the standard trade agenda has widened to include two other "pillars" that have effectively been excluded from the FTAA agenda (Funabashi 1995:98–99): trade facilitation and development.

The United States has continued to conduct an active bilateral economic diplomacy in the region (Haggard 1995:ch. 3). However, it is not likely that it can offer either the inducements or credible threats that would move the region toward a trans-Pacific free trade area. First, it is far from clear that U.S. commitment to the idea is at all credible; opening the United States to Mexico generated a tremendous outcry; opening the United States to Asia would involve even more substantial political controversy. To the extent that Japan and China are interested in deeper integration, it is likely to focus in part on building dispute settlement mechanisms that would restrain the United States from pursuing its deep integration agenda (Yamazawa 1994)!

The explanatory purpose of this essay was to provide some tools for understanding the patterns of regional organization that appear to be emerging in the Western Hemisphere and East Asia. It also had a broader theoretical purpose: to spark a debate about the utility of liberal institutionalist models of cooperation on trade. I have argued that the assumption that trade constitutes a PD is not only questionable, but has diverted our attention from building on other strands of economic theory, such as the theory of customs unions or models of bargaining. The liberal institutionalist school has also driven an undesirable wedge between the literature on international cooperation, on the one hand, and the well-developed literature on endogenous tariff policy on the other. Emphasizing the

distributive politics that surrounds all trade bargaining promises to introduce more politics into the study on international cooperation than is visible in the literature on collective action and transactions costs, and thus
to build stronger theoretical linkages between research on international
and comparative politics.

Acknowledgments: My thanks to Helen Milner, Joanne Gowa, Andrew MacIntyre, Ken Oye, Diana Tussie, and two anonymous reviewers for extensive comments on ear-lier drafts, and to John Richards for superb research assistance. This paper was first pre-sented at the American Political Science Association meeting, New York, September 1–4, 1994.

NOTES

1. Regionalization or regionalism has been used to refer to an *economic* process in which trade and investment within a given region—however defined—grow more rapidly than the region's trade and investment with the rest of the world (Frankel 1993). Regionalization in this economic sense should not be confused with regionalism as a form of *political* organization—the subject of this chapter—in part because the causal relationship between the two phenomena is unclear (Fishlow and Haggard 1992).

2. I do not examine the preferential arrangements that are either springing up or being revived among the developing countries in the two regions: the ASEAN Free Trade Area (AFTA), Mercosur, the Andean Pact, CARICOM, and the Central American Common Market.

3. Two works which attempt to play out the implication of a wider range of trade games are John Conybeare (1986) and Lake (1988). Realists have also been sympathetic to this no-tion, of course.

4. As a classical economist, Viner focused solely on the costs of production; attention has subsequently been paid to gains in consumption, economies of scale, and terms of trade effects (Krauss 1972).

5. The logic is simple but elegant. Imagine that the world is characterized by some degree of protection and a customs union forms that reduces all barriers among the parties. If the par-ties maintain—or even raise—their tariffs vis-à-vis the rest of the world, then trade diversion clearly takes place. However, it is possible to write a common external tariff which would permit trade with nonmembers to remain unchanged from its preunion level. A further implication is that there is "an incentive to form and enlarge customs unions persists until the world is one big customs union." (Kemp and Wan 1976:96).

6. New urgency was given to securing European support for the launching of a new round of GATT negotiations and the Plaza accord of September 22, 1985, initiated a new phase of international cooperation on exchange rates.

7. Korean restrictions on the entry of American insurance firms; Brazilian restrictions on American computer exports that resulted from its industrial policy in that sector; and Japanese restrictions on cigarettes.

8. Under so-called Super 301 provisions, the USTR was required to prepare an inventory of all foreign trade barriers, establish a priority list of countries singled out for action, set dead-

lines for compliance, and in the case that compliance is not forthcoming, retaliate. The 1988 Act makes specific reference to barriers to trade in services and restrictions on foreign investment, and a separate provision of the bill targeted barriers in the area of telecommunications. The so-called Special 301 provisions are similar, but address violations of intellectual property rights. The 1988 act also made explicit mention of workers' rights, export targeting, and systematic toleration of anticompetitive practices.

9. With Brazil the issue was import licensing. India was targeted for trade-related investment questions and barriers in services, particularly insurance.

10. The most significant were the 1986 softwood lumber cases, in which the U.S. industry obtained a ruling that Canadian stumpage practices were a countervailable subsidy, the 1987 shakes and shingles case, in which the U.S. industry obtained safeguards protection, and the controversy about Canada's Western Grain Transport Act, which subsidized transport costs for Western wheat growers.

11. The following paragraphs draw on U.S. International Trade Commission (1992); World Bank (1993a); Hufbauer and Schott (1994); Haggard (1995:ch. 3); Haggard (1996).

12. The one interesting exception to this pattern is Colombia, which undertook a major trade reform in 1990–91 in the absence of a manifest crisis.

13. The implications of the hub-and-spoke design for the participants has been explored in Wonnacott (1991).

14. The advanced industrial states obligated themselves to that goal by 2010.

15. The 1992 PECC declaration on "open regionalism" is a clear statement of the principle of nondiscriminatory regionalism (Cheit 1992).

THREE

The Political Economy of Currency Regions

Benjamin J. Cohen

Most studies of international political economy conventionally (and conveniently) assume that all money is effectively insular: each currency sovereign within the frontiers of a single state. In fact, nothing could be further from the truth. As a practical matter, cross-border use and competition between currencies are commonplace. The realms within which each money serves the standard functions of money (medium of exchange, unit of account, store of value) thus often diverge quite sharply from the legal jurisdiction of issuing governments. Where effective use or authority of a money extends beyond the frontiers of a single country, we may legitimately speak of a currency "region."

Currency regions, in this sense, differ substantially from the traditional notion of a currency "area" as developed by economists in the familiar theory of optimum currency areas (OCAs). In OCA theory, currency *areas* are the explicit product of state action and embody formal arrangements designed to merge separate moneys or link exchange rates. Synonyms include such institutional variants as exchange-rate unions, currency boards, monetary unions, and currency unions. Reflecting standard political geography, currency areas are understood to encompass the sovereign jurisdictions of participating governments and thus are defined in strictly territorial terms—tangibly distinct and mutually exclusive spatial enclaves; in effect, the monetary counterpart of customs unions or free trade areas in commercial relations. As in commercial relations, the countries involved need not be located in close physical proximity.

Currency *regions*, by contrast, are functional rather than geographic in nature—bounded not by territorial frontiers but rather by the range of each money's effective use and authority; and thus, as will be explained below, defined by market networks of domestic and transnational transactions rather than by legal agreements or formal institutions. Though not easy to visualize—they certainly cannot be drawn easily on a map—currency regions are both pervasive in practice and frequently extensive in scope. They are important because they pose a direct challenge to the presumed insularity of national moneys. The full implications of that challenge have been comparatively neglected by scholars and remain poorly understood in practice.

My purpose here is to explore the political economy of currency regions. The basic question asked is: What are the advantages or disadvantages of currency regions as seen from the point of view of a single sovereign state? The public sector orientation, focusing on the policy concerns of national governments, is consistent with the guiding spirit of OCA theory, which provides the inspiration and starting point for discussion here. But the analysis departs from standard practice of OCA theory in two critical respects—first, in the focus on regions rather than areas, which adds a market dimension to the determination of currency relations; and second, by incorporating noneconomic as well as economic considerations into the policy calculations of governments, thus adding a political dimension as well. Both extensions permit a more nuanced appraisal of state interests in alternative monetary outcomes.

The paper is organized as follows: the next section reviews the principal elements of OCA theory, with particular emphasis on both its contributions and limitations. The market dimension is added in the third and fourth sections and the political dimension in the fifth. The potential effects of currency regions are evaluated in the sixth section and state interests are summarized with some brief concluding remarks at the end.

OPTIMUM CURRENCY AREA THEORY

Dating back to the seminal work of Robert Mundell more than three decades ago (Mundell 1961), OCA theory has lately enjoyed something of a revival as a result of developments in the European Union and elsewhere.[1] In its first incarnation, the theory was strikingly apolitical. Following Mundell's lead, most early contributors concentrated on a search for the most appropriate domain of a currency irrespective of existing national frontiers. The globe, in effect, was treated as a tabula rasa. The only issue was finding the right criteria for the organization of currency space. But as the practical limitations of the so-called "criterion approach" (Tavlas 1994:213) became clear, an alternative—and politically seemingly less naive—approach eventually prevailed, focusing instead on costs and benefits of national participation in a common currency area. No longer an irrelevance, the existence of sovereign states now became the starting point for analysis. OCA theory was deliberately reincarnated in a presumably more policy-relevant form.

As developed over the last twenty years or so, OCA theory highlights the advantages or disadvantages, as seen from a single country's point of view, of abandoning monetary autonomy to participate in a currency union or its equivalent, a regime of irrevocably fixed exchange rates. Under what conditions, analysts ask, would a state surrender its right to alter the external value of its currency? The now standard approach identifies a number of key economic characteristics that may be regarded as instrumental in the government's decision. These include: wage and price flexibility, factor mobility, geographic trade patterns, the degree of commodity diversification, size and openness of economies, inflation trends, and the nature, source, and timing of potential payments disturbances. These particular variables are singled out because they all are assumed to influence, to a greater or lesser extent, material gains or losses for the nation as a whole. Exchange-regime choices are presumed to be based on a systematic calculus of both potential costs and benefits.

On the positive side, a common currency or equivalent is expected to yield certain distinct gains, including in particular possible improvements in the usefulness of money in each of its principal functions: as a medium of exchange (owing to a reduction of transactions costs as the number of required currency conversions is decreased), store of value (owing to a reduced element of exchange risk as the number of currencies is decreased), and unit of account (owing to an information saving as the number of required price quotations is decreased). Additional benefits might also accrue from a saving of international reserves due to an internalization through credit of what would otherwise be external trade and payments—effectively enhancing the foreign purchasing power of each participating currency—and from a broadening of the foreign-exchange market vis-à-vis third countries, decreasing currency volatility.

Against these advantages, on the negative side, governments are assumed to compare the disadvantages of the corresponding surrender of monetary autonomy: the potential cost of having to adjust to domestic disturbances or balance-of-payments shocks without the option of changing either interest rates or the exchange rate. In Paul Krugman's words (1993b:4), the question "is a matter of trading off macroeconomic flexibility against microeconomic efficiency."[2] Each of the variables identified by OCA theory arguably affects the magnitude of losses at the macroeconomic level by influencing either the severity of potential external imbalances or the ease of the consequent processes of adjustment. The basic premise is that, ceteris paribus, the lower the potential net economic cost to the country, the more willing governments should be to absolutely peg their exchange rates.

The contributions of OCA theory are considerable. In particular, the work serves to remind us that all money is *not* insular—that alternative spatial configurations of currency relations do (or could) exist, extending across the frontiers of individual states. However, OCA theory also seems limited in two fairly distinct ways, both reflecting the economist's propensity for the greatest possible parsimony in model-building. First, attention is directed exclusively to configurations of monetary space that are the result of government design (currency "areas"). Monetary configurations reflecting market forces (currency "regions") are effectively ignored. And second, states are pictured as rational unitary actors with invariant utility functions defined exclusively in terms of aggregate economic welfare (identified with the total volume of goods and services available for final use)—a logic borrowed directly from conventional microeconomic analysis and analogous to that of neorealist political theory, which also portrays states as rational unitary actors with fixed preferences defined in terms of a single goal, national security. Other possible influences on policy behavior are also effectively ignored. In both respects, the standard approach greatly simplifies reality. Currency outcomes, in practice, involve both a greater role for private markets and, typically, a more complex definition of policy objectives. Some sacrifice of parsimony, therefore, would seem called for in order to move analysis closer to the actual choices confronting governments.

THE ROLE OF MARKET FORCES

First, consider the role of market forces. Standard OCA theory tends to discount the influence of the private sector, by ignoring the existence of cross-border currency use and competition. The world is portrayed as comprised solely of insular national moneys, which either remain wholly independent or else may be formally merged into a currency union or its equivalent. Moneys, in effect, are treated like discrete building blocks, homogenous products of state sovereignty to be combined or remain independent at the whim of governments. But is this plausible? In fact, insular national money is a very special case—an exception rather than the rule.

Global Currency Competition

For any money to be truly insular, its functional realm would have to coincide precisely with the political jurisdiction of the nation-state. The currency would have to exercise an exclusive claim to all the traditional roles of money within the domestic economy. There could be no other currency accepted for transactions purposes or used for the denomination of contracts or financial assets. And the government would have to be able to exercise exclusive control over all aspects of the monetary system. In matters of commerce, the equivalent would be described as "autarky"—national self-sufficiency. In the real world, autarky is no more common in currency relations than it is in trade.

As a practical matter, cross-border currency use is commonplace. Several national moneys are widely employed outside their country of origin for transactions either between states (currency internationalization) or within foreign states (currency substitution). However, while both internationalization and substitution are familiar to technical specialists and frequently discussed in the theoretical economics literature,[3] their implications for the spatial organization of monetary relations are only rarely addressed.[4]

Currency internationalization ("international" currency use) occurs at two levels of operation: at the private level, as a medium of exchange (a "vehicle") for foreign trade, as a unit of account for commercial invoicing, and as store of value for international investments; and at the official level, as a reserve and intervention medium and as a peg (a numeraire or nominal anchor) for exchange rates. Currency substitution ("foreign-domestic" use) may be for any or all of the usual monetary purposes.[5] Both types of use emerge from an intense process of market competition between currencies—a kind of Darwinian process of natural selection in which some moneys come to be seen as functionally superior to others.

Analytically, the motivations for both phenomena can be easily appreciated. Internationalization derives from the economies of scale, or reduced transactions costs, to be gained from concentrating cross-border activities in just one or at most a few widely circulated currencies; or from cross-border variations of interest rates and currency expectations. Substitution typically occurs as a result of a high or accelerating inflation rate, which encourages a country's residents to turn to some more stable foreign money as a preferred store of value and, perhaps, ultimately, even as a unit of account and medium of exchange. Each represents a kind of Gresham's Law in reverse, where more attractive ("good") money drives out less attractive ("bad") money.[6] Neither is at all an irrational form of behavior. On the contrary, both internationalization and substitution may be regarded as quite natural responses to prevailing market structures and incentives.

Which currencies are likely to prevail in the Darwinian struggle? The principal qualities required for competitive success are familiar and hardly controversial (Cohen 1971; Tavlas 1991; Krugman 1992a). Two essential attributes, at least in the early stages of a currency's cross-border use, are widespread confidence in the money's future value and political stability in the country of origin. In addition, markets for the money should be sufficiently deep and resilient to ensure a high degree of liquidity and predictability of asset value. And perhaps most important of all, the money must be widely employed commercially, since nothing enhances a currency's acceptability more than the prospect of acceptability by others—what analysts refer to as the "network value of money" (Fratianni 1992) or its "network externalities" (Dowd and Greenaway 1993). None of these attributes, however, is a constant. We may also assume, therefore, that the outcome of the competitive process is quite likely to change substantially over time. No currency can be presumed to enjoy a permanent monopoly for either international or foreign-domestic use.

Empirical Evidence

How well are these cross-border uses documented? Although comprehensive statistics do not exist, partial indicators abound that provide some rough orders of magnitude for both currency internationalization and currency substitution around the world. Space limitations prevent their reproduction here. However, representative samples of data for recent years are available elsewhere (Cohen 1994; Thygesen et al. 1995); and these diverse data—no matter how imperfect—offer a composite picture that is strikingly at variance with the conventional assumption of insular national moneys.

Currency internationalization, for example, is evidently quite substantial in magnitude. Reflecting the economies of scale involved, however, it also appears to be highly concentrated in terms of numbers. Just a small handful of moneys accounts for the great bulk of use at both the private and official levels. The leading role of the U.S. dollar, though diminished from what it once was, is confirmed by its still dominant position in central bank reserves and interventions, commercial banking claims and bond issues, and wholesale foreign exchange market activity. Vying distantly for second place are the Deutsche mark, especially important in official reserves and exchange markets, and the Japanese yen, which ranks strongly in banking assets and securities. The only other international currencies of any particular significance are the pound sterling and French and Swiss francs, and beyond them the Netherlands guilder, Belgian franc, Italian lira, and Canadian dollar.

The main exception lies in the area of trade invoicing, where a noticeably less asymmetrical pattern of currency use seems to prevail. Ever since the pioneering empirical work of Swedish economist Sven Grassman (1973), it has been well known that the most favored vehicle for trade among industrial countries, particularly involving manufactures, tends to be the exporter's own currency.[7] Yet even for this purpose some currencies clearly remain more important than others. In bilateral trade between developed and developing nations, for example, the currencies of the industrial countries still generally predominate whatever the national identity of the exporter. Moreover, even within the industrial world, the importance of home money in export invoicing tends to vary quite sharply depending on the issuing country's relative weight in world trade: the smaller the country, the smaller the share of exports denominated in local currency. And in the vast area of trade in primary products (including, especially, oil), the dollar plainly remains the vehicle of choice. Though the selection of moneys for retail commercial purposes may be less asymmetrical than in the wholesale exchange market or global banking and bond markets, international use still remains quite highly concentrated in just a small handful of key currencies.

A complementary picture of asymmetry emerges from available data on currency substitution. Although less well documented than currency internationalization, the phenomenon of foreign-domestic use is known to be substantial in magnitude and also seems quite concentrated in terms of numbers. Only the most familiar and trusted international currencies tend to be used at all widely outside their own country of issue. On the other hand, the range of states where currency substitution occurs is apparently very broad, encompassing many of the economies of the developing world (particularly Latin America and the Middle East) and the former Soviet bloc. The sample of popular currencies whose effective range extends beyond their national frontiers may be small; the world of currencies whose legal jurisdiction is correspondingly penetrated certainly is not.

In short, evidence of the pervasiveness of global currency competition is overwhelming. Three observations stand out. First, the scale of cross-border currency use is obviously extensive. Autarky in currency relations truly is a special case. Second, the number of moneys actually employed for either international or foreign-domestic purposes tends to be rather small. And third, conversely, the number of moneys that routinely face effective competition at home from currencies orginating abroad appears to be quite large. The population of currencies is distinctly hierarchical. While all moneys enjoy nominally equal status as a matter of international law, some currencies (to paraphrase George Orwell) clearly are, as a matter of practical reality, far more equal than others.

THE NATURE AND DETERMINANTS OF CURRENCY REGIONS

From these facts emerge currency regions—each region grouped around one of a small handful of elite "key" currencies.[8] Contrary to OCA theory, governments cannot be assumed to be the sole determinants of the organization of currency space. Cross-border competition ensures that market forces too play a critically important role.

Currency Regions in Practice

If the available data are to be believed, it would seem reasonable to assume that currency regions in practice are quite ubiquitous (reflecting the sheer scale of currency competition). It would also appear that they are limited in number (reflecting the small handful of moneys actually employed outside their own country of issue) but frequently broad in scope (reflecting the large number of currencies routinely facing cross-border competition). The organization of currency space, in short, can be assumed to mirror closely the hierarchical structure of the monetary population. In an Orwellian world, a few key currencies hog the scene.

In fact, the list of regions is remarkably short. Topping the charts, of course, is the dollar, which remains by far the world's most popular money for both international and foreign-domestic purposes. In effect, the dollar's region spans the globe, from the Western Hemisphere (where the accepted synonym for currency substitution is "dollarization") to the former Soviet bloc and parts of the Middle East (where dollars circulate widely as a de facto parallel currency). And next comes the Deutsche mark, which clearly dominates currency relations within much of Europe, including East Central Europe and the Balkans (Tavlas 1991). In francophone Africa, a smaller region has long existed centered on the French franc (Boughton 1993); and in the Far East, a limited grouping may now be starting to coalesce around the Japanese yen.[9] Elsewhere, however, only a few "micro"-regions can be identified clustered around such locally influential currencies as the South African rand, Indian rupee, or Australian dollar; noticeably absent from the list is Britain's pound sterling, once the proud leader of an extensive region of its own, today no more than a pale shadow of its former self (Cohen 1992). In total, currency regions can be counted on less than the fingers of two hands.

The scope of some of these regions, on the other hand, appears to be remarkably broad. Though few moneys may be chosen to lead currency regions, many appear called to follow. It is the rare country indeed that remains fully insulated from the effects of cross-border currency competition. For most governments, therefore—not just the governments of the few key currencies actually used for cross-border purposes—state interests clearly are affected. The challenge for public policy is real. It is also more or less universal.

Defining Currency Regions

Can we define currency regions more formally? To do so, we need an appropriate analytical "metric" that we can use to distinguish and contrast the international competitiveness of individual moneys.

At issue is a fundamental distinction between physical and functional notions of economic space. Currency regions are market-driven, reflecting the choices of private actors at least as much as the preferences of public officials, and may never be formalized in legal or institutional terms. Based not on geography but on practice, they are delimited not by the territorial frontiers of sovereign states but rather by the range of each money's effective use and authority—"spaces-as-flows," in John Ruggie's language

(1993:173), rather than the more traditional "spaces-of-places." The key lies in the network externalities that are so critical to the competitive success of individual moneys. Currency regions are rooted in the networks of domestic and transnational transactions centered on a single key currency.

The distinction between physical and functional space is not a new one. Nearly half a century ago, economic historian François Perroux (1950) underscored the contrast between "banal" notions of physical space and more abstract ideas of *economic* space, defined in his language as a "field of forces." "Modern mathematics," he wrote, "has become accustomed to consider the abstract relations which define mathematical beings, and so to give the name 'spaces' to these structures of abstract relations" (1950:91). Economists, he continued, should learn to do the same. And among the most important of these abstract spaces of interest to economists, he maintained, was *monetary* space—a field of forces "seen more easily in terms of a 'network' of payments" (1950:98). Only recently, however, in a relatively new literature on the "economics of networks," developed largely in France, have theorists finally begun to explore seriously the implications of this alternative, functional approach to the organization of spatial relations.[10] Just two sources, to my knowledge, have as yet tried to apply the new network theory to the analysis of monetary relations as suggested here.[11]

A formal definition of currency regions can be readily constructed on the foundation laid by Perroux and the new network theory. Conceptually, what is at issue is what may be called the *authoritative domain* of each individual money. The term "domain" in this context refers directly to the range or network of transactions for which a given currency effectively performs the standard functions of money—its *economic space*, strictly speaking. But this is not the whole story, since currencies are still created and nominally managed by governments. No matter how important the role of markets may be, therefore, there is also a dimension of political authority to take into account. That is the purpose of the modifying adjective "authoritative," which refers to the range or network of transactions over which each issuing government is able to exercise effective control through its monetary and exchange-rate policies—the currency's *political space*, as it were. Both dimensions, the political as well as the economic, are integral to a comparative analysis of currency competitiveness.

To illustrate, consider a country where for one reason or another residents begin to favor a popular foreign currency for various international or even domestic monetary purposes. In effect, the economic space of home

60   *Benjamin J. Cohen*

money is correspondingly diminished. International competition has directly eroded its authoritative domain while enhancing the authoritative domain of the foreign currency. Much the same effect, however, will also be achieved even in the absence of overt currency substitution if external financial linkages are sufficiently strong. The more capital markets at home are functionally tied to a strong currency abroad, the more control over domestic monetary management is in effect ceded to a foreign central bank. Local money may continue to function for the usual purposes within the national economy, preserving its economic space. The money's authoritative domain is nonetheless once again eroded (and the authoritative domain of the foreign currency once again enhanced), owing this time to the shrinkage of its *political* space. Cross-border use and competition may influence either dimension of a money's international standing.

The concept of authoritative domain provides the basis for a more formal definition of currency regions. *Currency regionalism occurs whenever a money's authoritative domain extends significantly beyond the legal jurisdiction of its issuing government.* Admittedly, the concept of authoritative domain is not easy to operationalize for objective empirical purposes. The data simply do not exist to accurately capture every nuance and complexity of each currency's economic and political space. But it does at least provide a common, if subjective, standard for identification of currency regions like those centered on the dollar, Deutsche mark, and other key currencies. And it offers as well a useful focal point for the policy calculations of governments. Whether they recognize it or not, public officials mandated to manage a nation's money are speaking the language of authoritative domain.

The Role of Market Forces

What, then, determines the authoritative domain of currencies? Standard OCA theory assumes that governments are the dominant if not exclusive shapers of currency relations. Market forces enter into OCA theory only as input into the public decision process—exogenous considerations presumed to influence the costs or benefits of alternative currency choices. Assigning a central role to governments is a natural corollary of the notion of insular national money. In a world of extensive cross-border use, however, private actors are at least as important as the public sector in determining the authoritative domains of currencies, through the choices they make of what vehicles to employ for various monetary purposes. Configurations of currency space are by no means established at the whim of governments alone.

Governments may try, of course. States generally are no less concerned about the creation and management of money than they are about other dimensions of their putative national sovereignty; and within limits set by power capabilities and the strategic environment of interstate rivalry, most more or less do actively seek to preserve as much monopoly control over currency issue as possible. A national money is valued not only for its political symbolism or the macroeconomic flexibility it provides but also for vital public-finance reasons, as we shall see below. If governments had their way, monetary spaces would indeed be defined in strictly territorial terms, coterminous with national boundaries, and would be as numerous as states themselves.

Markets, on the other hand, prefer the efficiency benefits of a smaller number of moneys, as amply demonstrated by the pervasiveness of cross-border currency use. How small a number? For some theorists, such as economist Roland Vaubel (1977), the number might be as small as one, owing to the power of economies of scale. Unfettered currency competition, Vaubel argues, will lead eventually to a single universal money—the ultimate expression of Gresham's Law in reverse. "Ultimately, currency competition destroys itself because the use of money is subject to very sizable economies of scale. . . . [T]he only lasting result will be . . . the survival of the fittest currency" (1977:437, 440). Such a view, however, is highly deterministic, not to say simplistic, and appears to be contradicted by both empirical evidence and theoretical considerations. Markets may prefer to reduce costs by driving out "bad" money, but a multiplicity of currency regions seems the more natural selection than one single money.

Historically, the Darwinian process of currency competition has never shown any tendency to concentrate favor exclusively on a single money, even in the presence of competitive disparities as great as those, for example, between sterling and the dollar in the decades after World War I. In Paul Krugman's words: "The impressive fact here is surely the inertia; sterling remained the first-ranked currency for half a century after Britain had ceased to be the first-ranked economic power" (1992:173). Similar inertias have been evident for centuries, in the prolonged use of such international currencies as the Byzantine gold solidus or Spanish silver peso long after the decline of the imperial powers that first coined them (Lopez 1951; A. Andrews 1904); and they can still be seen today in the continued popularity of the dollar despite America's shrinking economic predominance. Such immobilism cannot be accounted for merely by residual political influences.

Network theory, on the other hand, provides a quite workable explanation for what has been called the "paradox of the non-universality of money" (Thygesen et al. 1995:41). Two distinct structures are recognized in the organization of "spaces-of-flows": the "infrastructure," which is the functional basis of a network; and the "infostructure," which provides needed management and control services. Economies of scale, by reducing transactions costs, promote a consolidation of networks at the level of infrastructure. At the infostructure level, by contrast, the optimal configuration is more decentralized and competitive in order to maximize agent responsibility. A natural tension exists, therefore, that is more likely to result in intermediate solutions than in either absolute centralization or decentralization—in short, currency regions rather than either a single universal money or insular national currencies.

A priori, no one intermediate configuration can be identified as optimal for all circumstances, as progenitors of network theory are the first to admit. More likely is the possibility of multiple equilibria—a conclusion consistent with other recent approaches to the analysis of international money (Krugman 1992a; Matsuyama et al. 1993; Hartmann 1994). Particularly influential is the self-reinforcing impact of "mimesis": the rational impulse of market actors, in conditions of uncertainty, to minimize risk by imitative behavior based on past experience. Once a currency gains a degree of acceptance, its use is apt to be perpetuated—even after the appearance of powerful new competitors—by regular repetition of previous practice. In effect, a conservative bias is introduced into the dynamics of the marketplace. As one source has argued, "imitation leads to the emergence of a convention [wherein] emphasis is placed on a certain 'conformism' or even hermeticism in financial circles" (Orléan 1989:81–83). In markets for money, as in other organized asset markets where choices are a function of interdependent expectations, any number of equilibrium configurations are in fact possible.

Ultimately, then, currency outcomes will depend on market psychology as well as political authority. While governments generally seek to preserve as much monetary sovereignty as possible, markets promote a greater consolidation of global currency spaces. Governments and markets thus both play a critical endogenous role, not only acting independently but also reacting strategically to the initiatives of the other—sometimes reinforcing one another's choices, at other times constraining the opposite side's behavior. Practical outcomes, in the form of currency regions, will reflect the balance of influence and ongoing dialectic between political authority and markets and must in the end be assumed to be both mutually determined and highly contingent.[12]

THE POLITICAL DIMENSION

Consider now the question of policy objectives. Neglect of market forces is not the only critical simplification in standard OCA theory. A second is its neglect of politics in the formulation of state preferences. Government motivations, in effect, are restricted to a single-minded concern for material gain. But that is hardly plausible either. Like insular national money, pure economic rationality in state behavior is also a special case. Policy calculations in practice generally take a far broader view, incorporating multiple interests and goals. In currency relations specifically, international politics and domestic distribution are likely to matter at least as much as aggregate economic welfare.

International Politics

Currency relations can have significant consequences for international politics—in particular, for the distribution of power between states. The very notion of regions, based on widely divergent authoritative domains of currencies, is political in nature, implying relationships of varying degrees of reciprocal influence; and since money *ex hypothesi* means command over real resources, these relationships can be expected to impact directly and substantially on the ability of states to achieve goals at home or abroad. Variations in the organization of currency space can greatly alter relative capabilities in the global arena. In an insecure world, governments can ignore these effects only at their peril.

How, in practice, are international politics affected by currency arrangements? Very few theoretical works exist that focus centrally on the role of power in currency relations.[13] OCA theory is absolutely silent on the subject. Some useful clues, however, are provided by historical and institutional studies of monetary hegemony, where the links between geopolitics and currency domains tend to be most visible. Admittedly, hegemony is something of an extreme in monetary history. Moreover, the sample of relevant cases is really quite small, with most serious analysis directed to just the two best-known examples: Britain in the late nineteenth-century and the United States after World War II (Eichengreen 1990:ch. 11; Walter 1991). Nonetheless, analysis of such cases does serve to highlight the principal channels through which reciprocal influences may be manifested in the context of currency relations.

Monetary hegemony, typically defined in terms of a country's ability to control the structure of global finance, manifests itself through the sway that the hegemon effectively exercises over economic conditions elsewhere—specifically, through the various roles that its currency may play, for example, as a source of long-term capital or international reserves, as a vehicle for foreign trade or exchange interventions, or as a nominal anchor for monetary policy. The dependence of others on these roles, all of which may be understood as indicators of the home money's expanded authoritative domain, confers substantial political benefits on the hegemon, both internally and externally. At home, the country should be better insulated from outside influence or coercion in formulating and implementing policy. Abroad, it should be better able to pursue foreign objectives without constraint as well as to exercise a degree of influence or coercion over others. The expansion of its currency's authoritative domain, in principle, translates directly into effective political power.

In practice, however, there are also likely to be distinct limits on the extent to which a hegemon is either willing or able to exploit its currency dominance. Constraints may be imposed by international institutions and regime structures, by security alliances, or by the country's own domestic politics or social values. Or they may be imposed by the very process through which its currency's cross-border roles evolve over time. A sizable postwar literature on the economic costs and benefits of being a reserve center[14] suggests that the material advantages of monetary hegemony are largest in the earliest stages of cross-border use, when the foreign popularity of a country's currency is greatest. Real-resource gains accrue to the local economy, reflecting foreigners' accumulation of domestic money, and the national government enjoys maximum latitude to pursue its own policy agenda. Eventually, however, much of that autonomy may be eroded insofar as an "overhang" of liquid liabilities piles up, gradually forcing officials to pay more and more attention to the maintenance of market confidence in the currency. Economically this process can become quite expensive, as interest rates must be kept sufficiently attractive to discourage capital outflows. Politically, it can impose an effective brake on the government's ability to act independently abroad or even at home.

Power, in short, does not come without cost. Losses as well as gains may ensue from a pursuit of dominance through currency relations. Accordingly, for any rational policy-maker, the challenge is the same as in OCA theory: to calculate the *net* benefit of alternative choices—not necessarily to *maximize* international influence but, rather, in some way to *optimize* the country's position within the overall distribution of currency power. Different configurations of monetary space clearly do imply very different political outcomes for individual states. Governments, it seems fair to assume, are not entirely indifferent to such implications when comparing alternative currency arrangements.

Domestic Distribution

Currency relations may also have significant consequences for domestic distribution. OCA theory assumes that alternative currency arrangements can generate sizable changes in the economic welfare of individual states. But there is no reason to assume that these impacts will be homogenous across sectors, industries, or regions. Quite the contrary, in fact. Effects on the income and wealth of specific groups are more likely to be differentiated to a greater or lesser extent; and these differences, in turn, may well exercise a distinct influence on domestic political processes through the actions or reactions of self-interested individuals and organizations. To paraphrase former House Speaker Thomas "Tip" O'Neill: All currency relations—like all politics—ultimately are local. Needless to say, few governments can afford to ignore such effects either.

In this context, two distributional issues stand out as particularly critical—one involving a potential conflict of interest between state and society (the public and private sectors); the other, a potential for a distinctive pattern of conflict within the private sector. Between state and society, the main issue involves the question of "seigniorage," also known as the "inflation tax" (Fischer 1982). Seigniorage, technically defined as the excess of the nominal value of a currency over its cost of production, can be understood as an alternative source of revenue for government (beyond what can be raised via taxation or borrowing). Since the cost of providing a non-commodity money is virtually nil, public spending financed by money creation in effect appropriates real resources at the expense of the private sector, whose purchasing power is correspondingly reduced by the ensuing increase of inflation.

The key to seigniorage is the lack of substitutes for domestic currency. It stands to reason, therefore, that for public finance reasons governments are always likely to be biased, ceteris paribus, toward preserving as much of their monetary control as possible. The larger the authoritative domain of a currency, the easier it is for public officials to divert resources away from private use. On the one hand, this helps to explain why most governments are so resistant to any threat to their monopoly power over currency issue. In the words of one source: "[I]t is the national bureaucracy who is the only loser from the loss of the right to devalue the national currency" (Jovanovic 1992:133). On the other hand, it also helps to explain why currency substitution so often occurs in highly inflationary economies. In the words of another source: "Few national currencies survive the destructive power of high inflation. . . . [T]he public turns to a foreign money in its quest for a healthy currency" (Calvo and Vegh 1993:34). The conflict of interest between state and society, in this respect, is direct and bound to color any debate over alternative currency arrangements.

Within the private sector, the critical issue is the familiar one of whose ox is gored: Who wins and who loses? The real incomes of many groups are directly dependent, for better or worse, on how a state organizes its monetary affairs, as recent research has begun to emphasize (Frieden 1991, 1994). Effects, however, are not always easy to predict (Giovannini 1993; Frieden 1993b). Producers and consumers of tradable goods, for example, as well as internationally active investors, are all apt to be favored by currency arrangements that maximize the stability and predictability of exchange rates. Currency volatility, for such groups, is an anathema. But cutting across this shared interest is a potential for conflict generated by the question of authoritative domain: Who determines the *level* at which the nation's money is stabilized? Exchange-rate stability attained via a renunciation of some degree of monetary control (e.g., a currency union or strict currency peg), inhibiting the state's right to devalue at will, is apt to disfavor exporters and import-competing producers (who would be hurt by persistent overvaluation) but not importers and consumers (who gain from overvaluation) or international investors (who are able to acquire foreign assets at lower cost). Stability attained via a widening of the domestic money's authoritative domain would, on the other hand, imply just the reverse. So would these various groups be more likely to unite in support of more predictable exchange rates or to diverge over how to achieve them? A priori, we cannot say. All that seems certain is that these issues too are bound to color any debate over alternative currency arrangements. As Jeffry Frieden argues, "domestic distributional considerations are also central to the choice of exchange-rate regimes" (1993a:140).

THE EFFECTS OF CURRENCY REGIONS

Keeping this broader view of public policy in mind, we can now broach the central analytical question of this paper: What are the advantages or disadvantages of currency regions as seen from the point of view of a single sovereign state? For this purpose, we must focus on consequences: the potential *effects* of alternative configurations of monetary space. Only if we comprehend *how* the spatial organization of currency relations impacts on individual nations (or how it is *thought* to impact on nations) can we begin to understand *why* governments might prefer one policy choice over another. In currency relations no less than in other dimensions of international affairs, calculations of state interest may legitimately be assumed to follow logically from a more or less well-informed assessment of potential results.

As in OCA theory, analysis may be structured as a dichotomous comparison of two alternative policy choices: national monetary autonomy versus participation in a broader currency region. As compared with the assumed status quo of an insular national money, three types of results may be considered: effects on (a) aggregate economic welfare; (b) international politics; and (c) domestic distribution. Going beyond standard practice in OCA theory, however, each effect in turn will be viewed from not one but two perspectives: that of the home country—the state whose currency (the key currency) forms the basis for a region; and that of host countries—the states whose moneys' authoritative domains are correspondingly reduced. For home and host countries, calculations of state interest are in fact likely to be quite different.

Aggregate Economic Welfare

At the microeconomic level, the broad impact of a currency region is likely to be much the same as predicated in OCA theory for a common currency or equivalent. The wider the authoritative domain of the key currency, the greater will be the savings on transactions, information, and hedging costs. The usefulness of money will be improved for all participants, whether in home or host country.

Such a result is not surprising. Currency regions are largely driven by the forces of market competition, which can ordinarily be expected (ceteris paribus) to generate some measure of efficiency gains. Indeed, if left entirely to themselves, market forces might conceivably maximize micro-economic efficiency, thus achieving in practice what Robert Mundell and other early contributors to OCA theory set out to identify in principle: the economically most appropriate domain of a currency irrespective of existing national frontiers. Refocusing analysis on currency regions rather than areas, ironically, suggests that the first incarnation of OCA theory may not have been so naive after all.

At the macroeconomic level, the main impact of a currency region will be felt in the mechanism for balance-of-payments financing. Economists have long contrasted the relative ease of adjustment to interregional imbalances within countries with the frequently greater difficulties associated with payments adjustments between countries. One major difference, early theorists pointed out (Scitovsky 1958; Ingram 1959), appears to lie in the high volume of equilibrating capital flows within countries made possible by a large stock of "generalized" short-term financial claims that can be readily traded between surplus and deficit regions. The development of these generalized claims, in turn, has traditionally been attributed to the existence of a single national currency, which removes all exchange risks. Such reasoning, of course, is based on the conventional assumption of insularity in national moneys. But the same logic applies even if that assumption is relaxed to allow for the possibility of a broader currency region. The wider the authoritative domain of a given money, the greater will be the range for equilibrating capital flows as well, taking the form of purchases and sales of generalized claims denominated in the key currency. Other things being equal, these flows should reduce the collective cost of payments adjustment.

This result too is unsurprising, since it largely replicates another of the benefits of a common currency or equivalent mentioned in OCA theory: the savings that accrue from internalization through credit of what would otherwise be external payments transactions. But there is a crucial difference here that tends to be obscured by OCA theory's narrow state-centric approach. If currency space can be assumed to be shaped predominantly if not exclusively by national governments, then it is not unfair to conclude that all participating countries are apt to share in this benefit commensurately. The same is not true, however, when currency relations are shaped in larger part by market forces, which promote a hierarchy rather than a merger of national moneys. In this case, the home country will almost certainly gain disproportionately, to the extent that the area within which its currency can be used to finance imbalances is enlarged. Its macroeconomic flexibility is in effect enhanced. Host countries, by contrast, will find themselves less able to rely on equilibrating capital flows denominated in their own national moneys. Their room for maneuver will be effectively constricted. Thus costs of payments adjustment may indeed be reduced, but most if not all of the benefit is likely to go to just one participant, the home country.

The gain of macroeconomic flexibility for the home country may not be costless, of course. In principle, increased use of a national money abroad could actually lead to welfare losses insofar as it causes a shortage of currency at home (Matsuyama et al. 1993). Likewise, monetary policy could conceivably be pegged to a misleading target (since a large but indeterminate part of the currency supply is in circulation abroad) or be destabilized by unanticipated variations of foreign demand for domestic money. On balance, however, the advantage here would appear to outweigh disadvantages.

For host countries, on the other hand, implications are more ambiguous. What is the significance of the constriction of their policy flexibility? At least two contrasting viewpoints are possible, as illustrated by some past and current discussions of the Euro-dollar in international currency relations.[15] On one side is an early contribution of my own (1963), focusing on the emerging European Community (now European Union), which emphasized the disadvantages of widespread domestic use of a foreign currency. Already by the 1960s, I argued, the Euro-dollar had acquired some of the characteristics of a de facto common currency for the Europeans—"the informal common currency of the Common Market" (1963:613). In effect, the Community had become part of a currency region centered on the dollar. But because this meant reliance for financing on a supply of assets managed by the Federal Reserve rather than by their own central banks, it appeared that the effectiveness of national monetary policies was bound to be reduced. "The problem," I wrote, "is not one of geography but of sovereignty . . . . Because the borders of the area within which the Euro-dollar circulates do not coincide with the borders of the Common Market, efforts to control liquidity within the union must inevitably [be compromised]" (1963:614–15).

The other side is illustrated by a more recent contribution by financial consultant James Meigs (1993), focusing on the emerging states of East-Central Europe and the former Soviet Union, which takes a more sanguine view of the potential role of the Euro-dollar. For these countries, Meigs notes, the challenge has been not to preserve monetary stability but to create it. And what better way might there be, he asks, than to "hire" a foreign currency for the job? "Using Euro-dollars, without exchange controls, would greatly speed up the clearing of international trade and capital transactions. . . . Evolution of the new trading and payments system would be market-driven [and] would provide an automatic, nonpolitical system for grading the republics on their performance" (1993:716–17). Quite clearly, there are indeed circumstances in which a loss of monetary autonomy may well be regarded as a blessing rather than a curse.

International Politics

At first glance, the implications of a currency region for international politics would appear to be much the same as suggested by studies of monetary hegemony. Expansion of a currency's authoritative domain should be expected to translate directly into effective political power vis-à-vis host countries. In fact, the broad impact on relative capabilities in the global arena is likely to be quite different.

It is true, of course, that expanded cross-border use of a currency may, at least initially, offer the home country both greater insulation from outside influence and a potential means for coercing others. An apt, albeit extreme, example was provided recently by the United States in its relations toward Panama, a country that has long used the dollar for most domestic monetary purposes. As part of its campaign of opposition to the regime of General Manuel Noriega, the Reagan administration in 1988 both froze Panamanian bank deposits in the United States banks and halted exports of dollar currency to Panama. The resulting liquidity shortage in Panama contributed directly to the subsequent weakening of the Noriega government and eventually to its removal in 1990. In the laconic words of econ-omist Lawrence Klein:

> Panama . . . uses US dollars for its monetary units. As long as relations remain cor-dial, this is not a bad arrangement. . . . But for Panama the risk price is very high for having the convenience of US dollars. The small country would be in a better and more independent position if it had not let some of its monetary actions be governed by foreigners.   (1993:8)

Expanded cross-border use, as indicated earlier, also results in a real-resource gain for the home country—the equivalent of a subsidized or interest-free loan from foreigners—so long as the national money con-tinues to be held or circulate abroad. Economists refer to this dryly as "international seigniorage" (not to be confused with "domestic" seignior-age, the inflation tax). Journalists have more colorful ways to describe the phenomenon:

> The United States has an advantage few other countries enjoy: it prints green paper with George Washington's and Ben Franklin's and Thomas Jefferson's pictures on it. These pieces of green paper are called "dollars." Americans give this green paper to people around the world, and they give Americans in return automobiles, pasta, stereos, taxi rides, hotel rooms and all sorts of other goods and services. As long as these foreigners can be induced to hold those dollars, either in their mattresses, their banks, or in their own circulation, Americans have exchanged green paper for hard goods.   (Friedman 1994).

The key to all these benefits, plainly, is the willingness of foreigners to *persist* in holding the key currency or using it for international or foreign-domestic purposes. Unfortunately, the continued competitiveness of a cur-rency can never be guaranteed. As already suggested, latitude for the home government is apt to be greatest in the earliest stages of cross-border use, when its money is most popular. Later on, material gains as well as policy autonomy are likely to be steadily eroded by the accumulation of an over-hang of liquid liabilities. Equilibrating capital flows may continue to pro-vide an extra degree of macroeconomic flexibility to deal with transitory balance-of-payments problems. Over time, however, policy will be increas-ingly constrained by the need to discourage sudden or substantial conver-sions into other currencies. Ultimately, effective political power on balance may well be decreased rather than increased.

The interesting question is: Where does the power go? It certainly does not go to host governments, which also suffer an erosion of policy autonomy through loss of monopoly control of their effective money supply. The greater the competition from currencies originating abroad, the less will public officials be able to rely on seigniorage, when needed, to extract resources from the private sector at home. In effect, the base for levying an inflation tax is shrunk. This not only means a deceleration of fiscal revenue, which for countries with underdeveloped tax systems could be a particularly acute problem (Tavlas 1993:673). Unless budgetary deficits are reduced it could also mean an acceleration of inflationary pressures, since to finance the same level of expenditures policy-makers would now have to speed up the rate of domestic money creation. The result might be "a vicious cycle of ever increasing inflation" (Brand 1993:46) that could, in the end, be reversed only by a severe curtailment of public spending.

Worst of all, host governments would now be deprived of an emergency source of revenue to cope with unexpected contingencies—up to and including war. Domestic seigniorage has been described as the "revenue of last resort" for governments (Goodhart 1995:452): the single most flexible instrument of taxation available to mobilize resources in the event of a threat to national security. Loss of that instrument surely impairs a state's capabilities in the global arena.

So where does the power go? Quite clearly, it goes from the public sector in general—home and host governments alike—to the private sector; in other words, from state to society. The capabilities of policy makers everywhere are reduced: in the home country, by the burden of a currency overhang; in host countries, by the loss of a base for the inflation tax. The capabilities of market actors, in the aggregate, are correspondingly enhanced. Through the choices they make in the Darwinian struggle among currencies, private entities can exercise a degree of discipline over public policy that goes well beyond what would normally be tolerated in direct state-to-state relations (as the 1995 Mexican peso crisis amply demonstrated). This is what economists mean when they describe the impact of currency competition as a "market-enforced monetary reform" (Melvin 1988); Meigs had the same idea in mind in referring to "an automatic, nonpolitical system for grading [policy] performance" (1993:717). Market forces not only help to shape currency space; they also exercise enormous influence over how governments behave within existing monetary arrangements.

In effect, therefore, the impact of currency regions is to amplify the shift

in relative capabilities from states to markets that is now commonly associated with the increase of global capital mobility in recent decades (Cohen
1996). Few scholars today dispute the proposition that, as David Andrews
phrases it, "the degree of international capital mobility systematically con-
strains state behavior by rewarding some actions and punishing others"
(1994:193). As true as that proposition is, however, it underestimates how
deeply the discipline of the market truly penetrates into domestic political
economies. A focus on capital mobility highlights just a part of the story,
relating solely to cross-border use of alternative moneys for store-of-value
purposes.[16] In fact, international currency competition is far more extensive, involving all the standard functions of money and penetrating to the
very core of what is meant by national political sovereignty. A focus on currency regions makes clear that much more is involved here than a few narrowly defined economic policies. It is, indeed, a matter of the effectiveness
of government itself.

Domestic Distribution

The distributional implications of a currency region follow directly from
the preceding discussion. To the extent that governments are deprived of
the option of domestic seigniorage, society gains (or retains) resources at
the expense of the state.[17] And within society, the actors who gain most will
be those with the greatest ability to switch readily between local and foreign moneys—generally, though not exclusively, higher-income groups
who can best afford the costs of currency conversion. The base for levying
an inflation tax is therefore not only shrunk. Domestically inflation's
impact also tends, on balance, to become increasingly concentrated on the
poorest and least adaptable elements of society. Overall, as compared with
the assumed status quo of an insular national money, participation in a currency region is likely to result in a distinctly more regressive income distribution at home (Brand 1993:72).

The purpose of this chapter has been to extend standard OCA theory in
two critical respects—first, by focusing on regions (in the specialized sense
of the term proposed here) rather than the traditional notion of currency
areas, thus adding a market dimension to the determination of monetary
relations; and second, by incorporating noneconomic as well as economic
considerations into the policy calculations of governments, thus adding a

political dimension as well. Analysis suggests two main refinements in conventional calculations of state interests.

First, it is clear that the calculus of potential costs and benefits is quite different for the home country and host countries. For the home country, material gains may be anticipated from cost savings at the microeconomic level as well as from enhanced macroeconomic flexibility and, at least initially, a real-resource benefit from international seigniorage; and also political gains, particularly from the opportunities that a key currency may offer to exercise effective influence over others. There are manifest advantages to issuing a key currency. For host countries, on the other hand, significant benefits emerge only at the microeconomic level. In other respects, economic as well as political, host governments can expect to lose insofar as they find themselves deprived of a large degree of policy autonomy. Only in circumstances where monetary stability needs to be created rather than preserved might the impact of cross-border currency competition be regarded as more advantageous than disadvantageous.

And second, it is clear that the big winners are not governments at all, whether home or host, but rather the markets—in particular, higher-income groups within the private sector. For host governments, the discipline of the markets is evident from the start. And even for home governments, despite early gains, policy autonomy is likely to be eroded eventually by a growing overhang of foreign liabilities. To the extent that the spatial organization of currency relations is driven by market forces, a significant shift occurs in the balance of influence between political authority and society. As "spaces-of-flows," currency regions may be more difficult to visualize than "spaces-of-places." Their impact, however, is unmistakable.

Notes

1. For recent surveys of OCA theory, see Masson and Taylor (1993); Tavlas (1993, 1994).

2. The loss of macroeconomic flexibility matters, of course, only insofar as monetary-policy instruments (the money supply or exchange rate) can be assumed to have a sustained influence on real economic variables (output and employment). In effect, there must be some lasting trade-off between unemployment and inflation (technically, a negative slope to the Phillips curve). Many economists, inspired by so-called rational-expectations macroeconomic theory, dispute this essentially Keynesian view of the world, arguing to the contrary that there is no such trade-off (no slope to the Phillips curve): money is instead said to be neutral with respect

to real output, influencing only prices. In the "monetarist" view, the only benefit of an independent currency is an ability to chose one's own inflation rate. Empirical evidence, however, suggests that the monetary neutrality argument is valid, if at all, only in the relatively long term. Over periods of time relevant to public officials, monetary policy does retain importance: its surrender does represent a cost. For more, see Krugman (1993b:21); Tavlas (1993:669–73).

3. For more on currency internationalization, see Krugman (1992a:ch. 10); Black (1991, 1993). For more on currency substitution, see Giovannini and Turtelboom (1992); Calvo and Vegh (1992, 1993); Brand (1993); Mizen and Pentecost forthcoming.

4. For an early exception, see Cohen (1963). For a much more recent discussion, see Thygesen et al. (1995).

5. Conceptually, two types of currency substitution may be distinguished. One is the more-or-less symmetrical interchangeability of assets denominated in different national moneys characteristic of financial relations among industrial countries. Substitution in this sense may be viewed as integral to the process of global portfolio diversification and should more appropriately be regarded as a part of the phenomenon of currency internationalization—cross-border use of money as a store of value. It is what economists normally have in mind when they use the term "capital mobility." The other type of substitution, more characteristic of many developing nations, refers to the asymmetrical situation where local demand for desirable foreign currency is not matched by a counterpart demand from abroad for the less attractive domestic money. Though technically also a form of capital mobility, this phenomenon is probably better described by the term "capital flight." It is this type of asymmetry that is most commonly associated with the term currency substitution, and is the sense in which the term is used here. For more on the definition of currency substitution, see Giovannini and Turtelboom (1992:1–3); Brand (1993:1–4).

6. Streissler (1992); Guidotti and Rodriguez (1992). The reversal of Gresham's Law in conditions of high inflation has been labeled "Thiers' Law" by Bernholz (1989), after the nineteenth-century French historian Louis Thiers, who noted occurrence of the pattern at the time of the French Revolution.

7. This pattern of home-currency preference is variously labeled the symmetry theorem (Carse et al. 1980) or Grassman's rule (Bilson 1983).

8. The term "key currency" was originated by economist John Williams at the end of World War II. See, e.g., Williams (1947).

9. Kwan (1994:ch. 9); Taguchi (1994). But cf. Frankel (1993); Frankel and Wei (1994).

10. For some discussion and references, see Aglietta and Deusy-Fournier (1994); Thygesen et al. (1995).

11. Aglietta and Deusy-Fournier (1994); Thygesen et al. (1995). In fact, these two sources might be considered one, since the relevant texts are virtually identical and owe their composition to one single scholar, Pierre Deusy-Fournier, who was a co-author of both publications.

12. For more on the determinants of the organization of monetary space, see Cohen (1994).

13. But see Kirshner (1995).

14. The literature is summarized in Cohen (1971:ch. 2).

15. Euro-dollars, part of the broader worldwide Euro-currency market, are dollars deposited in and lent by banks outside the United States (or, within the United States, by

International Banking Facilities which operate technically outside the reach of domestic U.S. banking regulation).

16. See note 5.

17. Note that this applies to the home country as well as host countries. In the earliest stages of cross-border use, when the authoritative domain of the key currency is expanding, the scope for home-country exploitation of seigniorage opportunities is of course undoubtedly increased. (This is, indeed, the basis for the benefit of "international" seigniorage.) But once a substantial overhang of foreign liabilities develops, the home government too must worry about competition from other currencies and curb its appetite for the inflation tax accordingly.

FOUR

Industries, Governments, and Regional Trade Blocs

Helen Milner

Regional trade agreements have flourished since the early 1980s. During the past decade, the European Union (EU) has completed the Single Market Act and passed the Maastricht treaty on European Monetary Union (EMU). In North America, Canada, the United States, and Mexico have formed a regional free trade area (NAFTA); and the expansion of NAFTA to Central and South America has begun. In addition, countries in South America have already formed several free trade areas, Mercosur being the most important. Finally, both ASEAN and APEC have agreed to create free trade areas. The sources of these agreements are numerous and complex. Changing international balances of power, shifting domestic power relations between capital and labor, changes in ideology, the failure of past policies—all of these and more could be cited as causes of the resurgence of interest in regionalism. This chapter explores a different issue. It asks why these agreements, although all are free trade areas or customs unions, are shaped differently. Why is it that each looks different in terms of the amount of liberalization accorded each economic sector?

The central hypothesis of this chapter is that the character of these regional agreements reflects the rational responses of governments to their *domestic* political situations. Authors of other chapters in this volume also stress how the character of regional institutions varies, but they focus on different explanatory variables (Grieco this volume; Haggard this volume). In particular I argue that governments craft regional trade agreements in an attempt to balance consumer (and thus voter) interests and pressures from their private economic agents—e.g., firms in industry, finance, agriculture, services, etc. Firms with certain types of industrial structures prefer regional trade liberalization and thus they affect governments' calculations of their optimal trade policies. Under certain circumstances, political leaders seeking reelection then may pursue regionalism as a way to maximize their utility. Moreover, crafting an agreement that gives some sectors greater liberalization than others is eminently rational for governments, since not all firms will prefer liberalization; as Grossman and Helpman (1995) demonstrate, excluding some sectors from a free trade agreement may make it more feasible.

The puzzle motivating my research is the fact that regional agreements have treated different economic sectors differently. For instance, NAFTA treats the textile and apparel industry differently than the telecommunications one. Trade liberalization within a regional context is very substantial and rapid in the latter and much more moderate and gradual in the former. Why do these differences in outcomes across sectors exist within the same regional agreement? If governments are motivated by factors at the international level—say, current account balances, political alliances, the distribution of capabilities, etc.—one would not expect any *systematic* differentiation of regional trade liberalization by economic sectors. In addition, these regional agreements tend to violate GATT rules. GATT Article XXIV permits regional trade agreements as long as two conditions are met: external barriers are not raised in the wake of such agreements, and all sectors are fully liberalized in the regional agreement (Bhagwati 1993; Eichengreen and Frankel 1993: 24). Why then if regionalism is a response to international pressures, does it treat sectors so differently? Why do regional agreements violate these GATT norms of equal treatment?

If one could show that particular industries should be more favorable to regional trade liberalization than others and that these different preferences account for the actual sectoral differences within the agreements, then one could provide support for a domestic sectoral explanation of the shape of regional trade organizations. Thus I first develop an argument explaining why certain industries may be more interested in regional trade arrangements than others. I point out what factors characterizing industrial sectors would make them more favorable (or opposed) to regional arrangements. I explore why these type of industries would prefer regional trade liberalization to both protection of the domestic market and multilateral trade liberalization. I discuss why certain industries may view regionalism as a more profitable strategy than the other two policies.

Second, I link these industry preferences to political leaders' policy choices. The argument shows why, given that regionalism may be in various sectors' best interests, it may also be the best choice available to political leaders. Hence it explores the interaction between industry preferences and political leaders' decision making. Finally, the third step is to show why *mutual* trade barrier reduction is preferred. This involves looking at the interaction among countries. The claim is that countries agree to regional trade barrier reduction because they can trade scale economies across industries.

I then test my three-step argument on data from the NAFTA accord.[1] Initially, it presents an analysis of seven key sectors and how they were treated in the agreement in terms of all trade barriers. This analysis, while preferred since all forms of trade barriers are included, is limited since data could be gathered on only seven sectors. To obtain a wider sample of industries, I examined data on tariff reductions only in the NAFTA accord. Here I regress the tariff reductions on a series of independent variables measuring salient industry characteristics. The key question asked is do industries with the characteristics predicted by the model actually obtain greater liberalization than other types of industries within regional trade blocs.

I further use data on the NAFTA agreement to show that holding other factors constant, the sectors that were most liberalized were also those with particular characteristics making them most favorable to regional agreements, in particular economies of scale. This is only an indirect and preliminary test of the argument. It does not reveal the mechanism by which firm preferences are translated into policy outcomes. Nor does it show that these types of industries preferred regional over multilateral liberalization. But it does establish that there is sectoral variation within regional agreements and that this can be accounted for systematically by examining various industry characteristics.

The argument here is important because it helps us understand the potential consequences of the regionalization of trade. As certain types of industrial structures become more prevalent globally, firms in these sectors will increasingly *demand*, and states will be more willing to *supply*, regional trade arrangements. An implication of this claim is that these demand- and supply-side dynamics may distinguish the protectionist and trade-averse regionalism of the 1930s from the more recent regionalism embodied in the Single European Act (SEA) and the North American Free Trade Agreement (NAFTA). If regionalism acts as a substitute for multilateral trade liberalization, then it could result in greater closure and conflict in the international economy. If, however, it is a complement to, and\or precursor of, greater multilateral trade liberalization, then its consequences may be more benign (Kemp and Wan 1976; Bhagwati 1993; Eichengreen and Frankel 1994). The argument proposed here suggests this latter view of new regional agreements. It sees them as extensions of firms' attempts to compete in world markets and governments' responses to altered economic conditions. The regional organization of trade relations is thus the rational response of firms and governments who are faced with changed industrial structures.

THE LOGIC OF THE ARGUMENT

Step One: Increasing Returns to Scale (IRS) Industries and Their Demand for Regionalism

Why would firms ever be interested in regional trade liberalization? More interestingly, when would they prefer it to both multilateral trade liberalization or domestic protection? This is equivalent to asking when will their profits be maximized by a regional strategy. Using the new international trade theory, it is argued that firms with increasing returns to scale (IRS) should be the ones who pursue a regional strategy. For these types of firms, profit-maximization can be achieved by attaining optimal production levels within a regional market because of the economies of scale they possess.[2]

Much of the "new" theorizing on trade policy making has drawn on the themes of imperfect competition. For industries that are characterized by conditions that distinguish them from perfectly competitive ones, scholars have shown that free trade may not be optimal for the firms or the countries (Brander and Spencer 1985; Helpman and Krugman 1985; Krugman 1984; Eaton and Grossman 1986; Helpman 1984; Venables 1985). Standard economic analysis demonstrates that for firms in perfectly competitive markets, the welfare-maximizing outcome is free trade globally. Moreover, even when markets are not perfect, much traditional analysis shows that trade barriers are at best a second- or third-best solution (Corden 1974; Bhagwati 1971). Recent work on imperfect markets, however, has challenged this conventional wisdom.

One type of market imperfection of importance is the existence of scale economies.[3] Economies of scale imply that firms face declining *marginal* costs as they increase their output. In this situation the cost of producing another unit of the good declines as production becomes more efficient with scale. Economies of scale can also arise if firms face very large fixed costs which they must undertake prior to beginning production (Krugman 1979). These fixed costs mean that the *average* cost of producing goods falls with each unit produced. That is, one can double the amount of output without doubling the amount of inputs. Hence there are declining average costs, not constant or rising ones. Increasing returns to scale, rather than the common assumption of constant ones, characterize both of these types of industries. Because of these scale economies, the industry will not be exposed to perfect competition. Scale economies create a situation where the optimal number of firms in an industry may be small, or in the extreme only a single firm (a "natural monopoly").[4] In these industries achieving the optimal scale is essential to maximizing profits, and hence having only a few firms that have very large outputs may be most efficient. Having a larger number of firms producing smaller quantities each will be both inefficient and fail to maximize profits, since the firms will not be able to travel down their cost curves to the minimum. Hence the market structure in these industries will tend to be oligopolistic or monopolistic (Chamberlin 1962; Dixit and Stiglitz 1977) .

These types of firms also gain scale economies by concentrating their production in a single location, and tend to locate near their largest market in order to minimize transportation costs. Thus, if two states have similar preferences and factor endowments and no trade barriers, the state with relatively greater demand may emerge as a net exporter of the product in question (Krugman 1990a:30–35). Moreover, direct foreign investment for them is often a second-best strategy since each plant requires a high fixed investment cost which may not be profitable given the size of the market. Firms with scale economies would rather export from existing plants to attain optimal scale than invest abroad.

In industries with economies of scale, some scholars have argued that protectionism might be the best policy for the firm and its home country. In one form of the argument, the claim is that for firms with scale economies import protection may be the optimal policy because such protection serves as export promotion. This can be labelled the Import Protection as Export Promotion (IPEP) argument (Krugman 1984; Brander and Spencer 1984; Dixit 1984; Venables 1985). The logic behind this argument is that when markets are protected a firm with scale economies can capture a larger percentage, or even all, of the home market. This allows it to move down its cost curve, becoming more efficient and reaping higher profits. In addition, this may allow it to become an exporter. The increased home production may also make it competitive in foreign markets. Gaining access to these markets will further drive down its costs, assuming it has not reached efficient scale yet, and will further enhance its profits. The externalities associated with this enhanced production may make protection beneficial for the entire nation. Protection maximizes social welfare in this setting.

This IPEP argument leads to the conclusion that both firms with scale economies and governments should prefer to protect their markets rather than open them to trade.[5] The argument here is different. Altering several assumptions upon which the IPEP claim rests, it shows that such firms may actually prefer regional liberalization to either protection of the home market or global liberalization. Their profits will be greater under regionalism than under either protection or multilateral trade liberalization.[6] What is argued is that, given a protected home market, firms with increasing returns to scale can reap higher profits by moving to a regional trade bloc than they can from either continued protection or multilateral trade liberalization.[7]

The argument about IRS firm profits being maximized by regional liberalization flows from the theory of custom unions. A customs union occurs when two or more countries abolish trade barriers among themselves and adopt a common external tariff (CET) vis-à-vis third countries.[8] Two aspects of this analysis concern us: first, the effect of customs unions on firm profits and second, their effect on consumer surplus. In the static analysis of customs unions (CU), economists have shown that their welfare effects may be ambiguous. Assuming that consumer surplus[9] is one element of a measure of welfare, customs unions can be either beneficial or detrimental depending on the balance between two forces. Viner's (1950) path-breaking analysis demonstrated that customs unions produce two opposing effects: trade creation and trade diversion. Trade creation occurs when the lowering of trade barriers among the partners stimulates new trade flows within the union which otherwise would not have occurred. Trade diversion occurs when the lowering of trade barriers among the partners eliminates trade that occurred previously with lower cost nonpartners. Diversion occurs when nonpartner imports are forced out of the CU market as liberalization within the union replaces them with partner imports. The balance between these two forces establishes whether a CU is beneficial. If trade creation dominates, then consumer surplus is on net enhanced and the CU is beneficial. The less countries raise barriers to third party trade when a union is formed, the more likely the CU is to be trade-creating on balance.

In perfectly competitive markets, all the gains from trade liberalization whether regional or not are reaped by consumers. The costs of liberalization are borne by firms which must give up their protectionist rents and the government which must give up its tariff revenues.[10] The gains of consumers may, of course, be redistributed by the government to other actors. The problem for the theory of custom unions is that when markets are perfectly competitive there is no *economic* rationale for CU. That is, a country can always do as well or better economically by unilateral trade barrier reduction as by creating a preferential trading area. As Pomfret (1989) and others have noted, only when markets are not perfect can one make a convincing economic case for why a country or a firm would ever be interested economically in a CU.

In imperfectly competitive markets, the effects of trade liberalization may be different from the standard analysis. As will be argued, under certain conditions firms may actually benefit when barriers are lowered. The analysis used here follows Corden's (1972) and Pearson and Ingram's (1980) discussion of customs unions in the presence of increasing returns industries.

When increasing returns are present, Corden has shown that to understand a CU one must add two effects to the standard analysis. In addition to trade creation and diversion, Corden puts forth the idea of cost-reduction effects. He also notes that one must add an account of both the production and the consumption effects that trade creation, diversion, and cost reduction produce.[11] *Cost reduction* refers to gains that come from realizing economies of scale in a CU. Imagine that countries A and B both produce a good X whose production is subject to IRS and which they protect. They decide to enter a preferential trade agreement. In this case, it is likely that one country's industry , say A's, will be more efficient and will take over all or part of the others market for X. The cost-reduction effect refers to the lower price and higher quantity of good X that is produced by country A. The industry in A replaces higher priced domestic production in country B, thus moving down its cost curve and gaining even higher scale economies. There is a production effect as the industry in A producing at lower prices elicits greater demand and thus produces more in both A and B. There is also a consumption effect as the extra production in B is achieved at a lower price. The second effect noted by Corden is the *trade suppression* one. Assume that B does not produce X domestically but imports it from a third country. Now in the presence of a CU, A's industry captures B's market, driving the third country's imports of X out. This is trade suppression.

Hence when moving from a protected domestic market to a preferential trade arrangement, firms with IRS may benefit. Both trade suppression and cost reduction may increase an IRS firm's profits. Three mechanisms can lead to this outcome. First, trade suppression may act just like trade diversion in the case of perfect competition to increase the profits of the industry in country A, even though it lowers prices in both markets. Krishna (1993) shows how under imperfect competition but constant returns to scale firms can increase their profits through bilateral versus multilateral trade agreements. Moreover, his analysis shows that the bilateral situation may be preferred to the multilateral one under such conditions. Extending this analysis to a situation of increasing returns to scale makes the conclusions easier to derive, since the firm's average costs will now also decline. As Haggard also points out in chapter 2 of this book, gains from trade diversion and suppression may tempt firms to demand regional FTAs.

Second, cost reduction when combined with product differentiation may allow IRS firms in both countries to increase their profits. Assume that before the CU was formed the countries had in place their optimal tariffs and each country had one firm producing a differentiated good.[12] The logic is that when trade barriers are lowered among the regional partners, for good X produced by country A's firm, it will face lower prices at home, but it more than makes up for this by the increased quantity it produces in both A's and B's markets.[13] Prices may fall but this increases demand and thus the firm produces increased quantity in both A's and B's markets, which thus reduce its costs further. Because the industry is not perfectly competitive, the firm is able to reap a surplus.[14]

What happens to firm profits in country A under multilateral trade liberalization? The results of multilateral liberalization depend on two factors: one is whether the firm in A is the only producer globally of the differentiated good and two, whether its economies of scale are still unexploited at the global level. If the firm in country A is not the only producer, then opening its market globally will lower prices, expand demand but may or may not increase its quantity sold. If imports from a third country are lower cost, they will enter the market in A and B. Hence firm profits may not rise in this case since quantity sold may not increase, or may even decrease. Also if the firm in A has economies of scale that are exhausted by a market somewhat larger than the national one but not very much larger, then even if it is the lowest cost producer it will not gain as much from global trade liberalization as it could from a regional agreement.[15]

Hence two factors are very important for understanding when the existence of increasing returns to scale will allow firms to reap higher profits in the presence of a regional trade agreement than with domestic protection or global liberalization. Both the size and extent of scale economies matter. If scale economies are very large so that marginal or average costs drops greatly as quantity produced rises, then profits will respond even more as the market expands.

Also the extent of the scale economies matters. Most economists assume that economies of scale are not infinite; that is, at some point increasing returns are fully exploited and the marginal or average costs of production begin to rise again. At some level of production firms may simply grow too large to be efficient, for example. If we did not assume this, then the number of firms in the industry globally should be one. This seems unreasonable. It is argued here that scale economies are significant but limited in range; increasing returns exist for a large amount of production but at some point returns begin to decrease.

The other side of this proposition concerns the size of the home market. It is the ratio of the size of the home market to the most efficient scale of production that matters. *If the home market is large, ceteris paribus, the pursuit of scale economies through regional agreements will be less important for firms since they may be close to efficient scale already.* The smaller the home market then, the more scale economies a firm should have unexploited and the more firm profits should rise under a customs union. Casella (1995) argues similarly for the effect that enlargement of a trade bloc has on small versus large countries under conditions of increasing returns to scale. This implies, for example, that in NAFTA Mexican and Canadian firms with IRS should be more interested (because they benefit more) in the agreement than are American firms.[16]

Third, in the general case of undifferentiated goods, IRS firms in countries A and B may gain from a CU in terms of cost reduction vis-à-vis third country (nonpartner) markets. If both countries have one firm producing a good before the CU, then after it is enacted prices will fall in both markets, demand will increase in the partner countries, and average cost will fall as production rises. In their own markets, the firms will be pitted against one another, and one or both may experience reduced profits. But the reduction in cost may allow them to expand or initiate exports to third country markets, thus displacing production by nonpartner firms in these third country markets. This third country effect may make the CU profitable overall for each firm in country A and B. Obviously, if trade were liberalized on a multilateral basis in this situation, then the third country firms would benefit from access to countries A and B's markets and the firms in countries A and B would receive no cost reduction effect relative to the nonpartner countries' firms. Imagine, for instance, that US firms care most about their worldwide competition with Japanese firms. NAFTA then may make sense for them since the enlarged "home" market it provides may drive them down their cost curves and allow them to gain market share not only in Japan but also in other non-NAFTA markets (via exports that displace Japanese production).

This section thus has shown that for three reasons a firm in an industry with scale economies may be able to reap higher profits from a regional trade liberalization than from either remaining protected at home or pursuing global trade liberalization. Because of this, these types of firms will prefer and advocate regional trade liberalization. These firms will lobby their governments for such agreements. Firms lacking scale economies should have different preferences. Firms with constant returns to scale (CRS) will tend to advocate either domestic protection or multilateral liberalization, depending on their ties to the international economy. If they are solely import-competing, they should desire the former; if they are export-oriented, they should prefer the latter (Milner 1988; Trefler 1993). Firm preferences are not the whole story, though. Governments make trade policies and negotiate regional or multilateral trade agreements. Hence we must look at what would motivate a government to undertake such a policy as well.

Step Two: Political Leaders' Trade Policy Preferences

In this model, governments make the ultimate choices about what shape a regional trade agreement should take. Thus one must examine their preferences. Under what circumstances, will they desire liberalization in a regional context? In this model, political leaders are utility-maximizers, who desire to remain in power most of all. Their utility comes from remaining in office, not from pursuing a particular trade policy. Their trade policy preferences are thus derived from their utility-maximizing position. They choose the trade policy that they believe will give them the highest probability of remaining in office. Can we show that their utility is under certain circumstances higher with a regional agreement than without one?

Political leaders' primary motivation is to remain in office; their policy choices reflect this motivation. Three factors help political leaders get reelected: consumer surplus, firm profits, and tariff revenues (Baldwin 1987; Grossman and Helpman 1994). Political leaders thus want to adopt trade policies that optimize their utility from each of these three factors. They should thus create regional agreements that reflect their domestic constraints; that is, they offer protection and liberalization to industries regionally to optimize the three components of their utility.

First, they depend on the public voting for them. In turn, voters in the leaders' eyes care about their economic situation. In terms of trade policy, leaders can improve the chances that the public will vote for them by generating greater consumer surplus. Consumer surplus is a gain in income for the voting public. More consumer surplus is in the eyes of political leaders better for obtaining votes than is less consumer surplus.

Returning to custom union theory, we can show how consumer surplus is affected by a regional agreement. Relative to a protected home market and multilateral trade liberalization, how does a CU fare in terms of consumer surplus? Economists have shown that multilateral trade liberalization generates at least as great or greater consumer surplus than does a CU. The reason is simply because trade diversion does not occur in a multilateral setting; hence consumer surplus must be as great or greater than in a CU.[17] Protection is, of course, the worst of the three alternatives from a consumer's point of view. Hence in democracies we would rarely expect to see political leaders giving protection to all sectors of the economy. This ranking of outcomes is important because consumer surplus affects political leaders' policy choices.

Second, political leaders have to worry about special interests. These special interests are important for they can help political leaders retain office by providing campaign contributions, getting out the vote, etc. Without this aid, leaders would have difficulty running their campaigns and getting reelected. In trade policy one key group of special interests are firms. Maximizing firm profits may be related to maximizing leaders' ability to retain office. Hence leaders may face a trade-off in trying to maximize their utility in trade policy. If the policies preferred by firms lead to reductions in consumer surplus, then leaders face a dilemma. For example, to the extent that firms prefer protectionism, political leaders will be confronted with pressures to sacrifice consumer surplus. Benefits for the general public—i.e., consumer surplus—may be expended appeasing special interests. But firms do not always prefer protection. As argued above, export-oriented firms and IRS ones may be very interested in freer trade.

In this case, political leaders are not caught in a trade-off situation. They can maximize consumer surplus and firm profits by opening markets. What political leaders will thus do is try to find the optimal balance between promoting special interests—i.e., firm profits—and maximizing public welfare—i.e., consumer surplus. They will craft trade agreements to realize this optimal combination.

Finally, political leaders care about tariff revenues. These are just another source of government revenue which can be redistributed to special interests or to the public and thus garner votes. Given the prevalence of non-tariff barriers which do not generate government revenues, one might question the utility of including this variable. In most developed countries where tariffs are low, tariff revenues are no longer a significant part of the government budget, but for some developing countries they still are.[18] To keep the model general then, tariff revenues are included. Moreover in the case of NAFTA, the loss of tariff revenues actually played an important role in American debates over the agreement. Because of the budget deficit agreement, the executive branch had to make up any tariff revenues lost in NAFTA through other means, and this posed problems for American political leaders.

Political leaders' utility can be seen as a function of three factors: consumer surplus, firm profits, and tariff revenues.[19] Optimizing each of these elements maximizes leaders' chances of remaining in office. Governments' decisions about trade policy will then reflect how different policy choices affect these three elements. Above it was shown that one term in leaders' utility—IRS firms' profits—may well be higher under regional liberalization than under domestic protection or global liberalization. If firm profits in increasing returns industries are highest under regional liberalization, then they will be a positive factor in leaders' decisions for regionalism. Political leaders should craft the regional agreement so that these IRS sectors realize the greatest amount of liberalization among all sectors. CRS industries, on the other hand, will be less benefited by regional liberalization and thus political leaders should seek to exempt them from such liberalization. The discussion of the theory of CU points out that consumer surplus will be greatest under global liberalization and least under domestic protection. In a regional trade agreement, consumer surplus can be greater than under domestic protection, but it will never exceed that under global liberalization. Hence for the second term in leaders' utility functions, we can show that regionalism is at least as good as protection. Finally, tariff revenues are more likely to be maximized under protection and minimized under multilateral trade liberalization.[20]

We can rank the payoffs leaders obtain from the three different possible policies in terms of their utility functions:

With a protected home market, $U_p = f(S_p, \pi_p, t_p)$

where S is consumer surplus, π is firm profits, and t is tariff revenues.

With a regional trade agreement, $U_R = g(S_R, \pi_R, t_R)$.

With a multilateral trade accord, $U_W = h(S_W, \pi_W, t_W)$.

Under most conditions, tariff revenues will be largest under a protected home market and least with multilateral trade liberalization, so $t_p > t_R > t_W$.[21] Firm profits in an IRS industry should be highest under a regional agreement and lowest under a multilateral one: $\pi_R > \pi_p > \pi_W$. If other sectors (i.e., non-IRS ones) are exempted from regional liberalization, then firm profits overall can be maximized. Finally, consumer surplus is greatest under multilateral trade liberalization and least under a protected home market; regional trade liberalization can produce a surplus somewhere between these two. Hence $S_W > S_R > S_p$. Thus firm profits for IRS industries will be highest in a regional context; consumer surplus for the regional agreement will be somewhere between that of the two other options; and tariff revenues should also be between those of the multilateral and the protectionist outcomes.

When debating among these three options, political leaders thus face several trade-offs. Multilateral trade liberalization, as in the GATT rounds, maximizes consumer surplus but will lower IRS firm profits and tariff revenues for governments. Protection, on the other hand, may hurt consumer surplus most but it may maximize tariff revenues and aid some firms' profits. Regionalism maximizes IRS firm profits, while lowering to some extent tariff revenues and maybe consumer surplus. *Regional liberalization targeting IRS industries can represent a middle way, which sacrifices less in consumer surplus and tariff revenues than the other two options, while emphasizing IRS firm profits.*

The central question is what type of regional liberalization will maximize the value of a political leader's utility function. Under what conditions, will political leaders pursue regional trade liberalization? There would seem to be at least four conditions:

developed countries

1. *When existing tariff levels are low,* then trade diversion in a regional agreement is likely to be minimal. The difference between consumer surplus under regionalism and multilateral liberalization may then be very small. Also in this situation the loss of tariff revenues for governments will be very small when any liberalization is achieved. In addition, as noted above, both IRS firms in undifferentiated goods markets may gain in the regional case when initial barriers are lower. On the other hand, when barriers are lower, trade diversion or suppression will be lower, making these less important sources of profitability for IRS firms. Hence regionalism may be preferred by leaders since it leads to a bigger gain in firm profits than the losses in tariff revenues or consumer surplus.

2. *Of course, the more important scale economies are to firms,* the greater the increase in firm profits from regionalism and hence, ceteris paribus, the more motivation for leaders to choose regionalism. Thus one would expect industries exhibiting substantial economies of scale to be more interested in regional trade agreements, while constant returns to scale industries would prefer either protection or multilateral free trade depending on their competitiveness.

3. *When political leaders can craft regional agreements that treat sectors differently,* they will be more likely to pursue a regional option. Their utility will be maximized if they can liberalize some industries (IRS ones), while not liberalizing others.

4. *The smaller the size of the home market relative to the optimal scale of production,* the more profits IRS firms will make under regionalism and ceteris paribus the more political leaders will prefer regionalism. Hence leaders in countries with relatively small home markets, low trade barriers, and extensive IRS industries will be most interested in regionalism and will try to negotiate agreements that differentiate among sectors, with IRS ones realizing the lion's share of liberalization. This is their utility maximizing strategy.

Step Three: Mutual Tariff Reductions in a Regional Agreement.

If under certain circumstances regional trade liberalization is a government's most preferred alternative, why don't we see countries unilaterally lowering their barriers within a region? After all the unilateral extension of trade preferences is a possibility. What leads to the *mutual* exchange of preferential trade arrangements in a region? Unilateral liberalization may be less politically advantageous than mutual, bilateral liberalization. Political leaders can maximize their utility by trading access to IRS industries across the countries. Gains from trade diversion and increased competitiveness in third country markets may allow firms in the same industries in both countries to increase their profits, and hence support a regional CU. Even where such gains are not possible, in industries with differentiated products, this swapping of markets across countries may be possible at low political cost. Firms in the same industry in different countries may simply readjust their production from one line of the product to another, rather than going out of business, as a result of the CU.

On the supply side, governments are more likely to negotiate regional trade arrangements if the potential member states have a significant number of such IRS industries. The logic is that regionalism essentially involves *trading scale economies* with other states. As Vousden (1990:244) has pointed out, regional agreements may come about because there are "Additional gains (in the form of rents conceded by a country's union partner) from bilateral tariff swapping when compared with unilateral tariff reduction." This "market swapping" suggests that the greater the number of such industries among potential members of the regional bloc, the more likely states are to be able to agree on regional trade arrangements.

> It is possible that the two countries may agree to form a [customs] union if [country] B also has a decreasing cost industry which can expand its sales to [country] A when tariffs are removed. This would be the case, for example, if there is intra-industry trade in differentiated products; however, it is a possibility in any situation in which both union partners have potential export industries exhibiting economies of scale. Then, whether a particular country elected to join the union would depend on whether the increase in its rents from exporting to its partner was sufficient to offset the loss of tariff revenue on its (diverted) imports. (Vousden 1990:245–46)

Exchanging market access is the crucial aspect of this game. In our model above, both countries begin producing the good behind their optimal tariff walls. A CU then leads to one country 's firms taking over the entire market for the differentiated good in the union, forcing the other country's firms out of that line of business. Thus one might expect a more nuanced relationship between scale economies and trade liberalization. Certainly those firms that believe that they will take over the regional market should favor the most liberalization. Those firms that are IRS but uncertain of their fate in a regional market may well be more reluctant about liberalization. Indeed those IRS industries facing strong competitive pressures before any CU is signed may be less disposed toward it. Nonetheless, the industries with IRS and competitive products should be strong proponents of the CU.

Thus the existence of complementary industries with IRS among the union partners is important.[22] All the states can gain from a regional agreement if they trade access to these industries as long as each has some industries with scale economies that will benefit. As Pearson and Ingram note:

> Economies of scale and domestic divergences [such as imperfect competition] offer an important scope for gains from industrial integration. . . . In this context, swapping of industries is *politically* practical and negotiable provided that both prospective partners can retain and expand some industrial production. Hence, emphasis on *production* effects of economic integration is crucial since either country could always achieve consumption gains by simply [unilaterally] reducing protection of inefficient industries.   (1980:1006–7, emphasis added)

Can this explain the interest of "small" countries like Mexico and Canada in the creation of such regional markets?[23] In IRS industries located in countries with "small" home markets, opening regional markets may allow those industries to gain advantages and maybe dominate the entire regional market in their differentiated good. In the absence of a regional agreement, they would be forced to produce at higher marginal or average cost since they could not exploit their economies of scale. For small countries, access to a regional market may allow them to more fully exploit the economies of scale in their industries. For large countries, the same industries may be much nearer optimal scale within the domestic market and thus less interested in regionalism.

This may help explain why small countries overwhelmingly support, if not provide the initiative for, regional trade agreements. For instance, Canada and Mexico were responsible for initiating NAFTA; and small countries like Benelux were prime movers in the SEA. This hypothesis contrasts with argument that small countries just want to ensure that large, nearby markets remain open; in other words, that all they do is worry about rising protectionism in large markets such as the United States. This more defensive argument is supplemented by the more "offensive" one presented here.

For instance, assume Canada has a competitive telecommunications firm or industry; that this industry demonstrates large scale economies and that the Canadian market alone is too small to achieve efficient scale. If the U.S. market is closed to Canadian exports, then the Canadian firms have the option of trying to locate in the United States if they desire to gain the advantages of the large U.S. market. But IRS firms will find DFI very costly (and probably unprofitable). If they locate in both the United States and Canada, then they may be operating at even more inefficient levels. Thus gaining access to the American market so that the Canadian firms can continue to produce in their home market but also begin exporting to the large U.S. market and other countries as their costs decline may be the best solution for both the Canadian firms and the Canadian government. The ratio of the extent of economies of scale to the size of the domestic market is the crucial factor here in motivating firms' interests in regionalism. One implication then is that IRS firms in "small" countries may be more interested in creating regional markets than those in "larger" countries.

If one assumed that the industry with IRS was producing a homogeneous product, trade liberalization in the CU would lead to the entire loss of the industry in one partner country. But if, as is more realistic, the industry produced differentiated goods, then the governments would not be trading entire industries but rather parts of industries. For instance, if aircraft production were highly differentiated, then firm A in country X after opening might produce short-range aircraft while firm B in country Y would produce long-range ones. This exchange would involve trading access to various sectors within an industry (intraindustry), rather than the whole industry (interindustry). Given the prevalence of intraindustry trade among the developed countries, this seems to be a reasonable assumption (Grubel and Lloyd 1975).

The key point, however, is that governments will be interested in regionalism when they each have IRS industries which can trade access to each other's markets. Trading access to different IRS industries will make regionalism a *politically* feasible policy.

Some Alternative Arguments

There are a few arguments that explain the shape of regional trade liberalization. Perhaps two stand out—one political and one economic.[24] On the political side, Gowa (1994), Gowa and Mansfield (1993), and Mansfield and Bronson (1994) have shown that preferential trade areas are more likely among countries that are political allies. They claim that trade creates gains that countries do not want to share with their enemies, actual or potential. This argument would suggest which countries should cooperate to organize regional trade areas. It would also suggest that the changing of political alliances should lead to the changing of regional trade partners. They, however, do not attempt to explain either when allies will form regional trade areas or what those regional agreements will look like. This argument is not that helpful in explaining either NAFTA or the SEA. The United States, Mexico, and Canada have been allies for most of the twentieth century and before. Why Mexico and Canada just now changed their policies toward the United States is unexplained. The end the cold war, in fact, would seem to imply that there might be less cooperation among these one-time anti-Communist allies. The situation in Europe is the same. Why did the Single Market come about in the mid-1980s? Most of the EU countries had been allies against the Soviet Union for about forty years. Again the end of the cold war seems to suggest less impetus for regional trade cooperation in the 1980s than before among these countries.

The second argument is one made by Grossman and Helpman (1995). They argue that regional trade areas will form under three different conditions. First, if the FTA must completely liberalize trade in all sectors, then governments will agree to them only under two conditions: 1) when the aggregate gains for consumers from the agreement are very large and industries are unable to cooperate in their opposition to it; and 2) when the agreement creates higher gains for exporters than it does losses for import-competing industries and for consumers. This is the case only when all sectors are completely liberalized by the agreement.

The third condition that makes regional trade cooperation possible is when governments can "exclude" certain sectors from complete liberalization, i.e., that they can treat sectors differently. In this case, their main conclusion is that "Each government would wish to exclude from the agreement those sectors whose inclusion would impose on it the greatest political costs. Political costs reflect either the fierce opposition of the import-competing interests or the harm that would be suffered by the average voter in the face of inefficient trade diversion" (1995:687). This means that "exclusions are granted to industries for which a weighted sum of the political benefit of market access in the exporting country and the (possible) political cost of more intense import competition in the importing country is most negative. Both the political benefit and the political cost are measured by a weighted sum of the change in industry profits and the change in average welfare in going from the status quo to bilateral free trade" (1995:687). These costs and benefits depend on the balance between export and import-competing industries in each country, on the organizational capabilities of the two groups, and on their relative campaign contributions. This argument is potentially interesting and in the next section we will examine some variables that might capture these political characteristics of each industry.

TESTING THE ARGUMENT: THE HYPOTHESES, VARIABLES, DATA, AND FINDINGS

The argument here suggests that there should be systematic differences in the trade barrier reductions achieved by different industries in regional trade agreements. Industries with substantial scale economies should be more interested in and likely to obtain regional trade liberalization. Note that this hypothesis contrasts directly with the argument of Froot and Yoffie (1991). They argue that IRS industries will favor protection over regionalism.

Two points stand out about U.S.–Mexican and U.S.–Canadian trade. First, tariff barriers among the countries were by the mid-1980s quite low. U.S. and Canadian barriers had been progressively lowered through the GATT negotiations, and Mexico began a unilateral liberalization program in the early 1980s, which was then accelerated later by its accession to the GATT. Hence while Mexico had the largest barriers, even these were down to less than 10 percent by the mid-1980s. In terms of the argument above this suggests that a CU should pose fewer tradeoffs for the governments. Tariff revenues would be less affected, and trade diversion relative to a multilateral agreement would be less.

Second, intraindustry trade among the three countries is very substantial. Despite the fact that Mexico is a developing country, intraindustry trade with both Canada and the United States has been very significant. For example, three of the five most important commodities traded between Mexico and the United States in 1994 were the same. U.S. exports to Mexico and imports from there were largest for electrical machinery and vehicles, with telecommunications equipment in third or fourth place (*NYT*, Feb. 14, 1995:D-1). High levels of intraindustry trade suggest that firms were producing differentiated goods. Hence trading scale economies across such differentiated sectors among the countries was very possible.

IRS firms in each could specialize in a different line of production of the same goods. Politically, this structure lowers the cost of trade liberalization for governments.

As a preliminary test for the hypothesis, I examine seven industries that have been singled out by Hufbauer and Schott (1992, 1993) in their two studies of the NAFTA agreement—one pre-NAFTA and one post-NAFTA, assessing its results. The dependent variable is coded by evaluating the extent of all trade barrier reduction achieved for the industry. The measure includes a qualitative assessment of how all barriers to trade within the industry were treated. It also weights these reductions by their time frame of implementation. That is, an industry whose tariffs were lowered 50 percent over one year in the agreement would be coded as more liberalized than one whose tariffs were lowered 50 percent over fifteen years. A scale indicating the degree of liberalization (restriction) is then the dependent variable; see the appendix for the construction of this ranking.

For this subset of industries, a measure of the independent variable was also constructed. This variable was based on the work of Robert Hall (1988a, 1988b), who has estimated an index of returns to scale for a variety of industries. Using his work, we can see that for the seven industries examined, there appears to be a fairly strong correlation between scale and trade barrier reduction in NAFTA. Table 4.1 shows the industries and their values on these two variables. The correlation between these two variables is 0.83 ($p=.022$). Therefore, there seems to be some preliminary evidence that industries exhibiting scale economies received greater trade liberalization in the NAFTA accord.

In a more systematic but limited analysis, I examine 4-digit SIC industries in the United States and see how much liberalization they realized in the NAFTA accord. This analysis has at least two obvious limitations. Given the argument above, I expect the weakest relationship between scale economies and regional trade liberalization for American industries. Since the American market is so large, firms there should be much nearer optimal scale than are Canadian and Mexican ones. If I constructed the same model for these smaller countries' industries (which I hope to do in the future), they should demonstrate a stronger connection between scale and regional trade liberalization.

The second problem relates to the dependent variable. While a multiple regression technique allows us to hold other factors constant and survey a wide range of American industry, it is limited however since only data on *tariff* reductions could be examined. In the NAFTA agreement,

TABLE 4.1

Industry	Index of scale economies[a]	Trade barrier reduction
Telecommunications	2.237	7
Automobiles	2.261	6
Financial services	2.830	5
Transport equipment	2.261	4
Textiles and apparel	1.07	3
Agricultural products	0.0	2
Energy	−3.236	1

[a] This measure comes from Hall (1988a), table 4 and 5, the third column indicating "the reciprocal of the estimate." The greater the number, the higher the scale economies present in the industry. He has no estimate for agriculture, but it is usually assumed to have very insignificant economies of scale. The estimate for financial services comes from the more aggregate information in table 4.4.

much of the liberalization involved nontariff barriers, and these are not captured here. The dependent variable then is the degree of tariff liberalization among American industries in the regional trade agreement.[25] The predicted post-NAFTA tariff rates are our central focus; the dependent variable, DIFFTAR, measures the percentage change in tariffs from 1991 to 1998 due to NAFTA. The test used is similar to most endogenous trade policy arguments. It is a cross-sectional model using industry characteristics as its right-hand side variables. There is an extensive literature using this approach (e.g., Caves 1976; Baldwin 1985; Lavergne 1983; Ray 1981; Trefler 1993). The key independent variable for this study is that indicating the industry's extent of scale economies. Measures of this variable are problematic (Scherer 1974; McGee 1974). Here we use Caves' measure of minimum efficient scale, MEPS, as presented in Trefler (1993). We include two terms to capture this variable. The measure of minimum efficient scale, MEPS, should be positively related to regional liberalization. In turn, the interaction term of scale and import penetration, MEPS2, should be negatively related to the change in tariffs. This interaction term catches the fact that those IRS industries which lack competitiveness prior to the CU (and hence face high levels of import competition) are going to be far more hesitant about the CU than are the more competitive ones.

In addition to scale economies, several other factors are included in the regression. As earlier endogenous trade policy studies claimed, Grossman and Helpman (1995) also suggest that in addition to the industry's external orientation, political characteristics will be important. Hence the regression includes export-orientation and import penetration to reveal the industry's external orientation and thus its preferences toward trade policy. Several other variables that capture the industry's economic condition are included. It is anticipated that past levels of tariff protection should make industries less desirous of any liberalization. Hence the tariff in 1991 should be negatively related to the degree of liberalization. Using this variable also lets us hold constant the initial level of tariffs while examining the effects of the other variables. This implies that industries that begin with a higher level of protection should realize less liberalization in NAFTA, all other factors held constant. The industry's degree of capital stock can be used to measure the extent of its barriers to entry. The higher the stock, the greater the barriers and the less the need for protection. Thus capital stock should also be positively related to liberalization. The percent of scientists and engineers relative to total employment can be used as a proxy for human capital intensity; it should also be positively related to liberalization. In addition, the change in the value of industry shipments, which measures the rate of growth, should be positively related to liberalization. Unfortunately, no measure of the degree of product differentiation was included because none was available; this omission is likely, given our argument, to be significant.

Also included are variables to proxy certain political characteristics. Grossman and Helpman (1995) suggest deductively that the industry's capacity to organize is important; typical measures for this include the degree of seller concentration and their geographic concentration. More concentrated industries should be better able to organize and resist trade liberalization.[26] Geographic concentration has an ambiguous relationship to liberalization; some (Ray 1981) argue that greater concentration reduces free rider problems and increases the potential for protection by making representatives intensely supportive, while others (Pincus 1977) point out that greater spread of the industry makes a larger number of representatives willing to vote for its position. The independent variables included thus are scale economies, the interaction of scale and import penetration, import penetration, export-orientation, human capital intensity, capital intensity, seller concentration (c_4) ratio, geographic concentration, past tariff rates, and industry growth. Table 4.2 shows the indicator used for each of these and the expected sign of the relationship to the NAFTA tariff reductions.

TABLE 4.2

Variable	Measure Used	Sign
Past tariff, TAR91	Calculated tariffs on Mexican goods, 1991	−
Capital intensity, KSTOCK	Capital in industry	+
Scale economies, MEPS	Minimum efficient plant size	+
Human capital, OCCUPS	Scientists and engineers as % total employment	+
Import penetration, M80	Imports as % consumption	−
Export orientation, X	Exports as % consumption	+
Seller concentration, SCONC	Four-firm concentration ratio	−
Industry growth, VS79–83	Change in sales, 1979–83	+
Geographic concentration, GEOG2	Value added by industry in each state relative to pop. of state as % total pop.	−/+
Interaction of scale • import penetration, MEPS2	(MEPS • M80)	−

NOTE: The data for these variables comes from Trefler (1993). He very generously agreed to share his data.

Evidence

The OLS regression reported in table 4.3 shows the results of our test of the NAFTA data. As noted above, this is only a weak test of the data.[27] The regression shows that scale economies are positively and significantly related to trade liberalization, as expected. Those sectors with greater scale economies received greater trade liberalization within NAFTA, ceteris paribus.

The other major factors in explaining tariff liberalization within NAFTA are the past tariff level, export-orientation, geographic concentration, and the interaction term. These variables also display the expected signs. High levels of past protection mean less liberalization in NAFTA; this could result from the fact that such industries are highly effective politically or because they are in bad shape economically. Geographic concentration allows firms to prevent liberalization; they are more efficacious politically than dispersed industries, it appears. Scale economies in industries lacking competitiveness also are able to block liberalization; facing

TABLE 4.3
Regression Results

Variables	Parameter Estimates
intercept	1.037***
past tariff, TAR91	−0.017*** (5.535)
seller concentration, SCONC (log of)	−0.008 (0.414)
scale economies, MEPS	0.156** (2.048)
scale • import penetration, MEPS2	−4.516*** (4.404)
geographic concentration, GEOG2	−0.141** (2.031)
export orientation, X	0.213*** (2.966)
import penetration, M80	−0.067 (0.577)
human capital intensity, OCCUP5	0.347 (1.162)
capital stock, KSTOCK	−0.093 (1.200)
industry growth, VS79–83	−0.070 (1.304)
R^2 = .26 Chi-squared = 106.660***	N = 227

NOTE: Parameter estimates are unstandardized OLS estimates. Figures in parentheses are the absolute values of t-ratios, computed using White's heteroskedastic consistent standard errors. The White procedure produces asymptotically consistent estimates. With a large sample size, tests of significance are based upon an asymptotic normal distribution. The t-ratio is equivalently the square root of the chi-squared value.

** indicates significance at $p < 0.05$ for two-tailed tests.

*** indicates significance at $p < 0.01$ for two-tailed tests.

high import competition, these industries intensely prefer and demand protection. On the other hand, high levels of scale economies in competitive industries and high levels of export-orientation promote liberalization within NAFTA. The other variables are not significant, but they (import penetration, human capital intensity, and seller concentration) do take on the expected signs. Capital stock and industry growth, however, are not significant and take the opposite sign from that expected.

These results should be treated cautiously, as providing suggestive evidence for the argument.[28] They imply that American industries with scale economies systematically obtained greater trade liberalization in NAFTA than others. The data here do not show that these industries were liberalized more regionally than multilaterally, but I intend to conduct future tests on the results of the Uruguay Round to see if this is the case. If the argument is correct, one would expect the relationship between scale economies and tariff liberalization in the Uruguay Round to be less strong than those reported here. Tests on the Mexican and Canadian cases also seem important. In part the argument above suggests that the relationship between IRS industries and regional trade liberalization should be stronger in the Mexican and Canadian cases than in the United States.[29] Given the large size of the American market, its firms may be closest to optimal scale already; Canadian and Mexican firms should be more concerned with access to the large American market, given their relatively small markets. Finally, this argument can be extended to the European Union. Was the Single Market an exercise in swapping scale economies across states? The very preliminary results here, if generalized, suggest that this might have been the case.

In the preparation for the negotiation of the Single Market, the EC Commission (1985) released a report that examined the costs and benefits of regional trade liberalization within Europe. Its central conclusion was that the greatest benefits would accrue to industries who would be able to achieve greater economies of scale in a unified European market. This chapter echoes the argument made in that report. Industries with scale economies should be the demanders of regional trade liberalization. They benefit from it because of their increasing returns to scale. Hence demand for regional liberalization should grow as more industries in a country face rising scale economies. The shape of regional agreements then should reflect these domestic pressures.

Governments, however, make the final decisions about the terms of such agreements. They are more likely to respond favorably to industry demands for regional liberalization when 1) existing trade barriers within the region are already low; 2) they can tailor regional agreements to exclude certain sectors and target others; and 3) when firms profits increase greatly as a result of changes in the scale of their production. Finally, countries will be most able to negotiate such agreements when each possesses differentiated industries with scale economies that they can exchange. Swapping markets will make regionalism feasible politically.

The data here lend some credence to this argument. First, they suggest that, in contravention to article XXIV of the GATT, the NAFTA accord treated sectors differently and did not liberalize all of them completely. Second, for a few important sectors there seems to be a strong correlation between the extent of their economies of scale and the trade barrier reduction (NTBs included) in the NAFTA agreement. Finally, the multiple regressions showed a positive and significant relationship between IRS industries and NAFTA tariff liberalization, controlling for other factors.

On a final note, McKinnon and Fung (1993) point out that regional free trade areas are more likely to arise if countries can effectively stabilize their exchange rates. They note that "the tendency for the world to break down into regional trading blocs—within which more stable exchange rates based on a common monetary standard can more easily be established—has been greatly strengthened. For economies closely integrated in foreign trade, a zone of exchange rate stability now seems necessary to preserve free trade in goods and services while reducing investment risk" (241). Hence regional trade agreements may be more likely and more sustainable when exchange rates among the regional partners can be stabilized. This may help explain the pressure for EMU in Europe after the single market was enacted and the recent American aid to Mexico in the wake of the NAFTA accord. If this argument is correct, industries who gain from regional agreements—i.e., ones with large scale economies—should also demand exchange rate stabilization within the region. Thus the argument here might be extendable, helping explain both regional trade policy and exchange rate coordination.

APPENDIX:
DATA ON VARIOUS U.S. INDUSTRIES

Key sectors identified by Hufbauer and Schott (1992 and 1993) were liberalized in the following fashion:

1. Energy: very limited liberalization
   Oil sector in Mexico kept closed;
   Some liberalization in petrochemicals, coal, oil and gas field
      equipment, natural gas, and electricity.
2. Automobiles: major liberalization in all sectors
   All duties to be phased out on cars in 10 years, trucks in 5 years;
   Auto parts tariffs to be phased out in 5 years;
   NTBs on cars in Mexico and Canada to be eliminated over 10 years;
   New, stringent local content rules to be imposed;
   No Common External Tariff (CET) for 10 years.
3. Textiles and apparel: limited liberalization overall
   Quotas on Mexican textiles and apparel to be eliminated;
   Imports free as long as they meet stringent new local content
      requirements;
   Tariffs on Mexican textiles and apparel items to be phased out over

10 years;

Stringent new local content requirements to be imposed on all goods;

Safeguard measure added so that in case of serious damage during transition period NAFTA countries may increase tariffs.

4. Agriculture: 15-year phase-in of free trade in agriculture

U.S. and Canada to open their horticultural sectors in exchange for Mexican liberalization of field crops;

Elimination of wheat barriers in Mexico over 5 years;

All NTBs converted over time into tariffs;

Sugar not affected now but quotas eliminated over 15 years;

No liberalization of coffee;

No change in U.S.–Canadian farm agreement from CAFTA.

5. Financial Services: gradual but important liberalization

In Mexico foreign banks can expand gradually over 10 years;

In Mexico foreign companies can sell insurance increasingly over 10 years, but foreign investment limited for first 10 years;

Same arrangement applies to the securities industry;

Mexican industry remains protected to some extent.

6. Transport: gradual liberalization in a number of sectors

Over 10 years a phase-in allows truckers to move cargo from country to country, but movement is still limited;

Over 10 years agreement allows U.S. and Canadian investment in Mexican bus and trucking companies;

Technical and safety standards to be coordinated;

No liberalization in ocean or air transport.

7. Telecommunications: extensive liberalization in most sectors

In Mexico, immediate elimination of most tariffs and NTBs on telecom equipment (after 5 years all barriers to go);

Standards in telecom equipment harmonized to some extent;

Lifts Mexican restrictions on DFI in all products but telecommunications networks (i.e., local and long distance telephone services excluded;

Radio and TV stations not liberalized in any of the 3 countries.

From this overview, the following ranking of the industries as to their degree of liberalization was made. Based on three factors: the amount of trade liberalization, the timing of the liberalization, and the percentage of the sectors within each industry covered by the liberalization, in descending order, the most liberalized sector was

1. Telecommunications
2. Autos
3. Financial services
4. Transport
5. Textiles and Apparel
6. Agriculture
7. Energy.

Acknowledgments: I would like to thank Marc Busch, Jerry Cohen, Joe Grieco, Joanne Gowa, Stephan Haggard, Robert Keohane, John McLaren, Edward Mansfield, Pier-Carlo Padoan, Dani Rodrik, Ron Rogowski, B. Peter Rosendorff, and David Baldwin for their helpful comments on this paper.

NOTES

1. It is hoped that in the future a test could be done using the European Union (EU) and the single market directives. One could examine the extent of liberalization created by the harmonization that was accepted in each industry's directive.

2. It need not be the case that the free trade area is geographically contiguous. The reason why geographic proximity matters is due to transport costs. For nongeographically contiguous free trade areas, the advantages of scale may be eliminated by the costs of transport.

3. Increasing returns to scale contrast with the neoclassical economics assumption of constant returns. In increasing returns industries, efficiency improves with the level of production; as the number of units produced increases, their cost decreases. It also often implies that firms who are "first-movers" in their markets have strong competitive advantages, since they move down the cost curve first. Firms in increasing returns industries can thus drive their competitors out of business if they can reach optimal scale first.

4. The discussion here is about economies of scale internal to firms or industries. External economies also exist, and some have argued that they are even more important than internal ones (Caballero and Lyons 1990 and 1991). In this case, these industries generate externalities for the entire national economy. That is, their value to the economy is not just from their own production but also from the other outputs they provide. These include all of the spillover effects of their production, such as the training of skilled labor, the investment in R&D and the diffusion of new technologies. The backward and forward linkages between these sectors and other parts of the economy make them unusually important—or "strategic."

5. A number of authors have challenged this claim; using different assumptions, they show trade liberalization might be preferred over protection (e.g., Baldwin and Gorecki 1983; Venables 1987, 1988; Horstmann and Markusen 1986; Dick 1994). In contrast to the argument here, these authors see multilateral liberalization as being either in the best interests of the firms or country.

6. The assumptions that are made here are : 1) that firms internally face increasing returns to scale up to a certain level; 2) that monopolistic competition prevails; 3) that barriers to entry exist; and 4) that the good produced is differentiated. Hence, firm profits will not necessarily be

zero because the industry is monopolistic and there is not free entry and exit of firms. It is sometimes assumed that scale economies create barriers to entry. This may or may not be the case. For instance, if firms face declining average costs, the high fixed costs of entering into the market need not constitute barriers to entry. Only when those costs are sunk will they be barriers to entry. High fixed costs alone are not barriers to entry as long as the assets can be sold to other firms. Sunk costs, not fixed ones, create barriers to entry and exit. As Helpman (1984) and others have noted, the results of these types of trade models are highly dependent on the assumptions used.

7. In fairness to the IPEP argument, however, it should be noted that while its main thrust is that the optimal trade policy in terms of social welfare is protection, it acknowledges that some trade is better for firms than is no trade at all. Hence in this way the argument here is similar to the IPEP one.

8. A Free Trade Area (FTA) is slightly different than a customs union. It implies abolition of trade barriers among the members but no common external tariff. Each country may keep its own trade barriers against third countries. This of course creates opportunities for third countries to use one market to gain access to all the rest of the FTA, and it induces a demand for rules, like local content provisions, which prevent such arbitrage. In the analysis we note where the difference between and FTA and a customs union (CU) makes a difference. For a more general term, one can use the notion of a preferential trade arrangement (PTA), which includes both CU and FTA.

9. Consumer surplus is one element of the standard measure of welfare used in international trade theory. Consumer surplus represents the area under the demand curve but above the price, where in monopolistic competition price is set by dropping a perpendicular from the intersection of the marginal revenue and the marginal cost curves to the demand curve. That is, it is the quantity of consumption that consumers are able to buy at a lesser price than they would actually offer to pay.

10. If firms are protected by nontariff barriers (NTBs), then they may reap all of the gains from these barriers. The government may not gain revenue from them as they would with tariffs. To the extent that firms are protected by nontariff barriers, then the government does not lose revenue from trade liberalization.

11. See Lipsey (1960) for the original addition of production and consumption effects to the Vinerian model; see also Collier (1979).

12. Elsewhere Milner and Sivaramayya (1996) show that with undifferentiated products firms in both countries cannot gain from bilateral (regional) liberalization unless initial tariffs are low enough—or, at least not prohibitive. If they are low, then both firms can gain even without product differentiation and hence regionalism might be preferred.

13. The key assumption here is that the price elasticity of demand in both markets is high, or at least high enough to elicit an offsetting increase in demand when prices fall.

14. If the industry were perfectly competitive, then the firm would not be able to capture these gains. Instead they would go to consumers. Firm profits (above normal ones) would have to be zero.

15. If its scale economies extended over a vast or infinite range, then of course the firm would profit most from global liberalization, if it were competitive at this level.

16. Thompson (1994), however, shows that in Canada the opposite seems more the case. Canadian "firms operating in industries where the average plant scale is small relative to their U.S. competitors were anticipated to be more likely to experience losses as a result of the FTA than were firms operating in industries where the relative average plant scale is large" (23). The more disadvantaged Canadian firms were with respect to scale, the more they were likely to lose in CAFTA.

17. Kemp and Wan (1976) have demonstrated that under certain conditions a CU will always be trade-creating. That is, if external tariffs are set at an appropriate level no member outside the union will lose from the CU and if transfers can be made among the members then at least one and maybe all of them can gain. Hence in terms of consumer surplus, a CU can be shown to generate losses for none and gains for at least one state. Thus a CU may not always be less trade-creating than a multilateral trade agreement.

18. It is interesting to note that Russia recently said it might increase its tariff protection because the central government was lacking revenue. Hence even for some more developed countries, tariff revenues may be important for political leaders.

19. This is a common assumption in the economics literature. See for example Brander and Spencer (1984); Grossman and Helpman (1993, 1994, 1995).

20. If trade barriers are raised to prohibitive levels, then this is not true because there will be no imports and hence no tariff revenues. It is assumed that domestic protection implies less than prohibitive tariffs.

21. Under more extreme conditions, tariff revenues may not be greatest with domestic protection. If tariffs are prohibitive, then there will be no imports and hence no revenues.

22. If we assumed that the good produced in our model was differentiated, then this result would be even more likely since in this case countries would not lose an entire industry, just various segments of it. The assumption of a homogeneous product leads to this more extreme case.

23. Small and large here refer to the size of the domestic market—the extent of demand for a good. Both population and GNP per capita would be relevant measures.

24. There are a slew of arguments about why the EC was formed, or why EMU, SEA or NAFTA was agreed to, but these are either ad hoc discussions or explain only one particular case.

25. The data for the dependent variable come from Robert Shelburne (1994).

26. Because of multicollinearity problems, the seller concentration variable (SCRCONC) was put in log form, as SCONC. This seems to have alleviated some of the collinearity problems.

27. A tobit analysis was also done because the values of the dependent variable are truncated. This analysis showed that the signs of the coefficients remained the same. But I was unable to correct for heteroskedasticity in this model and hence the coefficients are unbiased but not efficient. That is, as in the OLS equation the t-statistics are likely to be insignificant. Indeed, the MEPS coefficient is not significant at the .10 level.

28. The regression was done using OLS and the parameters estimated and reported are OLS ones. But a White test of the model revealed significant evidence of heteroskedasticity. White (1980) has devised a method for estimating a consistent parameter covariance matrix even when the errors are heteroskedastic. The results in table 4.3 use this estimator.

In addition, a Wald test was used to test the joint significance of all the coefficients in table 4.3. This statistic has an asymptotic chi-squared distribution with degrees of freedom equal to the number of independent variables in the equation. This figure is reported as the chi-square statistic in table 4.3, and is statistically significant ($p=0.000$).

29. Thompson (1994) argues that this does not hold for Canadian industry.

FIVE

Regional Agreements as Clubs: The European Case

Pier Carlo Padoan

Stephen Haggard (1994) observes that the "question of number" has not been clearly understood in the debate about regional integration: success of a regional agreement is not related to the small versus large numbers issue.

A starting point of this paper is that the number of participants does matter. A regional agreement determines who joins and also who is excluded; a number, therefore, must be determined. To put it differently: regionalism is much a question of cooperation as it is of exclusion. When is the "optimal number of members" reached? Why does it change over time? Collective action theory offers topics for discussion (see Haggard 1994:1); economics can provide some insight on this topic as well.

In this paper I summarize the costs and benefits of integration in the theoretical debate. I then present some empirical evidence about the characteristics of the trade and monetary integration process in Europe. I finally offer an exploratory framework that brings together both economic and noneconomic factors affecting integration and the way they determine the collective behavior of states involved in the process, with special reference to the European experience. That framework is based on the assumption that integration agreements are partially excludable public goods and applies club theory to the issue.

Benefits and Costs of Integration: A Brief Summary

Traditional trade theory gives a precise answer to the question of number: the optimal size of a trade agreement is the world. Short of full liberalization, however, partial elimination of barriers following integration will improve the allocation of resources and hence welfare. Although the welfare gain might be partially curtailed by trade diversion, which could offset gains from trade creation, reallocation of resources generated by the integration process allows the exploitation of national comparative advantages. Differences in national resource endowments will lead to a deepening of specialization patterns that will benefit all countries involved in the integration process. Factors of production within each country will be allocated in sectors where the country enjoys a comparative advantage while production in other sectors will stop or will be reduced. Such a process will, of course, involve adjustment costs and temporary unemployment, the severity and duration of which could be alleviated through appropriate financial support. Once reallocation is completed, interindustry trade, i.e. trade of goods belonging to different sectors (like, e.g. textiles and food products) within the region will increase. Note that the benefits of integration, in such a framework, could be equally obtained by the reallocation of factors among countries, i.e., by migration and/or capital movements.

Within traditional trade theory the reason why the organization of international trade falls short of global liberalization, once the adjustment process has been completed, is usually found in the presence of special interests that, given imperfect political markets, have the resources and the ability to obtain protection from national or regional governments.

"New trade theory" has pointed at another possible source of gains from integration, deriving from the exploitation of (static and dynamic) gains from trade.[1] The larger market generated by integration would allow (oligopolistic) firms to exploit increasing returns. This would lead to further specialization within the same sectors as competition would rest on both lower costs deriving from expanded production and from product (quality) differentiation. Intraindustry trade, i.e., trade of similar goods between countries, would be generated. Welfare gains from integration would ensue from lower costs and broader quality range as well as the exploitation of dynamic returns to scale generated by the learning process following the introduction of new technologies.

In this case, too, costs from integration could emerge, however they would be permanent, rather than temporary. In addition to the standard adjustment costs, economies of scale could generate agglomeration effects as factors, both capital and labor, would concentrate in specific areas, leading to permanent core-periphery effects within the region. Employment opportunities would concentrate in some areas exacerbating the asymmetrical distribution of net benefits (Krugman 1992b).

The increasingly popular "gravity model" of trade flows suggests that countries are more likely to trade with each other the closer are their per capita and absolute income levels. This intuition can be given theoretical foundations according to the "new trade theory," which stresses economies of scale and diversity as a source of (intraindustry) trade (see Baldwin 1994: para. 3.1.1). The gravity model also assigns an important role to distance, predicting that geographical proximity will enhance the probability of trade between countries, ceteris paribus. While the economic justification of this element is related to transport costs, it can also be suggested (Alesina, Perotti, Spolaore 1995) that geographically close countries also share similar preferences about the provision of common policies, thus increasing the incentives to integrate.

In general, trade integration would increase both interindustry and intraindustry trade and, in both cases, increased competition would activate pressures to resist adjustment and/or demand for compensatory measures on the part of countries and regions most severely hit by the asymmetric distribution of net benefits.

The emergence of inequalities generated by the process of integration brings forward the notion of "cohesion" which may be defined as "(a principle that) implies . . . a relatively equal social and territorial distribution of employment opportunities, of wealth and of income, and of improvements in the quality of life that correspond to increasing expectations" (Smith and Tsoukalis 1996:1). An important implication is that, without cohesion, political support to a regional agreement is likely to fail.

Consensus to the regional agreement, and ultimately its size, will then depend on the cohesion among its members. Cohesion problems will be larger the larger the asymmetric distribution effects, and therefore the larger the impact of scale effects generated by integration. These effects, in turn, will be larger the larger the diversity among members of the integrating region. Once the costs for cohesion management (i.e the costs that must be borne to offset the asymmetry effects) exceed the benefits from integration the widening process will come to an end. A number will be determined.

Monetary integration too, both when it implies fixing exchange rates and when it takes the form of full monetary union, can produce an asymmetric distribution of net benefits. Economic benefits from monetary integration stem from three sources:[2] the elimination of transaction costs, the elimination of currency risk, the acquisition of policy credibility for inflation-prone countries. The first two benefits can be fully obtained only with monetary union. The third benefit has to be weighted against the costs of real appreciation which hits high inflation countries once they credibly enter an exchange rate agreement (Krugman 1990b). If the latter are also the peripheral countries from a trade point of view, adverse effects of real and monetary integration will cumulate, leading to further demand for compensation.

Low-inflation countries, on the other hand, would be adversely affected by entering a monetary agreement with excessively expansionary partners, ultimately refusing permission to join to the latter (Alesina and Grilli 1993). In both cases the extension of the monetary agreement will stop short of global integration.[3] Again a number must be determined.

Economics can provide several elements to the understanding of the number problem, however a satisfactory theory of regional integration should explain the "optimal number" of members through the interaction of economic, institutional and political variables.

REGIONAL INTEGRATION AND DIVERSITY IN EUROPE

The history of European integration offers a unique case for the application of a multisided approach to the problem of regional integration. Indeed it would be hard to understand, e.g., the making of the European Monetary System and its (possible) development into monetary union, or the decision to proceed with the European Single Market (SM), relying only on the prescriptions of the theory of optimal currency areas (see Cohen 1993) or the benefits of industry liberalization. The two programs are also deeply interconnected with one another, both in their practical evolution and in the strategy of the supporters of European integration, the EC Commission in the first place (as captured in the "One market One money" formula). Both projects, in addition, cannot be understood without considering the political aspects behind both the negotiation processes (e.g., Cameron 1990) and the interaction between the evolution of the two initiatives (e.g., Garrett 1993; Martin 1993). The current trend toward global regionalism (see, e.g., De Melo and Panagarya 1993) has added a new dimension to the dynamics of European integration as the incentives to deepen and widen European agreements have been influenced by the uncertain evolution of global trade relations.

A second feature of the European (and not just European) experience in regional integration is that it proceeds in a highly "nonlinear" fashion, presenting phases of acceleration, slowdown and setback resulting in wavelike movements rather than in a smooth path toward a final structure of international relations. In such a process the attitude and choices of the actors involved, nation-states, do not reflect just their individual preferences, responses to incentives, and distributional issues, but are characterized by interactions where individual choices leave the way to collective behavior. The optimal number, therefore will be the result of—often highly complex—collective interaction.

European integration is a process that will probably involve, in a decade or two, twenty-five to thirty countries. This will necessarily increase the diversity of members. Diversity will bring benefits, through a more efficient division of labor, but will also increase costs, stemming both from adverse effects of specialization, such as those recalled above, and from the increasing costs of assuring the cohesion of a larger and more varied community.

In what follows I present some empirical evidence of the increasing differences among European countries, related both to current and future members of the European Union (EU).

Comparative Advantages

A first piece of evidence is presented in table 5.1, which offers a synthetic description of the distribution of revealed trade comparative advantages (RCA) in Europe defined so as to include both current and (some of the) future members of the European Union plus Mediterranean countries, the probable candidates for future extension of the trade integration process in Europe.[4] The table offers information about two interrelated issues: which countries are in the best position to exploit the benefits from scale effects; and which member countries are likely to gain from, or be hit more severly by, enlargement insofar as this will redirect trade within the Union according to the distribution of RCA.

Revealed comparative advantages (+) and disadvantages (-)[5] are com-

112   *Pier Carlo Padoan*

TABLE 5.1

Revealed Comparative Advantages in Europe and in the Mediterranean

	SB	SI	SS	T	Ag
Germany	+	+	+	−	−
France	+	+	+	−	−
Italy	−	−	+	+	+
Netherlands	+	+	−	−	+
BLuxembourg	−	+	−	−	−
UK	+	+	+	−	−
Ireland	+	−	−	+	−
Denmark	+	−	+	+	+
Spain	−	+	−	+	+
Portugal	−	−	−	+	−
Greece	−	−	−	−	+
Norway	−	+	+	−	+
Sweden	−	+	+	−	−
Austria	−	+	−	+	+
Finland	−	+	−	−	−
Czechoslovakia	+		−	+	−
Hungary	−	−	−	+	+
Poland	−	−	−	+	+
Romania	−	−	−	+	+
Bulgaria	−	−	−	+	−
Maghreb	−	−	−	+	−
Egypt, Jordan	−	−	−	−	+
Israel	+	−	+	−	−
Libya, Syria	−	−	−	−	−
Gulf	−	−	−	−	−

SOURCE: Padoan, Pericoli (1993), Guerrieri (1995), and author's calculations.
SB=science-based; scale intensive; SS=specialized suppliers; T=traditional; Ag=agriculture

puted with respect to productive sectors grouped according to Pavitt's (1984) taxonomy. This taxonomy aggregates industrial sectors according to a number of elements focusing on the ability to produce innovations within the sector or the necessity to import innovations from outside and on the different ability to exploit static and dynamic economies of scale. It is, therefore, well suited to look at the issue of cumulative effects from integration. An additional feature of the taxonomy is that each of the groups into which manufacturing sectors are classified is dependent on different competitiveness factors. The groups (with the specific competitiveness factors and examples of industries included in each group in brackets) are: SB=science based (capacity to innovate, computers); SI=scale intensive (exploitation of economies of scale, motor vehicles); SS=specialized suppliers (product quality and differentiation, machine tools); T=traditional (price, textiles). International trade of the first three sectors is largely (if not completely) of the intraindustry type, while it is mostly of the interindustry type in the traditional sector. I have added the agricultural sector (Ag), given its obvious relevance in the European integration process.

Countries are grouped according to the different, past and future, enlargements. We start by considering the nine countries made up by the initial six and the ones included in the first enlargement. All of them, with the exception of Italy, show revealed comparative advantages in sectors (SB and SI) where gains from economies of scale may be relevant and where international trade is largely intraindustry. This explains, in part at least, why the first enlargement was relatively painless (Winters 1993). Adjustment costs have been lower and the scope for differentiation higher with respect to the case when trade is more of the interindustry kind. Product diversification within the same sector allowed industries to resist the competitive pressures brought about by integration.

Things looked different with the second enlargement, involving the three Mediterranean countries, Spain, Portugal, and Greece.[6] All three countries have their RCA in the traditional sectors and in agriculture, where cumulative scale effects have little relevance and the scope of competition through diversification is limited. A partial exception is the case of Spain, which exhibits positive RCA in scale intensive sectors. This, too, is an example of positive cumulative effects. The development of a scale intensive sector in Spain is largely the effect of an inflow of foreign direct investment following Spain's accession to the EC.[7] Largely because of this factor, the three Mediterranean countries became net beneficiaries within the redistribution mechanisms of the EC based on structural funds and on CAP transfers (CEPR 1992).

The next enlargement has involved three EFTA countries whose RCA are positive in scale intensive sectors (as well as specialized suppliers and traditional for Sweden and Austria respectively). From the point of view of adjustment capability and the exploitation of scale effects,[8] these countries represent no serious problem to enlargement, for the same reasons recalled above with respect to the first enlargement. Difficulties arise when one considers the role of agriculture (which includes fisheries). As all EFTA countries exhibit positive RCA in agriculture, this sector represents an element of friction with older EU members (most notably France and Spain).[9]

Let us now consider the prospects of the enlargement to Central and Eastern European countries (CEECs) by looking at the consistencies and inconsistencies derived from the structure of RCA.[10] The first thing to note is that the comparative advantages of the three largest Western European economies—Germany, United Kingdom, and France—are located in the sectors where the comparative disadvantages of the CEECs lie, and vice versa. From this point of view these two groups of countries are in a favorable position as far as the process of integration is concerned. The comparative advantages that the former enjoy in the science-based and specialized suppliers sectors suggest that they are in the position to produce and export the technology and equipment CEECs need to upgrade their competitive position, while they would become importers of the goods for which CEECs enjoy a comparative advantage.

But here is the conflicting part of the scenario. France has a comparative advantage in agriculture while, on the eastern side, Czechoslovakia (actually the Czech Republic) reveals a comparative advantage in the scale intensive sector. Problems are possibly more severe if we turn to the position of the southern members of the EU: Italy, Greece, Portugal, and Spain. Their comparative advantage lies in the traditional and agricultural sectors (with Spain acquiring one in the scale intensive sector), and also in the specialized suppliers in the case of Italy. As is well known, in order to accomplish full integration into the EU, markets still have to be liberalized for access in three crucial areas: agriculture, textiles and clothing, and steel, i.e., those sectors where protectionist resistance is the fiercest and where the action of the Community has been able, so far, to produce only a moderate amount of liberalization, but also where the liberalization agreed in the Uruguay Round will be relevant. Our evidence supports the view that liberalization in these sectors would favor the comparative advantage of the CEECs.

The structure of the RCA of the Mediterranean countries, with the notable exception of Israel, is in many ways similar to that of the Southern and Eastern European countries, suggesting that future liberalization toward the South, launched at the Conference in Barcelona in the fall of 1995, would pose similar problems as those raised by the future Eastern enlargement. Some have argued (Hoekman and Djankov 1995), however, that Mediterranean countries will be competing with Eastern European economies rather than with present members of the EU.

Protectionist policies implemented at EU level reflect sectoral, rather than national pressures. However the current situation of "suspended liberalization" in Europe seems to suggest that special interest group pressures are strong enough to influence nationwide and Community-wide policies. A fact that is quite common in regional trade agreements (De Benedictis and Padoan 1993; Leidy and Hoekman 1993).

TABLE 5.2
Per Capita Income Differentials in European Countries, 1990

Belgium	69.62	Netherlands	77.60
Denmark	98.92	Portugal	21.95
Germany (West)	100.00	UK	72.13
Greece	26.84	Finland	79.70
Spain	49.37	Sweden	72.40
France	87.32	Austria	58.30
Ireland	42.79	(Switzerland)	100.00
Italy	75.40	(Norway)	70.70

SOURCE: World Bank
NOTE: In percentage with respect to the highest GDP per capita (=100).

To summarize, the evidence sketched in table 5.1 suggests that only in few EU countries comparative advantages would not represent a source of conflict to a liberal policy viv-à-vis the CEECs. In fact only a few countries seem to be in such a position, notably Germany and the Benelux countries.[11] In general, if the crucial agricultural sector is left out, the southern members of the EU would the most hardly hit by the competition of CEECs, while the northern members would benefit most. The resistance to Eastern European enlargement of the EU finds, at least partially, its roots in differences in industrial specialization.

Income Distribution and Redistribution Mechanisms

Income distribution problems within the EU have not decreased over the past decade. Income disparities at the national level have increased (CEC 1991), and they are significant especially between northern and southern members of the EU (see table 5.2). In addition they are particularly relevant when one considers regions rather than countries. Table 5.3 offers a measure of per capita income disparities considering 166 regions within the European Union. Real per capita income of the 10 richest regions has increased from 1980 to 1988 while it has slightly decreased for the 10 poorest regions. Similar tendencies emerge if one considers the 25 poorest and richest regions respectively.[12]

The fact that regional integration generates disparities in Europe can be inferred from the redistribution of resources within the EU through the structural funds mechanism. Structural funds, as well as the newly established Cohesion Funds resources,[13] are distributed according to income per capita and share of agriculture in GDP. Following this prin-

TABLE 5.3

Disparities in Per Capita GDP:
Regions of the European Community 1980–88 in PPP values (EC12=100)

	1980	1985	1988
Average 10 richest regions	145	150	151
Average 10 poorest regions	47	45	45
Average 25 richest regions	135	138	137
Average 25 poorest regions	57	56	56

SOURCE: Commission of the European Communities (1991).

ciple CEPR (1992) and Baldwin (1994) show that net current beneficiaries include all southern members, with the exception of Italy and
including Ireland and the Netherlands, while estimated net contributions are positive for all EFTA members and negative for all Central and
Eastern European countries. This indicates that another, major, element
of friction generated by enlargement will be the distribution of structural
funds (Fratianni 1995).

Monetary and Financial Variables

The EMS faced a severe crisis in September 1992, when Italy and the
United Kingdom left the exchange rate mechanism and Spain and Portugal devalued with respect to the ECU. This episode came after a relatively
long period of stability, starting in 1987, during which no parity realign-
ments had occurred and which was universally believed to be the first step
toward full monetary union. Over this period increasing nominal (inflation) convergence had produced real divergence (real appreciation)
putting strain especially on the peripheral countries (see table 5.4). Also as
a consequence of this, the monetary agreements collapsed when the
macroeconomic environment deteriorated and unemployment soared,
severely undermining the credibility of the system (De Grauwe 1994).
One way to interpret these events is to note that the European monetary
arrangements did not pass the test of keeping together countries exhibiting different fiscal and monetary conditions. After all, the Maastricht conditions for convergence require precisely that (relevant) differences in fiscal and monetary performance be eliminated as a precondition for participation to monetary union.

The evidence above is consistent with the idea that the process of

TABLE 5.4

Real Effective Exchange Rates in European Countries (1987=100)

	1988	1989	1990	1991	1992	1993
Belgium	97.7	99.2	102.1	98.9	99.9	97.8
France	99.0	97.3	100.7	98.2	100.0	101.4
Germany	98.5	96.6	100.3	99.7	103.4	105.0
Netherlands	98.0	97.6	99.0	96.6	96.8	96.4
Italy	97.2	99.6	103.6	104.1	101.8	88.2
Ireland	97.3	95.8	97.1	93.4	96.6	94.4
Denmark	99.0	97.9	103.1	100.4	100.8	101.1
Austria	97.3	94.8	98.0	96.4	96.6	97.1
Spain	103.2	108.0	112.4	111.6	109.6	96.6

SOURCE: Bank of Italy.

regional integration in Europe, concerning trade, industry, and monetary issues, has been facing increasing difficulties stemming from the (also increasing) diversity of members. To offset the consequences of these diversities, compensation mechanisms had to be envisaged and financed. This, in turn, has generated resistance to liberalization and difficulties in the management of the agreement.[14] In short, in each integration wave, benefits from integration (both in the widening and in the deepening aspects) have been decreasing while the costs have been increasing, leading the integration wave to an arrest. The process, however, has resumed whenever new conditions have changed the incentives to the integration of both members and nonmembers. The Single Market program has accelerated the enlargement process to the southern members and later to the Eftan's. The fall of the Soviet empire will, quite probably, lead to a new enlargement and so will the opening up of the new "Mediterranean front," while yet to be fully understood are the consequences on European integration of the formation of other regional agreements. As a consequence, the optimal number problem finds, each time, a different solution.

REGIONAL AGREEMENTS AS CLUBS: A SIMPLE REPRESENTATION

In this and the following sections I offer a formal interpretation of regional integration, both in trade and monetary relations following a club theory approach. The economic analysis of clubs' formation started to develop in the 1960s with the contribution of James Buchanan (1965) and Mancur

Olson (1965) and has been applied since then to several economic and political issues such as community size, production of local public goods, two-part tariffs, congestion problems, political coalitions, and more recently to international organizations (Casella and Feinstein 1990). The literature has been surveyed by Sandler and Tschirhart (1980), Frey (1984), and Cornes and Sandler (1985).

Club theory deals with problems related with the establishment of voluntary associations for the production of excludable public goods. Optimal membership is determined by marginality conditions, when the spread between an individual member's cost and benefit is maximized. Marginal costs and benefits are functions of the size of the club, Q. In principle, this can be measured both by the number of countries involved and the extent of market liberalization within and between each member. We will consider the amount of club good (e.g., the amount of liberalization) produced as given, concentrating on the optimal number of members and assuming a continuum of countries.

Costs are, in our presentation, related to management and decision making activities, hence management costs should not be confused with congestion costs arising, e.g., from cumulative effects such as those already discussed and which will be considered as factors affecting the level of net benefits from club provision.

Marginal costs are increasing with the extension of club membership because management problems rise with an increase in the number of members. As Fratianni and Pattison (1982) stress, decision theory suggests that the addition of new members will raise the costs of finding agreements in a more than proportional manner.[15] Costs will also rise more than proportionally for organizational reasons and because, for political balance, each new member will have to be given equal opportunity, irrespective of its economic size, to express its viewpoint (Ward 1991).[16] Institutional arrangements alter the behavior of costs. For example a shift from a unanimity rule to a majority rule in decision making within the club lowers marginal costs.

On the other hand, individual members' marginal benefits are decreasing, assuming that the equal-sized share of total benefits from integration increases at a decreasing rate with respect to the number of members because congestion deteriorates the quality of the club good. We will specify this point later as the nature of benefits is different in a trade and in a monetary club.

From a static point of view optimal club membership is obtained when marginal benefits (B) equal marginal costs (C). What we are interested in, however, is not just the determination of optimal club size—the extension of the area of integration—but also in its change, i.e., we want to look at the issue of the waves of integration as they represent a peculiar characteristic of the European (and not only European) integration process.

Consider the following simple rule. The incentive for a change in the extension of an integration agreement arises whenever there is a discrepancy between marginal benefits and marginal costs of the club. Note that this allows us to consider possible (and not at all unrealistic) contractions in the size of the club. In other words the number of club members changes whenever B and C differ, formally

$$DQ = z(B - C), \qquad (5.1)$$

where D is the derivative with respect to time and z is a positive parameter indicating that the adjustment toward new a club size is a lengthy—i.e., not instantaneous—process (determined, e.g., by the characteristics of the negotiation mechanism). Since both B and C are functions of the number of countries, Q equation (5.1) posits an evolutionary approach to institution formation (such as a club) as suggested, inter alia, by Witt (1989), where the size of the institution, and indeed whether the institution is to be formed at all, depends on the number of the individuals (countries) willing to participate.

The nature and shape of B and C functions differ with the nature of the club, trade or monetary, and give rise to different integration dynamics according to the degree of interaction between trade and monetary integration, which is the case of the European Union. In what follows I will first consider possible representations of a trade and a monetary club separately and then alternative formulations of "multiple clubs."

A Trade Club

A trade agreement responds to some of the crucial requisites for the definition of a club: it produces freer trade, virtually a public good, and it guarantees partial exclusion of nonmembers from free trade benefits and, in the case of a custom union, it guarantees the benefits of a common external trade policy.

The European Union is something more than a trade club. Its members share a common tariff policy and, with the completion of the Single

Market Program (SMP), a common policy, to replace national ones, has to be implemented also with respect to other trade policy instruments (such as quantitative restrictions). But there is more to this. The SMP requires the definition of common competition rules and standards within the EU, thus providing additional public goods to its members. In this respect the EU offers an example of an "industry club" in the sense that it provides to its members a number of public goods to guide both their internal and their external behavior. At the same time EU membership implies that countries participate, either as net donors or as net recipients, to the redistribution of resources through structural and cohesion funds.

We start by considering a simple trade club. Marginal benefits of a trade club (Bt) may be thought of having three components:

$$Bt = a - bQ + cY. \qquad (5.2)$$

The first component, a, is a fixed component, which captures the "security" effect of trade agreements. This implies that membership in a trade club is more valuable in the presence of a possible outside threat. This may be a genuine military threat as Gowa and Mansfield (1993) have argued.[17] The present global environment may present other forms of threat, i.e., those deriving from the formation of regional and aggressive trade blocs. In such a case the incentive for joining a trade club does not only lie in the trade creation and/or scale effects benefits, but also in the "insurance" that club membership provides against the harm that a trade bloc war could produce to small, isolated countries (Perroni and Whalley 1994, see also Baldwin 1993). Note that a larger club membership will benefit existing members as well as new entrants. If the size of the alliance increases it reinforces resistance to the outside threat. This implies that the value of a rises with the degree of conflict in the global system.

Another way of interpreting a is to consider purely political benefits from trade agreements, i.e., the fact that members will be admitted to the club insofar as they share the same political beliefs of the incumbents, like the full acceptance of democratic rules. This element has played a crucial role in the enlargement of the European Community to the southern countries, Greece, Portugal, and Spain (Winters 1993) and will play a similar role in the enlargement to CEEC.

The second component, bQ, is related to club membership. Since b is positive, marginal benefits decrease with club size because of rising congestion problems in club formation. I have earlier discussed why this is likely to be the case for the European experience.[18] If a deepening process takes place, i.e., a move from a custom union to a single market, the value of b decreases as the same number of members will produce larger integration benefits.

The third component in equation (5.2) posits that marginal benefits increase, ceteris paribus, with the level of economic activity. The pressure of rising inequality due to integration will be lower the more sustained is the level of economic activity as more sustained growth will benefit all club members although in a less than proportional way. Another way of looking at this component is to recall that protectionist pressures increase with depressions.[19] It is widely recognized that the pressure to enlarge the EU eastward has been slowed down by the recession that has hit Europe during the first part of the decade.

Marginal costs take the following form:

$$Ct = d + eQ. \qquad (5.3)$$

Marginal costs include a fixed component and a component depending on club size. As e is positive, Ct increases with club size. Marginal costs are generated by management problems. In the case of the EU, as Baldwin (1994) describes (see also Widgren 1994), voting rules are complicated by the increase in the number of members, and hence by the increasing diversity of preferences, as each member-country will use its voting power to increase the welfare of its citizens. Thus it is unlikely that the EU can successfully enlarge without a change in the voting procedure. As Fratianni (1995) stresses, the entrance of the CEEC in the Union will make the formation of a blocking minority much easier, given the current voting system. We can capture this effect by assuming that the parameter e takes decreasing values as the decision rule in the club takes less stringent forms, e.g., from unanimity to majority voting.

The fixed component d can be thought of being associated with the amount and quality of international cooperation already existing among club members in other areas, i.e., if other institutions linking countries involved in trade agreements already exist this will facilitate the formation and management of new institutions. While several reasons can be advanced to support such a claim, a fact well established in international relations theory is that institutions provide information about other actors' behavior, thus facilitating communication and information exchanges.[20]

Substituting equations (5.2) and (5.3) into equation (5.1) and assuming $z = 1$, one obtains the following:

$$DQ = -(b + e)Q + cY + (a - d). \qquad (5.4)$$

Equation (5.4) is a phase diagram which takes the form represented in figure 5.1 (Trade Club). If, at any moment the number of club members is less than Q^* there will be an incentive to enlarge the club up to Q^*, vice versa if club membership is larger than Q^*. To clarify the mechanism it is useful to reconsider the role of the endogenous and exogenous factors explaining regionalism.[21] Formally, the model presented here contains only one endogenous variable, the number of club members Q, however, the equilibrium size of the club varies because other magnitudes, such as the state of macroeconomic conditions, Y, and the degree of institutional agreements, d, change. While these are treated, in this model, either as exogenous variables or parameters (thus capturing the "structural characteristics" of the international system), they can be considered as endogenous to the environment within which the evolution of regional agreements takes place, in the sense that the evolution of regionalism feeds back on them. The logic of the model, as it is presented here, all the same, is necessarily simpler. Whenever a change in either an exogenous variable or a parameter occurs, what was once an equilibrium club size becomes a nonequilibrium and, hence, a dynamic adjustment process starts (as described in general terms in equation [5.1]) leading to a new equilibrium.

Starting from Q^* optimal club membership will vary according to a number of factors which change the value of optimal club membership. In particular we will witness an enlargement process if: macroeconomic conditions improve (Y increases); a deepening process, such as further removal of barriers within the existing club, takes place (b decreases); the degree of outside conflicts increases, thus raising the insurance value of membership (a increases);[22] the strength and efficiency of institutional arrangements among members other than trade relations increases (d decreases); the voting system becomes more flexible (e decreases).

As suggested by Mansfield and Bronson (1994) the presence of a leader (or k-group) may increase the degree of cohesion of a regional trade agreement. The above formulation can take into account the role played by a regional leader, or by a k-group. The condition for a club to exist is $cY + (a - d) > 0$. If, abstracting from macroeconomic conditions, the security

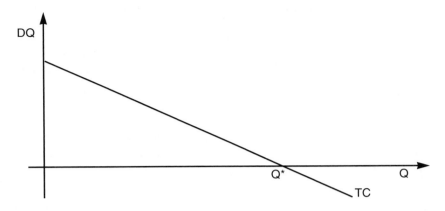

FIGURE 5.1.   Trade Club

benefit from the agreement is smaller than the fixed management cost given the low degree of international cooperation, i.e., $a - d < 0$, the club will not be formed. In such a case the presence of a leader (or a k-group) could fulfill the above condition with a positive sign. This could be formalized by adding a parameter k to the Ct function entering with a negative sign, i.e., leadership would increase the amount of international cooperation thus making the formation of the club possible.

A Monetary Club

A monetary agreement, both in the form of a currency union and of an exchange rate agreement, also responds to the requisites of a public good. The public good nature of a single currency is well established in the literature. In the case of an exchange rate agreement such as the European Monetary System—or rather its Exchange Rate Mechanism (ERM)—the public good involved is monetary stability extended to the participants of the ERM. Common intervention rules extended to members — not to unilateral peggers—allow for, at least partial, excludability of the good.

Marginal benefits of a monetary club can be expressed as follows,[23]

$$Bm = fQ^2 - gQ + hY + 1. \quad (5.5)$$

The squared component reflects the presence of economies of scale generated by the expansion of the monetary club. These may be enhanced with full capital mobility and deeper financial integration as these factors increase the desirability of monetary unions as a protection against destabilizing capital movements (Eichengreen 1994). The second component reflects the fact that members of a monetary club must fulfill appropriate requirements (e.g., in terms of financial stability, witness the well-known "Maastricht conditions") in their national economies and that, conversely, new members may deteriorate the quality of the public good if their monetary and fiscal policies follow non converging courses.[24]

The third component takes into account the fact that more favorable macroeconomic conditions make it easier to implement the policy stances that are necessary to be part of a monetary club. The final component considers the "noneconomic" benefits of monetary membership which play a relevant role in the success, or failure, of monetary agreements (see Cohen 1993).

Marginal costs can be assumed to take a linear form as in the previous case:

$$Cm = m + nQ. \qquad (5.6)$$

The meaning, however is slightly different. While the term associated with club size, nQ, refers to the decision-making process, itself dependent on the voting procedure,[25] the fixed component m represents one of the most widely debated points about monetary unions, the costs associated with the loss of monetary sovereignty as perceived by club members.

As above, we substitute equations (5.5) and (5.6) into equation (5.1) and we obtain the following phase diagram, assuming $z = 1$:

$$DQ = fQ^2 - (g + m)Q + hY + (l - m). \qquad (5.7)$$

Equation (5.7) takes the form as in figure 5.2 (the MC curve). Equilibrium club size may take two different values:

$$Q^* = [g + n - ((g + n)^2 - 4fH)^{1/2}]/2f$$

$$Q' = [g + n + ((g + n)^2 - 4fH)^{1/2}]/2f$$

where $H = hY + l - m$.

As the figure also shows, only one of the two solutions, the smaller one, is stable. This representation is consistent with the historical evidence that

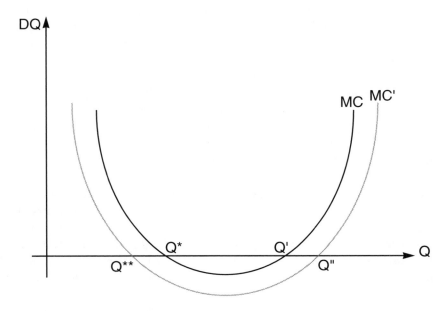

FIGURE 5.2. Monetary Club

monetary arrangements have often collapsed from a large to a smaller dimension. Examples are the crisis of the European Snake in the 1970s and the more recent crisis of the ERM.

Equation (5.7) and figure 5.2 also suggest why club membership may shrink as a consequence of a currency crisis. A shift in the parameter values of equation (5.7) could shift the MC curve downward, in *MC.* If, for whatever reason, a monetary club had been established at Q' this would no longer be an equilibrium position and the new club size would collapse to Q^{**}, i.e., after a crisis only a "core" group of countries would continue to participate in a monetary club.

There are several possible causes of such an outcome. A deterioration of the macroeconomic environment (lower value of Y); more rapidly decreasing benefits of new membership which would increase resistance by old members (higher value of g); a lower value attached to non economic benefits of monetary union (lower value of l); a higher cost attached to the loss of monetary sovereignty (higher value of m); a weaker effect of increasing returns to scale from monetary union (lower value of f).[26]

Figure 5.2 also sheds some light on the feasibility of a two-speed strategy to monetary union. Assume that the initial downward shift in the curve is generated, other things equal, by a prolonged recession (as the one generated by the response to German unification in 1991) represented by a decrease in Y. Once macroeconomic conditions have been restored on a more favorable course and Y is set onto its initial level, the equilibrium of the monetary club would not return to Q' and it would settle on its "core group" value Q^*. Starting from Q^* any enlargement of the club would require a change in any one of the parameters discussed above so as to produce an upward shift of the MC schedule.

Alesina and Grilli (1993) have argued against the feasibility of a two speed strategy to monetary union on the argument that, once a group of inflation-shy countries has set up an agreement to exploit the benefits of monetary stability they would vote against the entry of inflation-prone countries, thus preventing the possibility of enlarging the union through successive steps. In the representation suggested here once a crisis has pushed the club away from what was an "ex-post" unstable equilibrium, there is no incentive to bring the club back to its original size, even if the status quo ante has been restored. Once the status quo has been restored, club equilibrium shifts from Q^{**} to Q^*.

MULTIPLE CLUBS

"One market one money" (CEC 1990) aptly describes the strategy that the European Community intended to follow at the end of the past decade to accelerate the pace of integration. In terms of our approach this can be considered an experiment of multiple clubs, i.e., simultaneous membership in both a trade and a monetary club. The rationale behind this strategy is that membership in one club will enhance the benefits of participating to the other.

The economic theory of integration has not yet fully clarified this point. While it is widely recognized that monetary integration will enhance the benefits of market integration and, vice versa, market integration will bring forward more favorable conditions for the formation of a currency area,[27] it is not clear how widening (enlarging the size of one club) will favor deepening (the establishment of another club).

As mentioned at the beginning, traditional economic explanations of the benefits of a single currency are related to arguments such as the elimination of transaction and of currency risk. There is, however, skepticism (De Grauwe 1992) about the relevance and magnitude of such benefits for trade and industrial integration. Surveys of firms' responses to the perspective of monetary unification in Europe (Santos 1993) suggest that firms are willing to increase their investment activity in an area where monetary unification is associated with full market liberalization, not just because of reduced transaction costs but, more importantly, because a fully integrated area (monetary union and single market) represents an attractive business location in that agglomeration economies generated by a single market are enhanced by the advantages of monetary stability.[28]

Also note that while national economies would interact when the two clubs are formed, the management costs of the two clubs would be kept distinct as the decision-making bodies would be institutionally separated (short of full political union and perhaps not even in that case). As we have seen above there no is reason why the equilibrium size of the two clubs should be the same. In general, and in the current phase of European integration, this will not be the case but, for simplicity's sake, let us assume that the countries involved in the integration process must opt for simultaneous membership in the two clubs. To discuss the implications I will distinguish two cases: additive benefits and multiplicative benefits.

The first case is straightforward. If (marginal) benefits are additive, national economies will benefit from both club goods with little mutual interaction between them. In such a case the marginal benefit (B_{ma}) function will be:

$$B_{ma} = fQ^2 - (b + g)Q + (c + h)Y + (a + l), \quad (5.8)$$

and the marginal cost (C_{ma}) function will be:

$$C_{ma} = (d + m) + (e + n)Q. \quad (5.9)$$

The corresponding phase diagram will be:

$$DQ = fQ^2 - (b + g + e + n)Q + (c + h)Y + (a + l - d - m). \quad (5.10)$$

Equilibrium club size may take two different values:

$$Q_a^* = [g + n + b + e - ((g + n + b + e)^2 - 4fK)^{1/2}]/2f$$

$$Q_a' = [g + n + b + e + ((g + n + b + e)^2 - 4fK)^{1/2}]/2f$$

where $K = (c + h)Y + l - m + a - d$.

The graphic representation of equation (5.10) is similar to that of figure 5.2 and is not reproduced here. Obviously we will have two equilibria and only one stable one. This implies that if countries join both clubs at the same time the instability inherent in the monetary club will eventually lead to the collapse of a trade club whose dimension has been set at Q_a'.

It is perhaps more interesting to look at the value of the stable equilibrium Q_a^* and confront it with Q^*, the stable equilibrium value in the monetary club. In principle we cannot ascertain whether $Q_a^* \gtrless Q^*$, however the multiple club will be larger, ceteris paribus, the larger the value of a, the parameter associated with the noneconomic benefits of a trade club. So it is possible that, for some value of a, the multiple club will be larger than the monetary club. In other words, if the insurance or political incentive to join a trade club is particularly strong, this might overcome the resistance to join an international institution that requires, among other things, a loss in national sovereignty such as a monetary agreement (i.e., a high value of m).[29]

Let us now turn to the case of multiplicative benefits of multiple clubs. Marginal benefits (B_{mm}) become

$$B_{mm} = (fQ^2 - gQ + hY + 1)(a - bQ + cY) \quad (5.11)$$

while marginal costs (C_{mm}) become

$$C_{mm} = (d + eQ) + (m + nQ). \quad (5.12)$$

Solving (5.11) and introducing (5.11) and (5.12) into (5.1) the corresponding phase diagram becomes

$$DQ = -GQ^3 + MQ^2 - NQ + R \quad (5.13)$$

where: $G = fb$; $M = gb + cfY + af$; $N = (bh + cg) Y + bl + ag + e + n$;

$R = chY^2 + (cl + ah) Y + al - d - m$.

Equation (5.13) cannot be solved analytically. We know however, that its behavior follows a path like MUC in figure 5.3, given appropriate parameter values.

In the case of multiplicative benefits the multiple club has three possible equilibria of which Q_1 and Q_3 are stable and Q_2 is unstable. This representation is overly simple; it provides, however, some insight about the process of integration and enlargement. If, for example, the number of

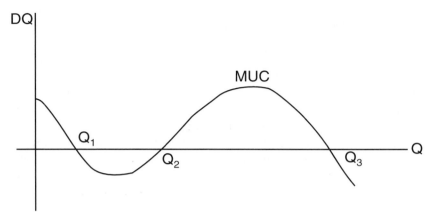

FIGURE 5.3.   Multiple Clubs

club members becomes larger than Q_2, then new members will join the club until Q_3 is reached. The opposite happens if the number of members is smaller than Q_2. This is consistent with the "threshold" analysis of institutions (see, e.g., Witt 1989). An institution will develop if a critical dimension—Q_2 in our case—is reached. If this happens countries originally outside the institution will find it profitable to join while existing members will also increase their welfare from enlarged membership.[30]

Our representation also gives some insight about the causes of successive waves of integration. If, starting from an initial equilibrium, which might be the unstable value Q_2, the MUC curve shifts upward, the incentives for enlargement appear. Of course the opposite may happen, determining a contraction of club membership.

Rapidly going through the elements entering equation (5.13) one can find a number of reasons why a wave of enlargement may come about. Note, for example, that improved macroeconomic conditions, and/or larger noneconomic benefits from trade and monetary integration will determine a shift upward of the MUC curve. The other elements discussed in the previous case will also produce such an effect. This is not dramatically different from what was found in the previous cases. The new insight is that if one assumes multiplicative benefits from multiple clubs, then integration does appear to follow a path of successive waves. In this case, too, one may consider the role of leadership. A leader, or k-group, may shift the position of the phase diagram so as to surpass the critical dimension for enlargement.

Regional agreements imply both a decision to include and a decision to exclude countries. In this respect regionalism requires the solution of a number problem. The "new" economic theory of integration provides some insights on why benefits from regional integration may be decreasing and, hence, why an "optimal" number of members will be reached. The European experience suggests that, while there is always an optimal number of members in a regional agreements, the number changes in response to changes in the international environment, of which global regionalism is a relevant example, as well as to forms of institutional deepening, of which the Single Market is one.

European regionalism, on the other hand, involves both trade and monetary integration and the two policies have been conceived as parts of a unitary strategy. This makes the number problem more complex as it will be determined by the interaction of the two integration processes.

I have presented a formal analysis of the formation of a regional agreement as a club problem, i.e., as an excludable public good. I have shown how noneconomic factors may explain the change in the optimal number of club members both in the case of a trade and of a monetary club. Many of these factors are crucial in explaining the evolution of regional integration in Europe. I have also presented an exploratory solution to the problem of multiple clubs (i.e., when members are required to participate in both a trade and a monetary club). In such a case multiple stable solutions to club size may be present and, according to changes in one or more factors, club size may shrink. This case mimics well the events following the crisis of the EMS in September 1992. The framework also sheds some light on the reason why regional integration may proceed in waves (as is the case of Europe). The shift from one stable dimension to another, larger, dimension, requires that a critical threshold in club membership be reached. This in turn may require an outside impetus to regional agreements, which may be provided by a regional leader or k-group.

Full economic and monetary integration in Europe may be represented in figure 5.3 by Q_3. The current state of affairs may be represented by Q_2, the unstable solution. It was not clear, at the beginning of 1996, whether Europe will move to the right of this value so as to reach Q_3. Negotiations for full membership of the Central and East European countries are still a long way from conclusion while two EFTA members, Norway and Switzerland, have voted themselves out of the integration process and the the United Kingdom and Denmark may use the "opt out clause" from Monetary Union. Austria has joined the exchange rate mechanism of the EMS, but Italy and the United Kingdom have left it although the former may be reentering it. Greece remains far away from joining it.

If full integration (Q_3) may be out of reach, then the other stable solution, Q_1, may gain some small, but positive, probability of being reached. A core group monetary union would include countries that are homogenous also from the point of view of the trade structure[31] and exclude most of the current southern members of the EU. More realistically, in such a case forms of "flexible integration," involving clubs of different size (see, e.g., CEPR 1995; Fratianni 1995) would probably emerge. This topic, however, requires further scrutiny.

Acknowledgments: I would like to thank Jerry Cohen, John McLaren, Ed Mansfield, Helen Milner and the participants to the conference on "The Political Economy of Regionalism" for stimulating comments on an earlier draft. The usual disclaimer applies. I also thank the University of Rome, "La Sapienza" for financial support.

Notes

1. For a recent survey see Baldwin and Venables (1994).

2. See De Grauwe (1992) for a discussion.

3. A well-known result of the theory of optimal currency areas is that their extension is smaller than the world.

4. Norway is included for completeness while disaggregated data for the Czech and Slovak republics were not available

5. RCA are measured by the so-called Balassa index: i.e., the share of country i's exports in sector j over the share of its total exports. A value of the index larger (smaller) than 1 indicates that the country has a revealed comparative advantage (disadvantage) in sector j.

6. Actually the timing was different as Greece entered before the two Iberic countries

7. The initially favorable effect was largely offset by the strong real appreciation of the peseta after its admission to the exchange rate mechanism of the EMS. See later text. On Spain accession to the EC see Vinals et al. in Bliss and De Macedo (1990).

8. And given also their limited dimension with respect to the EU which makes them net gainers from the trade creation effect. See Baldwin (1993, 1994).

9. Dispute over fishery rights was one of the main reasons that led Norway to vote against EU membership.

10. For an extensive analysis see De Benedictis and Padoan (1993).

11. Several authors have noted that Germany would be, by far, the country to benefit most from a deeper trade integration with Eastern Europe (see, e.g., Collins and Rodrik 1991 and the literature reviewed in De Benedictis and Padoan 1993).

12. Note that this evidence is not inconsistent with other studies relating the evolution of income distribution in the European Community (Ben David 1993), which consider the case of the EC with the exclusion of the Mediterranean countries. Not surprisingly the RCA of the initial six, and then nine members, which show limited differences in per capita income, are concentrated in intraindustry sectors, while the RCA of the Mediterranean countries as well as those of the CEEC, certainly the poorest members of the current and future UE, are concentrated in the interindustry sectors.

13. The Cohesion Fund was established following a request from Spain to compensate southern members from the costs of EMU. Its meaning is not only substantial, in that it entails a larger transfer of funds to the weaker partners, but also has a visibility effect in that it was considered as a major result obtained by southern members in exchange for progress in economic integration. See Correia (1994).

14. For a description of the various phases of the integration process see, e.g., Winters (1993).

15. This may be regarded as one aspect of the "large number problem" recalled by Haggard (1994).

16. In the case of the European Union, countries receive different voting weights according to their size, yet this does not make decision making an easy task. For a recent assessment see Widgren (1994).

17. See Mansfield and Bronson in this volume for empirical evidence on the role of security ties in enhancing trade relations.

18. See also the survey in Santos (1993) for evidence related to EU.

19. It can be argued that the operation of an international trade regime is influenced by the operation of an international macroeconomic regime. See Guerrieri and Padoan (1988).

20. See Powell (1994) for a survey of the role of institutions in international cooperation.

21. I thank an anonymous referee for drawing my attention to this point.

22. Baldwin (1993) explains the request of EFTA members to join EU with the fact that the completion of the Single Market would have hurt the competitive position of countries left out of the agreement. This is equivalent to a decrease in the value of b.

23. As in the previous case we may assume that the presence of a leader increases the value of benefits from a monetary club. In the case of the EMS this is related to the well-known discipline element provided by the anti-inflationary stance of the German monetary authorities. This would imply the addition of a positive term on the right-hand side of equation (5.5).

24. This is also consistent with the view (Bayoumi 1994) that the incentives for nonmembers to join a monetary union are larger than the incentives for union members to accept new countries.

25. In the case of a monetary union this is closely associated with the organization of the supranational Central Bank.

26. A weaker leadership effect, e.g., Germany's policy targeted at the unification process and neglecting support of partner currencies, would produce the same effect.

27. Because, e.g., of higher factor mobility.

28. The same point can be stated by looking at the costs of having trade integration without monetary integration. EU members which are also members of the ERM (e.g., France) lament that excessive devaluations of the currencies of EU members that have left the ERM (e.g., Italy) distort the competition within the Single Market and have threatened to impose sanctions on them.

29. This is consistent with the widely held view that monetary union in Europe has mainly a political relevance.

30. This is relevant to understand the current phase of EU enlargement. It has been suggested (Baldwin 1994) that before becoming full members of the EU, CEECs should form a subregional integration agreement among themselves as this would facilitate their joint admittance. This is consistent with the idea of a "critical mass."

31. A condition that is favorable to the formation of currency areas.

SIX

Dispute Settlement in International Trade: Regionalism and Procedural Coordination

Beth V. Yarbrough and Robert M. Yarbrough

I feel ill at ease with that little word "We."
No man is at one with another, you see.
Behind all agreement lies something amiss.
All seeming accord cloaks a lurking abyss.
— Albert Einstein

The creation of new institutions, *particularly those related to governance and dispute settlement,* constitute essential elements of the two flagship cases of regionalism—the European Union and the North American Free-Trade Agreement.[1] Yet, the role of dispute settlement in regionalism remains underexplored.[2] More generally, the record of scholarship on regionalism suggests that the cart (that is, evaluating the potential *effects* of regionalism) may have gotten in front of the horse (that is, a careful *definition* of what we mean by regionalism and an understanding of the phenomenon's *causes*).[3] In this paper, we attempt to advance the horse a step by examining the links between (1) regionalism as a means of coordinating procedures for dispute settlement and (2) international cooperation in trade.

THE COOPERATION PROBLEM

All smoothly functioning societies require mechanisms for settling disputes, both to solve immediate disputes and to promote long-term societal goals. The society of states involved in international trade is no exception; but dispute settlement in the international arena can prove especially problematic,

Table 6.1

Nonrepeated Prisoners' Dilemma

		Player 2	
		cooperate	*defect*
	cooperate	b_1, b_2	d_1, a_2
Player 1			
	defect	a_1, d_2	c_1, c_2

Note: Payoff pairs report payoffs for players 1 and 2 respectively, where $a_1 > b_1 > c_1 > d_1$ gives player 1's preference ordering.

because of its potential conflicts with national sovereignty. Traditionally, the difficulty of enforcing agreements and settling disputes between states served as the key distinguishing feature of international relations.[4]

The fundamental role of dispute settlement is to facilitate and support cooperation. In the international trade arena, cooperation usually is interpreted as opening markets and thereby promoting enhanced productive efficiency among self-interested states. Economic theory implies that even unilateral trade liberalization generally serves a country's economic interest; however, domestic political pressures for protection imply that states sometimes prefer to limit access to their own markets while attaining unrestricted access to trading partners' (Baldwin 1985; Corden 1984; Magee, Brock, and Young 1989).[5] Thus, the basic impediment to cooperative opening of international markets often is represented as a Prisoners' Dilemma, shown in table 6.1, where $a_i > b_i > c_i > d_i$ represents player i's preference ordering. In any single-stage or nonrepeated Prisoners' Dilemma, each player has a dominant strategy: cheat; so cooperation fails and potential gains from international trade are lost.

Situations of Prisoners' Dilemma generally require one of two basic structures to achieve and maintain cooperation. First, with a combination of good information (in particular, the ability to recognize defection and identify the defector), infinite or uncertain repetition, and low discount rates, the threat of loss of future benefits from cooperation can suffice to deter defection (Axelrod 1984). For example, table 6.2 illustrates the case of a self-enforcing agreement, where the first term in each payoff denotes the outcome of current play and the terms following the summation signs denote appropriately discounted payoffs from future stages of the repeated game. Under the rules of a self-enforcing agreement, if either party defects in the current stage, thereby capturing its a_i payoff, both parties receive the

TABLE 6.2
Repeated Prisoners' Dilemma Under a Self-Enforcing Agreement

Player 2

		cooperate	*defect*
	cooperate	$(b_1 + \Sigma b_1),(b_2 + \Sigma b_2)$	$(d_1 + \Sigma c_1),(a_2 + \Sigma c_2)$
Player 1			
	defect	$(a_1 + \Sigma c_1),(d_2 + \Sigma c_2)$	$(c_1 + \Sigma c_1),(c_2 + \Sigma c_2)$

mutual defection payoff (c_i) for each future period (Telser 1980; Yarbrough and Yarbrough 1986, 1990a, b, 1995b). The benefits from defection $(a_i - b_i)$, the benefits from cooperation $(b_i - c_i)$, the expected time horizon, and players' discount rates combine to determine whether cooperation will emerge and persist in a particular relationship.

The second means of supporting cooperation relies on third parties in one of two basic ways. First, third parties can provide the information and incentives necessary to support reciprocity within ongoing relationships (Axelrod 1986; Greif, Milgrom, and Weingast 1994; Milgrom, North, and Weingast 1990; Yarbrough and Yarbrough 1995b). In this case, the game structure looks the same as in table 6.2, which assumed that parties themselves had the information necessary to support a self-enforcing agreement; but here a third party provides the needed information concerning the presence and identities of defectors. Table 6.3 represents a second, more obvious role for third parties: direct third-party enforcement. Here, defection results in the third party imposing a penalty (P) which, to be effective, must be large enough to destroy the dominance of the defection strategy.

Along with either self-enforcement or third-party intervention, reputation may play a role in supporting cooperation. In the case of a self-enforcing agreement, if the informational structure is such that the defector's reputation for untrustworthiness spreads, defection may result in not only punishment by the victim in one particular game but the breakdown of cooperation in other games with other partners (Axelrod 1986; Yarbrough and Yarbrough 1986, 1995b). In other words, horizontal linkages across issues, even those involving different partners, can play much the same role as the intertemporal linkage of repeated play in supporting cooperation. Similarly, in the direct third-party-enforcement case, defectors may suffer a loss of reputation in addition to any explicit penalty; for example, in the international trade arena they may be perceived as having violated their

TABLE 6.3
Prisoners' Dilemma with Direct Third-Party Enforcement

		Player 2	
		cooperate	*defect*
Player 1	*cooperate*	b_1, b_2	$d_1, a_2 - P$
	defect	$a_1 - P, d_2$	$c_1 - P, c_2 - P$

NOTE: P denotes the penalty imposed by the third party on defectors. A necessary condition for the penalty to be effective is that $(b_i > a_i - P)$, $(d_i > c_i - P)$, or both.

"international obligation" (Hudec 1990; Kovenoch and Thursby 1992; Lipson 1991).

The amount of cooperation observed in international trade indicates that some or all of these cooperation-facilitating mechanisms are effective, at least some of the time, on some issues, and between some trading partners. On the other hand, the amount of noncooperation in international trade suggests that no single cooperation-facilitating mechanism or combination thereof provides a panacea.[6]

This line of reasoning has been applied widely to trade agreements, their enforceability, and the prospects for cooperation in international trade relations (Conybeare 1987; Grieco 1990; Keohane 1984; Oye 1986; Yarbrough and Yarbrough 1992). However, many real-world "trade" disputes occur in a different, albeit similarly structured, game. Those disputes involve issues of compliance *with dispute-settlement and enforcement procedures themselves.* The disputes we have in mind are not about whether one party cheated substantively on a trade agreement (for example, imposed a 5 percent tariff when an agreement specified a 3 percent tariff, or imposed a quantitative restriction when such restrictions are prohibited) but about *whether a party cheated procedurally on an agreement's recognized dispute-settlement and enforcement procedure* (for example, failed to remove a measure ruled impermissible under the agreed procedure, or blocked formation of an adjudication panel). In other words, these disputes are one step removed from substantive trade issues; they are less *trade* disputes than *dispute* disputes.

When we shift our attention from trade disputes to dispute disputes, the underlying Prisoners' Dilemma structure remains appropriate, as each country may want its trading partner to comply with agreed-on dispute-settlement procedures, but may itself want to disregard them in two ways:

as a "defendant" by blocking adjudication procedures or refusing to bring its behavior into compliance with rulings and as a "plaintiff" by retaliating against nonexistent, or at least undocumented, violations.[7]

DISPUTE SETTLEMENT IN INTERNATIONAL TRADE

Robert Hudec, one of the foremost legal scholars on the GATT, speaks of "the three key elements of the GATT legal system—the substantive rules, the adjudication procedure, and the government commitment to compliance" (1990:188); but study of the first and last elements of the triad far outpaces that of the second. Despite the relative lack of attention to dispute-settlement issues in the literature on international trade cooperation, they have been at the epicenter of events in the world political economy. Perhaps the most often-cited complaint about the pre-Uruguay Round GATT was the ability of the losing party in its dispute-settlement procedures to block adoption of GATT findings. Remedying this perceived deficiency ranked high on Uruguay Round negotiators' agenda, because consensus-based systems that include both the plaintiff and defendant in the consensus requirement can provide only weak dispute settlement. Recent regional efforts at trade liberalization in Europe and North America, while accomplished through different institutions and with different political rhetoric, share an emphasis on dispute-settlement mechanisms and on institutions to support compliance with those mechanisms. When the European Union achieved a breakthrough in its internal market, a key factor was the move to qualified-majority voting that restricted individual countries' prerogative to veto unfavored decisions and determine unilaterally their Community obligations (Garrett 1992; Moravscik 1991; Sandholtz and Zysman 1989). Similarly, North American integration, including both the Canada–U.S. Free-Trade Agreement and the NAFTA, has been anchored by elaborate dispute-settlement procedures, including appeals processes and other features designed to deter noncompliance with those procedures.

These observations suggest that it may be appropriate to apply the well-developed framework of game-theoretic analysis of cooperation at an additional level: one at which countries decide whether to comply with a dispute-settlement procedure to which they have agreed.[8] Even more important for present purposes, states seem likely to face nontrivial problems in deciding *which* dispute-settlement and enforcement mechanism to apply in a particular relationship. We know, based on the simple game theory outlined above, that multiple such potential mechanisms exist—self-enforcement based on repeated play, third-party information provision, and third-party enforcement, among others. We also observe a variety of arrangements in actual trade agreements, ranging from self-enforcement to third-party enforcement. For each specific observation, we can explain the particular arrangement *ex post* as an efficient solution to the participants' cooperation problem (Lipson 1991; Williamson 1985; Yarbrough and Yarbrough 1992, 1994a, 1994b, 1995a, 1995b). But we know little about why or how one particular solution emerges in a situation where multiple solutions are possible (Garrett and Weingast 1993; Westhoff, Yarbrough, and Yarbrough 1996). Faced with incentives to overcome a *substantive* dilemma, how or when can "prisoners" converge or coordinate on one of several possible dispute-settlement and enforcement *procedures;* and how does that choice affect the prospects for compliance and cooperation, both procedural and substantive?

Dispute-settlement mechanisms, while differing along many margins, can be roughly approximated by a continuum running from pure self-help to pure third-party enforcement. Of the many possibilities along this continuum, several different mechanisms may be feasible in a particular relationship, while some may be infeasible for one reason or another (as has been suggested, for example, about pure third-party enforcement in the international realm). For purposes of our discussion, it will be useful to define four prototypical dispute-settlement mechanisms, while recognizing that the lines between them become fuzzy when analyzing actual trade agreements.[9]

Dispute-Settlement Mechanism I

Dispute-Settlement Mechanism I (DSM-I) utilizes a third party to provide both information on violations and dissemination of that information, but relies on retaliation as the only punishment and contains a norm that failure to retaliate against a violator constitutes a violation. Figure 6.1 illustrates the possible courses of a dispute under such a system. After a complaint, the designated third party investigates the defendant's alleged behavior and determines a finding of guilty or not guilty. A not-guilty finding ends the dispute—unless the plaintiff engages in unilateral retaliation not justified by the third party's finding. Under a guilty ruling, the third

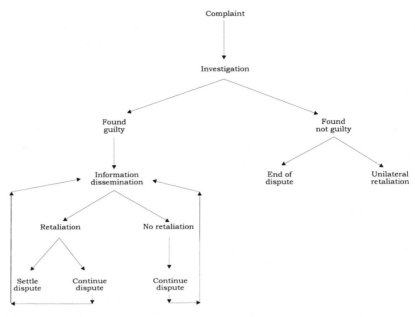

FIGURE 6.1.   Dispute Settlement Under DSM-I (third-party information provision).

party disseminates information to group members concerning the defendant's violation. Group members retaliate, after which the defendant either makes amends and settles the dispute or fails to, in which case the dispute may continue or ostracism may occur. If retaliation fails to provide a sufficient incentive for compliance or if group members fail to retaliate, the dispute continues.

Such a dispute-settlement mechanism has been suggested as a possible explanation for the existence of third-party institutions that lack any "real" enforcement power. Examples in international trade include the role of the medieval trade fairs and merchant guilds in facilitating the reestablishment of long-distance trade (Greif 1992; Greif, Milgrom, and Weingast 1994; Milgrom, North, and Weingast 1990). The fairs, with their private "judges," appear to have served as repositories and transmitters of information, providing the needed compliance information and creating incentives for traders to give evidence and retaliate against detected cheaters, thereby supporting reciprocity-based enforcement.

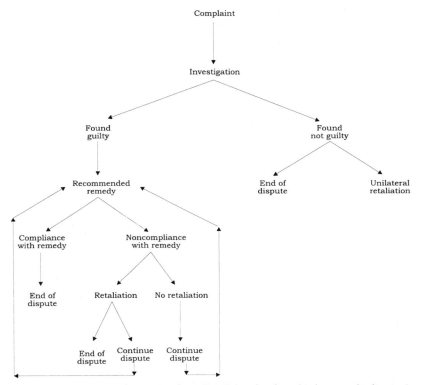

FIGURE 6.2.   Dispute Settlement Under DSM-II (nonbinding third-party adjudication).

Dispute-Settlement Mechanism II

Mechanism II (DSM-II) provides for nonbinding third-party adjudication in which the third party recommends a remedy, but, like DSM-I, establishes retaliation sanctioned by the adjudication as the only punishment. Figure 6.2 traces the routes a dispute might follow under such a system. A guilty finding is accompanied by a recommended remedy. Compliance with that remedy ends the dispute. Noncompliance sanctions retaliation. Once again, if retaliation fails to provide a sufficient incentive for compliance or if the plaintiff fails to retaliate, the dispute may continue. And, because the third party's finding is nonbinding, unilateral retaliation after a not-guilty finding is a possibility, leading to potential expansion of the dispute.

DSM-II resembles the procedure under NAFTA chapter 20, which covers all NAFTA disputes with the exception of dumping, countervailing duty, and investment cases (Horlick and DeBusk 1993; Hufbauer and Schott 1993; USITC 1992b). Disputes over interpretation of NAFTA treaty obligations, alleged violations of the agreement, or nullification and impairment of benefits all fall under chapter 20, which may be used by NAFTA members as a substitute for GATT dispute-settlement procedures. Dispute panels established under NAFTA chapter 20 issue a report and recommendations for a resolution, but the report can be overridden by a party to the dispute. Because compliance is not mandatory, there is no appeal procedure. Retaliation serves as the only recourse for a party who disagrees with the report and cannot otherwise negotiate an acceptable settlement.

DSM-II also approximates the dispute-settlement procedure under articles XXII and XXXIII of the GATT as it had evolved prior to the Uruguay Round.[10] Ideally, that process functioned as follows (Brand 1993; Hudec 1990; Jackson 1989, 1990). After a contracting party's complaint that a trading partner's violation of GATT obligations had nullified or impaired the benefits of the agreement, if consultations failed to resolve the matter, the GATT moved to establish an ad hoc arbitration panel.[11] This panel of three or five neutral members investigated and issued a report on the legal question underlying the complaint. The GATT Council then adopted the report. If it sustained the complaint, adoption of the report led to a GATT call for compliance by the defendant; and, in the absence of compliance, the plaintiff could request GATT authorization for retaliation.[12]

In practice, however, three separate points in the GATT process provided openings for the accused party to block the procedures. First, the defendant could refuse to permit formation of a panel, to approve its members, or to approve its terms of reference or charge; blockage here circumvented the process' move from "complaint" to "investigation" in figure 6.2. Milder versions of blocking occurred at this stage through strategic use of delays (Hudec 1990:182; Kovenoch and Thursby 1992).

Second, adoption of panel reports required consensus, so the accused party could block adoption (and thus publication) of the panel findings. This second type of blockage stopped the process flow at the "guilty-finding" stage in figure 6.2 . This occurred in approximately a quarter of GATT cases between 1975 and 1989 (Hudec 1990:183). The European Community blocked 5 reports, the United States 4, and Canada 3; but some of those disputes were settled by other means (Hudec 1990:184).[13]

Third, a defendant could block GATT's authorization of retaliation, halting the flow from "noncompliance" to "retaliation" in figure 6.2. This third type of blockage has been less important empirically, because requests for retaliation authorization have been rare; but blockage at this stage has been used. Overall, John Jackson (1990:67) estimates that 7 to 9 percent of GATT panel reports have not been followed. In addition, there have been cases of unilateral retaliation not backed by a GATT panel report, most notoriously by the United States.

The twin GATT weaknesses of (1) defendants' ability to block the dispute-settlement process, and (2) plaintiffs' unilateral retaliation were linked inextricably, as a judge of the European Court explains:

> The multilateral system excludes in principle unilateral action—but this is true only if the normal functioning of the multilateral system is not obstructed. If the multilateral system is not allowed to function, or, more precisely: if in a contentious process the defendant prevents consensus being attained, unilateral action becomes legitimate, as a last resort under general international law. . . .
>
> Such a situation may arise at any stage of the dispute settlement process: if a contracting party resists the institution of a panel and if, therefore, the procedure cannot be opened; if, a panel having been established, a contracting party blocks the panel procedure; if, a report having been presented by a panel, the losing party blocks adoption of the report by the Council; if, the report having been adopted, the losing party fails to perform obligations flowing from the Council decision. In all these circumstances unilateral action comes to the forefront because the multilateral system has not been allowed to function properly.   (Pescatore 1993:15)

This blocked-process/unilateral-action phenomenon is an inherent feature of DSM-II, but can be minimized by a shift to a third type of dispute-settlement mechanism.

Dispute-Settlement Mechanism III

Mechanism III (DSM-III), outlined in figure 6.3, specifies *binding* third-party adjudication, rules out retaliation after a not-guilty finding, and replaces the possibility of noncompliance after a guilty finding with an appeal process.[14] Unlike DSM-I and DSM-II, all permissible paths under DSM-III lead to resolution of the dispute.

Uruguay Round changes in GATT dispute-settlement provisions, embodied in the Dispute-Settlement Understanding of the World Trade Organization (WTO), represent a partial move from a DSM-II to a DSM-III system, largely at the behest of the United States and initially opposed

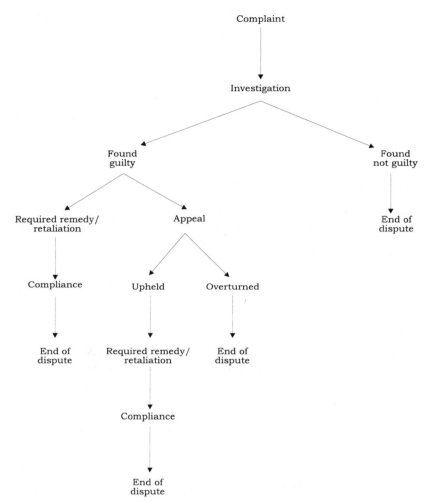

FIGURE 6.3.   Dispute Settlement Under DSM-III (binding third-party adjudication).

primarily by the European Community. Those changes include unification of dispute settlement so one procedure applies to all WTO cases, time limits to minimize delays, elimination of the defendant's ability to block formation of a GATT panel, and, most important, a shift from requiring consensus to *adopt* a panel report to requiring consensus to *block adoption* of a report (Brand 1993; Hudec 1990; Hufbauer and Schott 1993; Jackson

1990, 1994; Schott 1994; USITC 1992b). A country whose policy has been effectively challenged no longer will be able single-handedly to block adoption and publication of the panel report or authorization to retaliate.[15] A narrowly defined appeal procedure covering legal aspects of reports also has been added, along with time limits on each stage of the process, including compliance which now will be monitored. In cases where compliance with rulings is not forthcoming, authorization of retaliation will be more nearly automatic. The umbrella structure of the WTO also makes possible retaliation across multiple agreements; for example, a violation of the rules for trade in goods could be punished by retaliation in services trade.[16]

These changes move the GATT in the direction of the original post-World War II conception of the International Trade Organization (ITO). The ITO contained much of the institutional structure intended as a framework for international trade, but its ratification was blocked by the United States in 1948, leaving only the provisional GATT to fulfill a role for which it was not intended (Jackson 1989). In contrast to the GATT, the dispute-settlement provisions of the never-ratified ITO Charter included arbitration (mandatory in some cases) and reference to the World Court for legal opinions.

DSM-III also roughly corresponds to NAFTA chapter 19 procedures, which cover disputes related to antidumping (AD) and countervailing-duty (CVD) investigations (Horlick and DeBusk 1993; Hufbauer and Schott 1993; USITC 1992b).[17] Chapter 19 is of particular interest because it has been widely recognized that Canadian desire to constrain U.S. AD/CVD policies constituted the driving force behind Canada's decision to seek the initial Canada–U.S. Free-Trade Agreement, which grew into the NAFTA.[18] Predictably, the majority of actual disputes under the Canada–U.S. Free-Trade Agreement have been AD/CVD-related; and chapter 19 of the NAFTA follows closely chapter 19 of the original two-party agreement. The central innovation of NAFTA chapter 19 is its provision for *binational* panel review of disputed AD/CVD policies. This binational process substitutes for national judicial review and is to establish whether the disputed policies conform to the *national* law of the country whose policy has been challenged. Under the NAFTA, AD/CVD policies must conform to the implementing country's national law both in their finding of dumping or subsidies and in their determination of injury to the domestic industry.[19] NAFTA chapter 19 panel findings are binding. Under narrowly specified conditions, parties may challenge

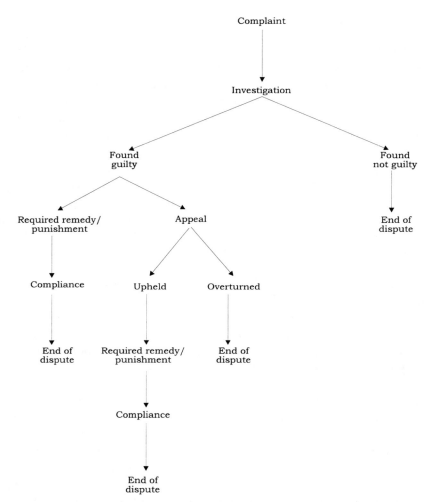

FIGURE 6.4.   Dispute Settlement Under DSM-IV (third-party enforcement).

panel findings by appealing to an Extraordinary Challenge Committee that can either uphold the original panel finding or establish a new panel to hear the case. In addition, chapter 19 contains provisions to prevent a party from interfering with the panel process itself. Charges of such interference go to a special committee that, should it find evidence of interference, can authorize retaliatory suspension of chapter 19 procedures or of other NAFTA benefits with respect to the interfering party.

Dispute-Settlement Mechanism IV

Mechanism IV (DSM-IV) represents the last step in our continuum of dispute-settlement mechanism prototypes. It specifies third-party enforcement of the type common in domestic legal systems and abolishes parties' right to retaliate. As outlined in figure 6.4, all permissible paths lead to resolution of the dispute, and an appeals process replaces the option of "legal noncompliance" from DSM-I and DSM-II.

As noted earlier, abundant examples of DSM-IV are conspicuously absent from international trade relations, an observation typically attributed to the anarchic character of the international arena.[20] Much of the attention devoted to the evolution of the European Union can be attributed to the group's largely unprecedented, though partial, shift toward DSM-IV-like dispute-settlement mechanisms. Garrett and Weingast, for example, note that "it is clear that the Community comprises at least two fundamental features normally associated with sovereign polities: majoritarian decision making and *an authoritative legal system to enforce decisions* so made" (Garrett and Weingast 1993:174, emphasis added). Most analysts agree that the key to the EC's 1992 project was the 1987 Single Europe Act's shift from unanimity voting requirements, that permitted a single country to veto, to qualified-majority voting on many but not all issues in the Council of Ministers (Moravscik 1991; Sandholtz and Zysman 1989; Taylor 1983; Yarbrough 1994; Yarbrough and Yarbrough 1992:89–99).[21] After all, consensus requirements, if defined to include both the "plaintiff" and the "defendant," severely constrain the potential effectiveness of any dispute-settlement system. But the second essential element is a Community legal system in which Community laws have direct effect in member states and in which members do not have the option of determining unilaterally the extent of their Community obligations.[22] The organizing precept of this legal framework is mutual recognition, under which goods have unrestricted access to all Community markets once they qualify for legal sale in one member state.[23] The overall result is a system widely acknowledged as more reminiscent of a domestic constitutional order than of a system based simply on international treaties (Burley and Mattli 1993; Garrett 1992).

Because Community law has direct effect in member states, suits alleging violation of Community law can be brought in domestic courts, with all their usual enforcement prerogatives. When individuals believe national law or a member state's behavior to be inconsistent with Community law, they may either petition through domestic courts for rulings from the European Court of Justice (ECJ) or request the European Commission to petition the ECJ directly for a ruling. The mere threat of such a petition may suffice to bring member-state behavior into compliance, or a ruling may be required. Either route can establish the supremacy of Community law.

Of course, the European Union remains a group of sovereign states. Therefore, both the decisions of the Council and the rulings of the Court are constrained ultimately by the willingness of member states to support them (Garrett 1995; Garrett and Weingast 1993; Mancini 1991).[24] The ECJ itself has few direct enforcement powers, although it can fine firms found in violation of Community law; rather, the Court depends on member states' national legal systems for enforcement. As described by an ECJ judge:

> Noncompliance with directives is the most typical and most frequent form of member-state infraction; moreover, the Community authorities often turn a blind eye to it and, even when the Commission institutes proceedings against the defaulting state under Article 169 of the Treaty [of Rome], the Court cannot impose any penalty on the offender. This gives the directives a dangerously elastic quality.
>
> (Mancini 1991:182)

However, the ECJ, by using the doctrine of mutual recognition to eliminate ambiguity concerning member states' responsibilities and performance under the Treaty of Rome and the Single Europe Act, does play a key role in supporting compliance, albeit imperfect, with those agreements. The Court serves the information-provision function that we saw in DSM-I as well as its more binding adjudicatory functions (Garrett 1992:540, 557). It is these roles of the Court, along with the direct effect of Community law in national courts, that render the European Union unique in the international realm in its placement near DSM-IV along the continuum of dispute-settlement mechanisms.

The Fundamental Trade-Off

All four classes of dispute-settlement mechanism are used in international trade; and each of the four exhibits strengths and weaknesses. DSM-I and II rely heavily on the benefits of the ongoing relationship to provide compliance incentives. Trading partners maintain their independence from third parties, but at the expense of ongoing disputes. A party might choose such mechanisms (1) if it is willing to endure occasional episodes of ongoing noncompliance by the partner in exchange for the right to engage in occasional noncompliance itself, (2) if it is willing to endure occasional unilateral retaliation, unsupported by a third-party finding of a violation, in exchange for the right to engage in occasional unilateral retaliation itself, or (3) if it fears that a third party, if given power to render binding decisions, would treat it unfavorably. DSM-III and IV, on the other hand, place more enforcement power in the hands of the third party, but provide more definitive resolution of disputes. These latter two mechanisms minimize cases both of noncompliance and of unilateral retaliation.

Jeffrey Schott summarizes the basic trade-off as it applies to the new WTO dispute settlement understanding (DSU): "In essence, DSU paragraph 23 involves a basic bargain: in return for the more expeditious processing of disputes and the more automatic right to retaliate after a panel ruling, WTO members are required to use and abide by the DSU provisions when seeking redress for any violation of WTO obligations" (Schott 1994:131).

Given this trade-off between rigor and opportunity for derogations (both offensive and defensive), it should come as no surprise that *different country groups choose different dispute-settlement mechanisms* or that *members of a single group may exhibit differing preference rankings over dispute-settlement mechanisms*. In fact, a single pair of trading partners may choose different dispute-settlement mechanisms for different issues. For example, we have seen that NAFTA's chapter 20 procedures (for most NAFTA violations) approximate what we have labeled DSM-II procedures, while NAFTA chapter 19 (for dumping and subsidy cases) coincides more closely with DSM-III.

If indeed different country groups prefer and choose to implement different dispute-settlement mechanisms for their trade relationships, this variation may provide an important explanation for minilateral groups, or regionalism, in the world trading system. This suggests a need to understand more about trading partners' choices of dispute-settlement mechanisms and how they affect the prospects for and the process of cooperation in international trade.[25]

The Coordination Problem

One simple way of approaching this issue is to recognize two requisite parts of the larger overall problem of procedural cooperation: (1) parties must *coordinate* on provisions for dispute settlement, and (2) each party must

TABLE 6.4

"Pure Coordination" Game ($b_i > 0$)

| | | Player 2 | | | |
		DSM-I	DSM-II	DSM-III	DSM-IV
	DSM-I	b_1,b_2	0,0	0,0	0,0
Player 1	DSM-II	0,0	b_1,b_2	0,0	0,0
	DSM-III	0,0	0,0	b_1,b_2	0,0
	DSM-IV	0,0	0,0	0,0	b_1,b_2

then decide whether to *cooperate* in the sense of complying with or defecting from those provisions.[26]

Consider a game between two parties choosing among the four possible dispute-settlement mechanisms for their relationship, as in table 6.4. The two parties must coordinate on a mechanism. Should coordination fail, no dispute-settlement mechanism is legitimated and the parties rely entirely on self-help, represented by the off-diagonal outcomes in table 6.4.[27]

In other words, we assume that recognition of a dispute-settlement mechanism other than pure self-help requires mutual acceptance. This mutuality is reflected in the fact that the dispute-settlement mechanisms of various trade groups (for example, the WTO, the EU, or NAFTA) apply only to member countries, that is, those that subscribe to the mechanism itself as well as to the group's substantive obligations. Of course, a member may not comply with the specified dispute-settlement procedure *in a particular case.*[28] But, as long as membership in the group continues, such an episode represents a case of noncompliance with a recognized procedure (in the later Prisoners' Dilemma or cooperation stage of the game), not a case of noncoordination or failure to agree on a dispute-settlement procedure for the relationship.

If each party valued all four dispute-settlement mechanisms equally and preferred any one of them to noncoordination, the result would be a "Pure Coordination" game. Pure coordination problems can be difficult to solve with no communication, but should be amenable to communication or announcements of intent (Schelling 1960, especially chapter 3). If either player announces an intention to support any one of the dispute-settlement mechanisms, the other player has an incentive also to support it—rather than risk an uncoordinated or off-diagonal outcome that is inferior for both parties. Third parties also can contribute to solving coordination problems by making regulatory announcements, as when governments regulate driving on the right- or the left-hand side of the road in their jurisdictions.[29] Such regulations focus and coordinate individuals' expectations (Schelling 1960; Ullman-Margalit 1977). Alternatively, one mechanism may be a Schellingesque focal point for other reasons.

BENEFITS AND COSTS OF COORDINATION ON DISPUTE-SETTLEMENT MECHANISMS

Regardless of the particular technique utilized to achieve coordination, the likelihood of successful coordination should vary directly with the cost of error or of failure to coordinate. If the b_i terms in a particular trading relationship are large, errors involve forgoing significant benefits; and parties are likely to put substantial efforts into communicating, supporting appropriate regulation, or otherwise discerning a focal point to coordinate successfully on a dispute-settlement mechanism for the relationship.[30] In other relationships, the b_i terms may be small; and the small cost of errors may lead parties to miss in their coordination efforts, leading to an uncoordinated outcome in which self-help prevails as a default.

In international trade, different pairs of parties face different benefits from successful coordination on dispute-settlement and enforcement mechanisms. Pairs of countries that engage in large amounts of trade, trade in politically sensitive sectors, and whose trade involves frequent need to adjust to unforeseen contingencies are likely to face the largest potential benefits from coordination on dispute-settlement mechanisms—because their trade transactions are likely to encounter frequent, politically important, and potentially difficult-to-resolve disputes (Garrett and Weingast 1993; Williamson 1985; Yarbrough and Yarbrough 1987a, 1987b, 1992). Large amounts of capital sunk toward servicing the partner's market places a premium on predictable and effective dispute settlement. So-called deep integration, in which trade-related activities impinge on sensitive non-border domestic policies, also can place greater demands on dispute settlement (Haggard 1994:14; Yarbrough 1994; Yarbrough and Yarbrough 1992). These relation-specific attributes are in addition to the individual preferences mentioned above in discussion of the rigor/derogation trade-off among the various dispute-settlement mechanisms.

Other things equal, successful coordination with trading partners involving higher benefits from coordination is more likely than with those involving lower potential benefits. But, other things typically are *not* equal.

TABLE 6.5

"Battle of the Sexes" Game

		Player 2			
		DSM-I	DSM-II	DSM-III	DSM-IV
	DSM-I	b_1^I, b_2^I	0,0	0,0	0,0
	DSM-II	0,0	b_1^{II}, b_2^{II}	0,0	0,0
Player 1	DSM-III	0,0	0,0	b_1^{III}, b_2^{III}	0,0
	DSM-IV	0,0	0,0	0,0	b_1^{IV}, b_2^{IV}

NOTE: Payoff superscripts refer to coordination on the respective dispute-settlement mechanisms. Rank ordering of b_1^j differs from rank ordering of b_2^j.

In particular, divergent preferences among trading partners over the different mechanisms for dispute settlement and enforcement introduce conflictual elements into the Pure Coordination game.[31] The result is a structure usually denoted the "Battle of the Sexes" game, as in table 6.5, where b_i^j denotes the benefit to player i from coordination on dispute-settlement mechanism j.[32] The incentive for coordination persists (both $b_i^j > 0$ for at least some j), but parties' different preference rankings over the four coordinated outcomes render coordination more difficult, as each party tries to steer the choice toward its own most-preferred outcome.[33] In addition, divergent preferences create incentives for parties to engage in strategic delays in the hope of attaining a more-preferred outcome.[34]

A third party still may be able to facilitate coordination by announcing a "standard," but such announcements will be more controversial than in the Pure Coordination game because of their distributional implications. Alternatively, a mutually discernible focal point may prevail. Or, the parties may reach an obvious compromise; for example, the two may coordinate on dispute-settlement mechanism DSM-II if $b_1^I > b_1^{II} > 0 > b_1^{III} > b_1^{IV}$ and $b_2^{IV} > b_2^{III} > b_2^{II} > 0 > b_2^I$, implying that each rules out the other's more-preferred outcomes by ranking them below a noncoordinated outcome.[35]

Obviously, the extent to which coordination requires forgoing one's top choices depends on the heterogeneity of parties' preferences across the dispute-settlement mechanisms.[36] For pairs of countries with closely matching preferences, the coordination problem takes its pure form. Such pairs are likely to coordinate successfully on a dispute-settlement system, since doing so is consistent with both attaining their first- or near first-choice mechanism. As heterogeneity of preferences rises, one aspect of the cost to a country of coordination (that of forgoing its own top

TABLE 6.6
Determinants of Net Benefits of Coordination on a Dispute-Settlement Mechanism

		Cost of compromise required by divergent preferences over dispute-settlement mechanisms	
		Low *(pure coordination)*	*High* *(battle of the sexes)*
Cost of coordination failure	*High*	High b_i	Medium b_i
	Low	Medium b_i	Low (or negative)b_i

choices) rises. For pairs of countries possessing very different preference rankings over dispute-settlement mechanisms, the Battle of the Sexes rages, and coordination requires deep compromise unless one country is powerful enough to impose its own first choice on the other.[37]

The likelihood of successful coordination on some dispute-settlement mechanism between any particular pair of trading partners, therefore, depends on the interaction of two considerations. One is a comparison of the on-diagonal (coordination) and off-diagonal (noncoordination) payoffs, or the cost of failure to coordinate. The other is parties' harmonious or divergent preferences over the on-diagonal (coordination) payoffs, without regard to the cost of failure to coordinate. Combining the two allows us to sort pairs of trading partners based on their net benefits from successful coordination on a dispute-settlement mechanism, as in table 6.6.

Pairs of countries can then be ranked according to their net benefits from coordination, as in figure 6.5, where the specific country pairs are for simple illustrative purposes only. At the left end of the ranking are pairs of countries with high net benefits from coordination, the result of high costs of coordination failure *plus* relatively harmonious preferences that allow both parties to achieve their first or near-first preferences among dispute-settlement mechanisms. Such pairs correspond to those in the upper left-hand cell of table 6.6. Further to the right in figure 6.5's graphical ranking are pairs with *either* lower cost of failure *or* higher cost of compromising across divergent preferences (corresponding, respectively, to the lower left-hand and upper right-hand cells of table 6.6). The United States and Japan, for example, face high potential benefits from more successful dispute-settlement in trade, but the very different styles and preferences of the two countries mean coordination would require substantial compromise, rendering such coordination difficult. Finally, pairs at the right end of the ranking represent trading partners with relatively little to gain from coordination *and* with highly divergent

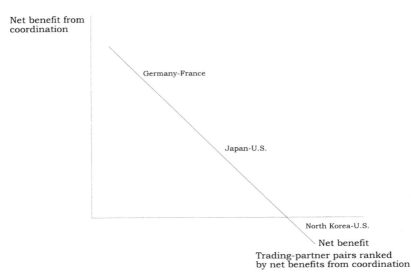

Net benefit from
coordination

Germany-France

Japan-U.S.

North Korea-U.S.

Net benefit

Trading-partner pairs ranked
by net benefits from coordination

FIGURE 6.5.   Country Pairs Ranked by Net Benefits From Coordination on Trade-Dispute Settlement.

preferences across dispute-settlement mechanisms, resulting in low or even negative net benefits and a deadlock in any coordination attempt.

Just as country pairs differ in their potential net benefits from coordination, the various possible dispute-settlement mechanisms in trade, represented by our DSM-I, II, III, and IV prototypes, differ in costs. Relevant costs include those typically subsumed under "transaction costs": negotiation, institution creation and financial support, monitoring and enforcement.[38] As a rough first approximation, we might expect these costs to rise with the extent to which the respective mechanisms require creation of new institutions and procedures. Basic international law and DSM-II-type procedures, such as those embodied in the (old) GATT, are available at relatively low cost. The relevant rules and procedures are already in place and can be used "off-the-shelf." More specialized or "customized" mechanisms such as DSM-III and DSM-IV require development of new and more extensive rules and procedures. This suggests that costs (per pair of countries) rise as countries move from DSM-I (third-party information provision) to DSM-II (nonbinding third-party adjudication), through DSM-III (binding third-party adjudication), and finally to DSM-IV (third-party enforcement), as in figure 6.6.

FIGURE 6.6.   Costs of Dispute-Settlement Mechanisms.

Combining the benefits to trading partners from successful coordination on a dispute-settlement mechanism and the various costs associated with the different mechanisms suggests an alignment of country pairs among the mechanisms, as illustrated in figure 6.7. Only those pairs with high costs of coordination failure *and* relatively harmonious preferences over the various mechanisms will have sufficiently high net benefits to con-

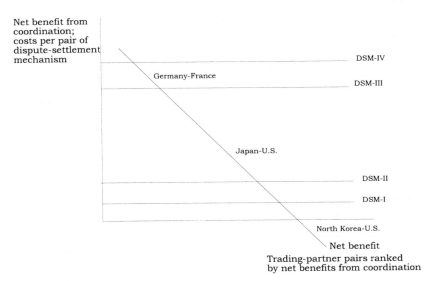

FIGURE 6.7.   Net Benefits from Coordination and Costs of Different Dispute-Settlement Mechanisms.

sider the more costly DSM-IV mechanism.[39] The implied *variation*, in the sense of different groups of countries choosing to construct different dispute-settlement mechanisms, is embodied in *regionalism,* which facilitates the preferred variation.[40]

CHANGES OVER TIME IN
DISPUTE-SETTLEMENT MECHANISMS

Using the basic framework outlined in figure 6.7, changes in the overall pattern of trade dispute-settlement mechanisms can occur for four reasons, each of which carries different implications for the observed pattern of dispute-settlement institutions. In particular, each source of change carries different implications for the extent of variation in pairs' dispute-settlement-mechanism choices and, therefore, for the extent of regionalism.

Changes in Benefits Facing a Specific Country Pair

A particular country pair may experience a change in its perceived benefits from coordination, shifting its position in the net-benefits ranking. This has been suggested widely as an answer to the "why now?" question concerning the EC-1992 project (Garrett 1992; Sandholtz and Zysman 1989; Yarbrough 1994; Yarbrough and Yarbrough 1992). Increased concerns about declining technology and competitiveness vis-à-vis Japan and the United States often are argued to have increased EC members' (particularly France's and Germany's) perceived benefits from an open internal market; and many analysts agree that moves to such an open market required the alterations in the institutional structure of EC decision making embodied in the Single Europe Act. Here, such changes would be represented by an increase in the Germany-France pair's b_i terms, due to perceived increases in the cost of coordination failure. As the pair moved up the net-benefit ranking, a shift from DSM-III toward DSM-IV became possible. A similar argument could be made for Canada and the United States: the perceived benefits of stronger dispute settlement grew as (1) Canada increasingly came to fear U.S. contingent protection, and (2) Canada's erratic policy toward inward foreign direct investment frustrated the United States. In such situations, we would expect to observe a change in the dispute-settlement mechanism selected by the particular country pair, while other pairs remained unchanged; in other words, distinct new regional groups may arise.

Shifts in the Entire Benefits Schedule

The entire net-benefit schedule also can shift. Trends toward both a higher share of economic transactions occurring across national boundaries and more capital sunk to serve particular export destinations place a premium on effective international dispute-settlement procedures.[41] Therefore, increased overall world trade would tend to shift the net-benefit schedule upward, as would efforts toward "deep integration" (Haggard 1994:14; Yarbrough 1994; Yarbrough and Yarbrough 1992). The result would be more success-ful coordination on all the dispute-settlement mechanisms. Increased har-mony in countries' preferences over the various mechanisms would have a similar effect, allowing each country to coordinate with its trading partners on a mutually more-preferred dispute-settlement mechanism.

In both these cases, we would expect to see increased use of specialized mechanisms such as the NAFTA and the EU *along with* growing member-ship in groups such as the GATT. Such shifts can also allow a pre-existing group to move from one dispute-settlement mechanism to another, as members' perceived net benefits from coordination grow. For example, we have suggested that the dispute-settlement accomplishments of the Uruguay Round, embodied in the new WTO, can be approximated as a partial move from what we have called DSM-II to DSM-III. The observed outcome following a shift in the entire benefits schedule—increased use of all dispute-settlement mechanisms by most countries—represents the pre-dictions of many proponents of regionalism, who see the phenomenon as a complement to other mechanisms such as the GATT.

Shifts in Relative Benefits

The slope of the net-benefits schedule can change, representing a change in the relative benefits of dispute settlement facing different subsets of trad-ing partners. The benefits schedule would become steeper if: (1) the net benefits from coordination rose for high-benefit pairs relative to those for low-benefit pairs, or (2) preferences over the mechanisms became more harmonious for already-harmonious pairs and less harmonious for already-contentious pairs. In these cases, we would expect use of DSM-III and

DSM-IV mechanisms such as the NAFTA and the EU to grow *relative to* or *at the expense of* DSM-I and II groups. This corresponds to the outcome feared by many opponents of regionalism. Conversely, harmonization of the benefits from coordination or of preferences across the various country pairs would flatten the net-benefits schedule and lead to growth in DSM-I and II arrangements, perhaps *at the expense of* DSM-III and IV.

Shifts in the Costs of the Various Dispute-Settlement Mechanisms

Finally, the costs associated with the different dispute-settlement mechanisms themselves can change. In particular, as the relatively rare DSM-III and IV begin to be used, the newly formed groups provide institutional models that can be copied and modified by others. This phenomenon reduces the set-up costs associated with those mechanisms and, other things equal, increases their relative usage. The cost of institutional development in NAFTA, for example, clearly was reduced by the prior existence of the Canada–U.S. Free-Trade Agreement. In this sense, dispute-settlement mechanisms in trade may exhibit positive feedback: use promotes more use.

FROM COORDINATION BACK TO COOPERATION

The outcome of trading partners' Coordination/Battle of the Sexes game over dispute-settlement mechanisms affects the likelihood of cooperation in two related but distinct ways. *First,* the outcome of the initial coordination stage of each trading pair's relationship—in which they choose a dispute-settlement mechanism—determines the benefits participants receive from their dispute-settlement agreement. Those benefits are reflected back to the b_i payoffs in the cooperation stage of the relationship, represented by the Prisoners' Dilemmas in tables 6.1 through 6.3, where each country must decide whether to comply with the agreed-on mechanism. In the case of highly specialized dispute-settlement mechanisms, cooperation or compliance is more likely as parties will not want to risk forgoing future benefits in order to attain the short-term gains from noncompliance with an unfavorable ruling.[42]

Second, the rules of the dispute-settlement mechanism itself, whether based on self-enforcement or on third parties, form an institutional layer that alters the structure of the compliance dilemma, as illustrated in the comparison of table 6.1 (single-play PD), table 6.2 (repeated PD under a self-enforcing agreement), and table 6.3 (PD with third-party enforcement).

It no longer is controversial to argue that institutions matter, especially in the international trade arena. In particular, we have good evidence that institutions can support cooperation. But cooperation in international trade (and, presumably, in other issues as well) does not mean just abiding by the barrier-reducing *substance* of trade agreements; it also means abiding by the dispute-settlement *procedures* that necessarily accompany substantive agreements. Thus, the larger process of cooperation requires trading partners to coordinate successfully on a dispute-settlement mechanism, which may include various elements of self-help and third-party enforcement.

Many recent institutional changes in international trade, including the NAFTA, the EU, and much of what has come to be viewed as a shift from multilateralism toward regionalism, can be approached usefully from the perspective of changing patterns of cooperation evidenced by new methods of dispute settlement. In particular, the deliberate creation of elaborate new governance and dispute-settlement institutions constitute key elements of the most important regional trade groups, especially the EU and the NAFTA.

Different dispute-settlement mechanisms provide varying combinations of rigor, definitive resolution of disputes, third-party prerogatives, and loopholes. Given the fundamental trade-off between rigor and opportunity for derogations, different country groups seem likely to choose different dispute-settlement mechanisms. If indeed different trading groups choose to implement different dispute-settlement mechanisms, this variation may explain important elements of the regionalism observed in the world trading system, because exclusively multilateral approaches preclude such variation. A dispute-settlement perspective on regionalism suggests that a single right answer to the frequently posed question, "Are regionalism and multilateralism substitutes or complements?" probably does not exist. However, to the extent that trends toward both a higher share of economic transactions occurring across national boundaries and more capital sunk to serve particular export destinations place an across-the-board premium on effective international dispute-settlement, we should expect regional institutions to thrive *along with* more multilateral institutions such as the new World Trade Organization.

160   *Beth V. Yarbrough and Robert M. Yarbrough*

Acknowledgments: We thank participants at the 1994 Annual Meetings of the American Political Science Association, at seminars at Princeton University's Department of Politics and Woodrow Wilson School and at Harvard Law School, and at the Columbia University Conference on the Political Economy of Regionalism, especially Giovanni Maggi, Edward Mansfield, John McLaren, Helen Milner, Ken Oye, and Anne-Marie Slaughter for comments on this paper. We also acknowledge Amherst College's support of our research, especially an Amherst College Faculty Research Award that supported revisions of this paper.

Notes

1. We take regional*ism* to be an *active* process in which policy makers differentiate between trading partners; this category includes free-trade areas, investment treaties, and factor-flow agreements. By contrast, we would use the term regional*ization* to denote a more *passive* process; this would include, for example, changes in trade patterns that occur because of changes in comparative advantage or transportation costs, as opposed to active policy choices. See also Haggard (1994:2–3).

2. Traditionally, international economists' work on regional trade groups has focused on their efficiency merits and demerits compared with universal free trade (Bhagwati 1993; Lipsey 1960; Viner 1950). Much of that work abstracts from the specific institutions through which trade liberalization is accomplished, whether regionally or universally. Internationally oriented political scientists, on the other hand, have examined the implications of trade regionalism for international politics and vice versa, but again with relatively little attention to specific institutional detail (for examples, see Gowa 1994; Mansfield 1994; Pollins 1989). Such approaches, at least when used in combination, may suffice for the study of many regional trade groups. After all, most groups currently function as (at most) simple free-trade areas or customs unions; that is, members lower their intra-group trade barriers and, perhaps, impose a common external tariff, but create little in the way of idiosyncratic institutions or specialized rules beyond this reduction of intragroup trade barriers.

On the other hand, the new institutions of regionalism, especially those underlying the European Union, and the processes by which they have been created have received extensive and detailed study, particularly by political scientists. However, studies of the actual institutions underlying these regional groupings have had a decidedly internal or intragroup focus (for examples, see Burley and Mattli 1993; Garrett 1992, 1995; Garrett and Weingast 1993; Moravscik 1991; Mattli and Slaughter 1995; Sandholtz and Zysman 1989). They tend to explain each group's institutions based on its unique history and not to take a comparative institutional perspective (in terms of either comparison across regional groups or comparison of regionalism with unilateral or multilateral alternatives); therefore, they have limited direct generalizability to the broader phenomenon of regionalism. Exceptions are Grieco (1994, this volume) and Haggard (1994, this volume), who compare the accomplishments and prospects of regionalism in the Western Hemisphere with that in Asia and Europe.

3. Haggard concurs (1994:2).

4. Milner (1991a) provides a useful discussion organized around definitions of "anarchy."

Implications of the resulting security concerns for regionalism play central roles in Kupchan (1994, this volume) and Mansfield and Bronson (1994, this volume).

5. Krugman (1995) ventures an alternative or additional explanation for observed trade policy: policy makers' preoccupation with military metaphors for trade and lack of understanding of fundamental concepts such as comparative advantage.

6. No doubt some failures of cooperation occur in situations in which the incentives for defection simply are too strong to be overcome, and thus the dilemma defeats the prisoners (D. Baldwin 1993; Grieco 1990).

7. The latter behavior is one interpretation of U.S. "aggressive unilateralism" in trade.

8. Garrett (1995) takes a step in this direction with application to the EC.

9. The four do not include pure self-help, which we take to be the default, or the outcome of failure to coordinate on an alternative.

10. Over the years, GATT practice evolved from a negotiation-oriented process with little emphasis on rules and their quasi-legal interpretation and application toward a more rule-oriented adjudicatory process. The change in dispute-settlement procedures from reliance on "working parties" (members of which represented governments of the parties involved) to more neutral "panels" is indicative of this general shift.

11. Increasingly frequent complaints of nullification and impairment based on *non*violations are even more controversial.

12. The GATT is unusual among international treaties in that violation by one party gives the aggrieved party the right to retaliate by withdrawing equivalent concessions, but *not* to discontinue its own performance under the agreement (Brand 1993:134).

13. In addition, a few panel reports were blocked by large numbers of countries because the reports were found to be in error; this functioned as an informal appeal process.

14. The "binding" in binding arbitration applies differentially to various countries, which utilize different constitutionally defined relationships between domestic and international law. In some ("monist") countries, their international law obligations automatically become a part of domestic law. In other ("dualist") countries, such as the United States, international law obligations generally have no domestic force unless they are given that force through implementing domestic legislation. For dualist countries, violations of international obligations that have not been incorporated explicitly into domestic law carry no domestic legal consequences (Jackson 1992). In addition, adopted GATT/WTO panel reports impose an international law obligation, but carry no power of precedent.

15. During the U.S. congressional debate on implementing legislation for the WTO and Uruguay Round results, opponents alleged these changes—instituted largely at the behest of the United States—constituted an infringement on U.S. sovereignty. Congress succeeded in introducing a process of domestic oversight of WTO decisions that could lead to congressional demands that the United States withdraw from the organization following three "improper" WTO panel decisions in a five-year period. Schott (1994) provides a useful discussion of the WTO's safeguards to national sovereignty.

16. The agreement recommends within-sector retaliation and sanctions retaliation across agreements as a last resort.

17. As we note below, despite their similarities, the WTO and NAFTA chapter 19 exhibit an important difference on another margin. The WTO adjudicates disputes based on *international* rules, that is, contracting parties' GATT obligations. NAFTA binational review panels adjudicate disputes based on members' *national* rules regarding imposition of antidumping or countervailing duties.

18. On the political economy of contingent-protection policies, including AD/CVD, see Westhoff, Yarbrough, and Yarbrough (1995).

19. National laws require both an affirmative finding of a nonzero dumping margin or subsidy and an affirmative finding of injury to the domestic industry before an antidumping or countervailing duty can be imposed.

20. While the degree of "anarchy" clearly differs between the domestic and international spheres, it is worth noting that third-party enforcement is far from perfect in a domestic context; otherwise, the producers of "America's Most Wanted" would lack for story lines.

21. Although provided for in the original Treaty of Rome, qualified-majority voting had been set aside from 1966 through 1985 under the so-called Luxembourg Compromise, in response to France's vehement opposition to some Community policies.

22. This was established in *Van Gend en Loos* (1963) and extended in *Van Duyt v. Home Office* (1974). The WTO plays an analogous role for the GATT by instituting membership as a "single undertaking"—that is, a prix fixe rather than an á la carte approach.

23. Mutual recognition was established by the European Court of Justice in *Cassis de Dijon* (1979).

24. Economists George Akerlof and Janet Yellen make a parallel point in a very different context (*Wall Street Journal* 1994). They argue that neighborhood crime control hinges on a critical level of community support. Without that support, law enforcement authorities are powerless to enforce the law, because members of the community withhold information, harbor fugitives, and fail to report criminal activity. The result is a delicate constraint on both criminals and law enforcement authorities. Criminals must engage in enough crime to earn profits, but not enough to lose the support of their community and cause a grassroots "get tough on crime" movement. Law enforcement authorities must enforce the law, but do so in a way that maintains the support of the community.

25. We assume throughout that states choose the dispute-settlement mechanisms for their trade. Private interest groups may affect these choices through their lobbying efforts, as emphasized by Milner (1994). We do not examine private parties' ability to contract for dispute-settlement mechanisms other than those chosen by their respective states. Cohen (1994) highlights the role of such private, market-driven arrangements in the monetary sphere. No doubt they are equally important in trade, providing, for example, one explanation of multinational enterprises, that can internalize dispute settlement for divisions operating in different nation-states.

26. Garrett and Weingast (1993:179–84) suggest a similar framework for analyzing the role of ideas in facilitating cooperation. Of course, the predicted outcome in the later PD/cooperation stage of the game will affect behavior in the earlier coordination stage, as well as vice versa.

27. We set the noncoordination (off-diagonal) payoffs at zero for simplicity, so that b_1 measures the benefits of coordination.

28. The distinction between compliance in a particular case and more general cooperation in a dispute-settlement mechanism is important. On the distinction in the European Union, see Burley and Mattli (1993), Garrett (1992, 1995), and Mattli and Slaughter (1995).

29. On alternative solutions to coordination problems in cases where announcement strategies are ineffective, see Yarbrough and Yarbrough (1995a).

30. Recall that, for simplicity, we set the off-diagonal or noncoordination payoffs to zero.

31. Haggard (1994:4, 15–18) and Kahler (1993) argue persuasively that many of the cooperation problems typically attributed to large numbers stem more fundamentally from divergent preferences (which, of course, become more likely as group size increases). See also Yarbrough and Yarbrough (1995a).

32. The classic story underlying the Battle of the Sexes game involves a couple who value spending time together (for example, an evening out or a week's vacation), but have different preferences over activities.

33. Krasner (1991) argues that the focus on Prisoners' Dilemma in the study of international relations has obscured the perhaps greater importance of Battle of the Sexes phenomena.

34. We thank John McLaren for pointing out the relationship between Battle of the Sexes and strategic delay. On delay tactics in international trade, see Hudec (1990), Kovenoch and Thursby (1992), and Lipson (1991).

35. This creates an incentive for parties to misrepresent their preferences.

36. By limiting our examination to the dispute-settlement mechanisms chosen by *pairs* of trading partners, we avoid some of the complex but important issues raised by the interplay between membership and rules. Padoan (1994), for example, highlights the role of the uncertainty about future membership in the debate over European monetary integration. See also Yarbrough and Yarbrough (1992).

37. In order to focus on the simplest relationship between the coordination and cooperation aspects of dispute settlement in trade, we ignore such power asymmetries, while recognizing that they clearly are important in many trading relationships.

38. We include only those costs that are not relation specific to particular pairs of trading partners. Items that are specific, including concerns over "loss of sovereignty," we include in the b_i terms.

39. Note that the predictions refer to the *type* of dispute-settlement mechanism selected by each pair of countries, not to the bilateral or multilateral nature of the dispute-settlement mechanisms themselves. For example, the GATT (a representative of DSM-II) is utilized by a large number of pairs, while NAFTA (DSM-II and DSM-III) covers only three: U.S.–Canada, U.S.–Mexico, and Canada–Mexico. On the interaction of bilateral and multilateral trade groups, see Westhoff, Yarbrough, and Yarbrough (1994).

40. Recall that we are using the "active" connotation of regionalism, as defined in note 1.

41. On recent changes in the nature of trade, see Yarbrough and Yarbrough (1996).

42. Garrett (1995) applies this argument to the case of EU member governments' compliance with ECJ decisions, especially Germany's with *Cassis de Dijon.*

SEVEN

Systemic Sources of Variation in Regional Institutionalization in Western Europe, East Asia, and the Americas

Joseph M. Grieco

As Edward Mansfield and Helen Milner point out in their introductory essay, countries in Western Europe, East Asia, and the Americas have initiated or redoubled efforts in recent years to promote regional economic integration through the establishment or strengthening of regional institutions.[1] The institutions that the nations of Western Europe and the Americas have built or are building differ significantly in their structures and goals, and the efforts to date of East Asian countries to construct such formal economic institutions have met with little success. The discussion below seeks to describe this variation, and to help account for it.[2]

Variation in regional economic institutionalization is likely to be the result of a wide range of factors that are discussed in this book. For example, Stephan Haggard in his essay demonstrates that the decision by many countries in Latin America to undertake domestic economic liberalization facilitated enhanced cooperation in that region, while continuing divergences in domestic political–economic structures hampered such cooperation among countries in the Pacific Rim. Helen Milner finds that the intersection of electoral interests of politicians and the market-expansion interests of large, politically important producers may have encouraged the formation of NAFTA.[3] Working at the systemic level, Edward Mansfield and Rachel Bronson demonstrate that the existence of political-military alliances may also promote regionalized trade cooperation. My essay seeks to complement such arguments by attempting to shed light on the variance in modern regional institutionalization through a focus on power-oriented variables operating at the regional level of analysis.

VARIATION IN REGIONALISM IN EUROPE, THE AMERICAS, AND ASIA

The process of institutionalization of economic relations in different parts of the world can be compared along at least three dimensions. The first is *locus of institutionalization*, the legal-organizational basis of association among partners. Possible modes of association include bilateral trade treaties, groupings composed of some but not all countries in the region, or a single regional entity. Following the lead of neofunctional integration theory (Schmitter 1969; Lindberg and Scheingold 1970), the second dimension is *scope of activity*, the number of issues covered by regional arrangements. The third dimension, and again following the lead of neofunctionalism, is *level of institutional authority*, which refers to whether national governments are jointly pooling a small or a substantial amount of responsibility regarding the activities covered by their regional arrangements.

Employment of these indicators allows for the observation of substantial variation in institutionalization in the three major regions. First, there are significant differences in the *locus of institutionalization*. The European Community (or, in regard to many issue-areas, the European Union) has emerged as the main focal point for economic cooperation in Western Europe.[4] When the six members of the original European Coal and Steel Community (ECSC)—France, Germany, Italy, Belgium, the Netherlands, and Luxembourg—formed the European Economic Community in 1957 (which in 1967 became the European Communities, or, more commonly, the European Community, or EC), Britain joined with Sweden, Finland, Norway, Switzerland, and Austria to form a more limited European Free Trade Area (EFTA). But the EC proved to be the more robust institution: Britain, Denmark, and Ireland joined in 1973; Greece did so in 1981, and Spain and Portugal acceded in 1986. Three other former EFTA countries—Austria, Finland, and Sweden—became EC members in 1995. Of the original EFTA countries, only Norway and Switzerland remain outside the Community, and such countries as Poland, Hungary, and the Czech Republic have emphasized that they very much wish to join the EC.

As described in studies by Milensky (1973, 1977), in 1960 eleven countries in the Americas attempted to create the Latin America Free Trade Area (LAFTA), but this effort ended in failure in 1969. Institutionalization is once again being pursued in the Americas (Whalley 1992; Edwards 1993), but is proceeding at least to date on the basis of a number of discreet trade liberalization pacts among subsets of countries in the region. For example, the Canada–U.S. Trade Agreement (CUSTA) of 1987 liberalized trade between these two key economic partners, and the North American Free Trade Arrangement (NAFTA), ratified in 1993, binds together the United States, Mexico, and Canada.

Another important new Latin American regional trading arrangement, the Common Market of the South (Mercosur), was agreed to in March 1991 by Argentina, Brazil, Paraguay, and Uruguay (Manzetti 1992; Hinchberger 1993; Pena 1995). It seeks to create a customs union among these countries, i.e., both to reduce intraregional tariffs and to establish a common external tariff. Intra-Mercosur tariff cuts proceeded between 1992 and 1994 so that when the agreement came into force in January 1995, approximately 90 percent of trade among the members was free of duties (Long 1994). The Mercosur members have had less success in formulating a common external tariff. The partners agreed that beginning in January 1995 each could exempt up to 300 products from the common tariff (399 for Paraguay). Moreover, in the face of an import boom, Brazil in the spring of 1995 asked for and was granted the right to increase its list of exempted products to 450, and Argentina, in an effort to stave off a similar problem, unilaterally raised tariffs on all imports from outside the region by 3 percent.[5] Still, by mid-1995 Mercosur was becoming a significant new institutional force in South America.

Colombia, Mexico, and Venezuela (the Group of 3, or G-3) are also pursuing a trade liberalization program, but its prospects are less certain than Mercosur's. At first the G-3 countries set January 1992 as the starting point for tariff cuts to be implemented over three years. However, the January 1992 starting point was missed; a new plan, formalized in a free trade agreement signed in June 1994 and entering into force in January 1995, is to reduce tariffs over ten years, and to do so in the sensitive auto sector over twelve years.[6] Finally, the Andean Pact countries (Bolivia, Colombia, Ecuador, Peru, and Venezuela) have sought again in the early 1990s to liberalize regional trade, but in light of past experience (Middlebrook 1978; Vargas-Hildago 1979; Hojman 1981) it is difficult to be confident that such efforts will yield significant results.

In sum, diplomatic efforts to date in the Americas are producing, in the words of John Whalley (1992:126), "a patchwork quilt of trade arrangements." It is unlikely that these arrangements will coalesce into a single institutional focal point. Yet, there are a few signs that the arrangements might expand and that some might establish linkages with one another. For example, at the December 1994 Summit of the Americas the NAFTA partners initiated talks with Chile aimed at its accession to that agreement.[7] In addition, Mercosur has undertaken negotiations with each of the five members of the Andean Pact to extend the former's trade preferences to the latter ("Venezuela Wants Free Trade Zone" 1995). Chile has had discussions with Mercosur that might result in some form of association short of full membership, but it is clear that Chile's primary goal at present is to join NAFTA ("Chile Wants Free Trade" 1995). In addition, the Mercosur countries signed a "framework agreement" with the United States in June 1991 that could serve as the basis for later negotiations for a trade agreement (Dandeker 1992). The United States has indicated that the NAFTA agreement might be opened to other countries besides Chile. However, such an effort to create a broader free trade area is unlikely to be pursued until well into the next decade; although at the December 1994 Miami Summit the attending states announced talks aimed at a free trade area for the entire region, they also indicated that such a free trade zone would come into effect no earlier than the year 2005.[8]

Trade integration through formal institutions has intensified in both Europe and the Americas, albeit along different paths with respect to loci of institutionalization. In contrast, in spite of several efforts the countries of East Asia have not achieved significant formal institutionalization of economic relations. The six members of the Association of South East Asian Nations (ASEAN)—Brunei, Indonesia, Malaysia, the Philippines, Singapore, and Thailand, with Vietnam joining as the seventh member in 1995—have long sought to provide preferences for intermember trade, but these efforts have had a negligible impact on actual trade patterns (Langhammer 1991; Yamazawa 1992; Kurus 1993). The ASEAN countries agreed in February 1992 to pursue intraregional trade liberalization on their own over a period of fifteen years through the mechanism of AFTA—the Asian Free Trade Area (Kandiah 1991; "Fortress Asia?" 1992). However, by the spring of 1995 very little progress had been made in starting the implementation process for AFTA.[9]

In addition, Malaysia's government began in December 1990 to solicit support for the formation of what would have been called the East Asian Economic Group, or the EAEG (Low 1991). The EAEG, according to the Malaysian government proposal, would have included the ASEAN countries as well as Japan, Hong Kong, South Korea, and Taiwan. The Malaysian government argued that such a grouping could serve as a pressure group within the Uruguay Round and, more significantly over the longer run, as a possible framework for enhanced regional trade liberalization. However, the Malaysian government was unable to garner the support even of its partners in ASEAN, and in the face of U.S. opposition and Japanese indifference the EAEG idea failed to materialize. Malaysia was able to persuade its ASEAN partners in October 1991 to try to form a weaker East Asian Economic Caucus (EAEC), but it was unable to win the support of other East Asian countries for this proposed arrangement and an ASEAN partner, Indonesia, lost interest in the proposal.[10]

To date the only regional trade grouping that involves the East Asian countries is a broader trans-Pacific process called Asia-Pacific Economic Cooperation, or APEC. The result of a 1989 Australian government proposal, it brings together officials of the United States, Canada, Mexico, Chile, Japan, Australia, New Zealand, China, Taiwan, Hong Kong, and the ASEAN countries (Elek 1991; Funabashi 1995). At a summit in November 1994 in Bogor, Indonesia, the leaders of the APEC countries said they would remove barriers to trade in manufactured goods and in investment flows among the advanced partners by 2010, and that such liberalization would be achieved by the developing-country members by 2020. However, the summit statement is nonbinding, and a subsequent summit at Osaka also produced only nonbinding unilateral commitments to liberalization on the part of the APEC participants (Hughes 1991; Crone 1993; Schott 1995; Grieco 1996a).

Turning to *scope of activity*, the members of the EC have widened the Community's responsibilities substantially in recent years through the Single Market Program of 1985 and the Single European Act of 1987. In addition, the EC countries are seeking to move the Community beyond trade liberalization, for with the Maastricht Treaty of December 1991 they initiated a process that, while currently seriously offtrack, might eventually end in Economic and Monetary Union, or EMU. Finally, with Maastricht the EC countries have sought to move more aggressively toward the establishment of common policies in social affairs and even defense and foreign policy.[11]

While there has been a marked expansion of tasks covered by EC institutions, Mercosur is concerned almost exclusively with the reduction of barriers to trade, and in particular the reduction of tariffs. NAFTA seeks to begin to address such trade-related matters as the protection of intellectual property rights and the environment. However, compared to the EC's efforts to establish a single currency, a common social policy, and a common defense and foreign policy, the current scope of regional economic arrangements in the Americas remains narrow.

ASEAN is supposed to have a substantial range of economic and even political responsibilities. However, as noted above, these formal responsibilities have not been translated into significant regional integration or cooperation. The scope of APEC's activities are at the same time moderately wide but thin: the members have established work teams on several issues, including trade, technology, energy, and telecommunications, but these are engaged for the most part solely in the gathering and exchange of information. To date, no government commitments regarding these issue areas have been undertaken as a result of the APEC process.

Finally, the European Community again provides evidence of a high and growing *level of institutional authority*. Its member-states have invested substantial responsibility in the Commission of the EC. The EC countries have also accepted that the European Court of Justice (ECJ) may have an important voice in both Community and therefore national economic regulatory policy (Burley and Mattli 1993). In addition, the Single European Act provides that the EC members, in regard to most Single Market Program issues, may proceed on the basis of majority voting (Garrett 1992). Moreover, if the European Community countries attain EMU over the next decade, then they will cede to an independent Community-level European Central Bank wide powers regarding monetary policy.

The level of regional authority associated with cooperative arrangements in the Americas is much more modest than in Western Europe. CUSTA has entailed the establishment of cross-national conflict resolution boards. Moreover, NAFTA and Mercosur envision the establishment of similar dispute settlement arrangements. However, these agreements are strictly intergovernmental accords with little aspiration to significant forms of supranational authority as in the EC case.

There is even less supranationalism in Asia. For example, discussions taking place over more than one year were required before the APEC countries were able to agree to establish a small secretariat for the group, and this was not accomplished until February 1993 when an office was opened in Singapore. It was not until April of that year that the members selected an executive director for that secretariat.[12] Perhaps most tellingly, it was a highly controversial matter within APEC as to whether the members' heads of government should meet at the November 1993 meeting of the group in Seattle, and not just the foreign and trade ministers: the proposal for such a high-level gathering met the opposition not just of China because of its concerns about the status within the group of Hong Kong and Taiwan, but also some of the ASEAN countries.[13]

Thus, in contrast to Europe and the Americas, Asia presents a case of the absence of significant institutionalization in economic affairs. Efforts—most notably the Malaysian proposal for EAEG/EAEC—have been made to create a stronger institutional manifestation of regional ties, but these efforts have either failed or face uncertain prospects at best. As Albert Fishlow and Stephan Haggard have observed of the Pacific region, "There has been a flurry of new proposals and initiatives in the last two years, but to date, the puzzle with reference to the Pacific is not to explain the progress of regional initiatives, but their relative weakness" (1992:30).

ACCOUNTING FOR THE VARIATION: FUNCTIONALIST AND HEGEMONIC LEADERSHIP EXPLANATIONS

In Western Europe we observe significant increases in regional institutionalization centered around the EC; in the Americas there have been several steps—especially through the construction of NAFTA and Mercosur—toward such institutionalization; but in East Asia the countries that were eligible to become members of the proposed EAEG and the EAEC elected not to pursue either, the ASEAN/AFTA scheme has modest prospects at best, and APEC is transregional in composition and is rather stunted in its goals and structures. Why do we see this pattern of differentiated regional institutionalization? The discussion below suggests that systemic-level arguments presented by functionalists and hegemonic leadership theorists are helpful but not fully satisfactory as we seek to understand this variation in contemporary economic regionalism.

Why should countries accept the costs (in terms most importantly of freedom of unilateral action) associated with the establishment and maintenance of an international institution?[14] One basic argument is that governments are most likely to do so if and as the latter meets specific functional needs arising from some form of international interaction.[15] From the viewpoint of this functionalist line of inquiry, as economic interactions within a particular region increase, governments in that region may find that there is a functional need to work more closely together through institutions, and to pay the autonomy costs associated with the latter, to ensure that such interactions continue and expand but do not unduly erode national economic policy autonomy to an even greater degree than would be entailed if they worked together through institutions. In the same vein, if economic integration is not increasing within a region, then this absence of a functional need for institutionalization would translate into little or no increase in the preferences on the part of states to establish such arrangements. Overall, then, the functionalist orientation to international political economy might suggest that we ought to see a positive relationship between the growth in intraregional economic interactions and efforts at regional institutionalization, with the former creating a functional need—and hence serving as a motor or catalyst—for the building of regional institutions.

This argument has an important level of empirical validity in regard to contemporary regional institutionalization, but it also has empirical problems. One key type of data that may be reflective of intensification of regional economic integration is that of trade encapsulation, defined here as the percentage of all exports by countries of an actual or proposed regional arrangement that go to other countries in that actual/proposed arrangement. As noted above, the specific functionalist expectation might be that as trading ties deepen among a group of countries, the latter will have a greater common interest in managing and perhaps also in accelerating that growth in intragroup trade through institutions. To the extent that trade encapsulation is in fact a valid indicator of deepening economic integration, then we should observe greater institutionalization of economic relations among those groupings of countries that have experienced greater levels of trade encapsulation, with the former induced by the latter.

To observe whether this functionalist-posited relationship obtains, table 7.1 presents data on trends in regional trade encapsulation between 1970 and 1990 in the European Community, two of the groupings of countries in the Americas (NAFTA and Mercosur) where institutionalization is taking place, and the three groupings in Asia and the Pacific where such institutionalization was proposed but rejected (EAEG/EAEC) or has modest prospects (ASEAN/AFTA and APEC).

A very high level of trade encapsulation developed among the member countries of the European Community during the past twenty years: encapsulation of exports among EC countries increased from a level of 50 percent in 1970 to 61 percent by 1990. Functionalists could look at these

TABLE 7.1

Trade Encapsulation Within Selected Actual and Proposed Regional Arrangements,
1970–1990

Intraregional Exports as percent of All Exports (all figures in percent)

Actual/Proposed arrangements	1970	1980	1990
EC	50	56	61
NAFTA	36	34	41
Mercosur	9	12	14
ASEAN	21	18	19
APEC	54	55	66
EAEG/EAEC	31	36	40

SOURCES: International Monetary Fund, *Direction of Trade Yearbook*, various years; Council for Economic Planning, *Taiwan Statistical Data Book*, various years.

data and make a strong case that the intensification of EC institutionalization during this period was driven by the functional challenges created by these very large increases in regional trade. Functionalists might also find support for their general argument in NAFTA: while export encapsulation among Canada, Mexico, and the United States was roughly one-third in 1970, it reached 41 percent by 1990.

However, contrary to functionalist expectations, in some areas of the world there have been increases in intraregional trade without a corresponding increase in institutionalization. For example, among the countries in East Asia that would have constituted the aborted EAEG/EAEC, there was an increase in regional trade encapsulation from 31 percent in 1970 to 40 percent in 1990, i.e., almost the same level as was attained in North America.[16] Similarly, the countries that form the very weakly developed APEC reached an even higher level of trade encapsulation by 1990 (66 percent) than had the EC countries by that time (61 percent).

Moreover, in some cases we can observe growth in institutionalization, or at least attempts at such institutionalization, in the absence of increased trade encapsulation. For example, the ASEAN countries have been making efforts—including the conclusion of an agreement—to establish AFTA even though trade encapsulation has not changed appreciably during the past twenty years (and was less in 1990 than in 1970). Finally, in the case of Mercosur we observe modest regional institutionalization in the absence of markedly enhanced regional trade encapsulation. Thus, while the EC and NAFTA cases support functional arguments, the cases of Mercosur,

ASEAN/AFTA, EAEG/EAEC, and APEC do not seem to be in accord with the functionalist perspective.

Similarly, regionalization both presents challenges to and can be partially explained by the second major systemic-level approach to world politics, neorealist international theory and its hegemonic leadership thesis. The general argument that neorealists such as Robert Gilpin (1971, 1975) and Stephen Krasner (1976) have brought forward about international economic cooperation is that it is heavily dependent on the presence and efforts of a hegemonic leader such as Britain in the nineteenth century and the United States after World War II. The hegemon, in this line of analysis, bears the costs associated with providing political-military and diplomatic resources needed to establish the institutions through which such interdependence can be attained. Further, according to this perspective, the hegemon plays a key commercial and financial role in sustaining economic openness, including serving as a large market and providing emergency liquidity in the face of currency crises.[17] From the viewpoint of this thesis, we should observe regionalism developing more fully in those areas of the world in which there is a local hegemon able to create and maintain regional economic institutions, and we should observe regionalism advancing at a less pronounced pace in those areas where local hegemonic leadership is less visible.

One key way to determine whether a single regional hegemon has been present in the actual or proposed groupings described above is to examine the distribution of intraregional *overall national capabilities*, while another is to examine the distribution of *issue-specific capabilities* (Keohane and Nye 1977:49–54; Keohane 1980). Both types of data are presented in table 7.2. Part A of the table employs as a measure of overall regional hegemony the relative share of Gross Domestic Product (GDP) of the largest state in each of the six major actual or potential regional arrangements in Western Europe, East Asia, and the Americas.

The cases of the United States/NAFTA and Brazil/Mercosur would appear to be in accord with the expectations of the hegemonic leadership approach. However, the cases of Germany/EC and Japan/EAEG/EAEC both seem to cut against that approach. In the former instance there is the combination of the lowest concentration of regional economic capabilities among the groupings under review and the highest level of achieved regional institutionalization, and in the latter case there is the combination of a very high concentration of economic capabilities but failed regional

TABLE 7.2

Hegemonic Leadership in Western Europe, East Asia, and the Americas, 1990

Part A: Overall Capabilities Method: Share of regional
GDP originating in largest regional partner

Country	Actual/Proposed Arrangement	Country GDP/Regional GDP (%), 1990
Germany	EC	24.8
U.S.	NAFTA	86.9
Brazil	Mercosur	80.9
Indonesia	ASEAN/AFTA	33.2
U.S.	APEC	51.6
Japan	EAEG/EAEC	72.5

Part B: Issue-Specific Method: Share of total exports from
regional trading partners going to largest regional trading partner

Country	Actual/Proposed Arrangement	Share of total exports to largest regional partner, (%), 1990
Germany	EC	18.3
U.S.	NAFTA	74.4
Brazil	Mercosur	14.9
Indonesia (1)	ASEAN/AFTA	2.1
Singapore (1)	ASEAN/AFTA	10.0
U.S.	APEC	33.3
Japan	EAEG/EAEC	14.6

SOURCES: Part A: World Bank, *World Bank Atlas* (1972, 1983, 1992); United Nations, *Statistical Yearbook of the United Nations* (1982, 1990/91); International Monetary Fund, *International Financial Statistics Yearbook* (1992); Central Intelligence Agency, *World Factbook 1992* (1992); and Central Intelligence Agency. *Handbook of International Economic Statistics* (1992). Part B: International Monetary Fund, *Direction of Trade Annual* (1968-72), and *Direction of Trade Yearbook* (1983 and 1993); *Taiwan Statistical Databook* (1994).

NOTE: While Indonesia is the largest country in ASEAN/AFTA in terms of overall GDP, Singapore is the largest ASEAN recipient of exports from other ASEAN members.

institutionalization. Hence, the presence of an overall regional hegemon appears to be neither a necessary nor a sufficient condition for the emergence of regional economic institutions.

The alternative approach to the question of hegemony and cooperation—focusing not on overall but rather on issue-specific capabilities—is pursued in part B of table 7.2, which provides data on the importance to regional partners of the largest national recipient of exports in each actual or potential institutional grouping of countries (in the case of ASEAN/AFTA, also reported is the significance to its partners of the grouping's largest country, Indonesia, as measured by its share of regional GDP).

As the issue-specific hegemonic leadership approach would anticipate, the United States is vastly more important to its trading partners in

NAFTA than Japan is to its trading partners in the proposed EAEG/
EAEC.[18] Moreover, this approach could point out that the modest success
of ASEAN/AFTA may be due to the low level of ASEAN exports received
either by the major ASEAN recipient of such flows (Singapore) or the
largest ASEAN economy (Indonesia), and it could suggest further that the
importance of the U.S. market to its partners in the Asia-Pacific may not
be sufficient to ensure the vitality of APEC. Yet, probably confounding
issue-specific hegemonic leadership expectations is the finding that Japan
is about as important to its potential EAEG/EAEC partners as a recipient
of goods and services as Germany and Brazil are to their respective partners
in the EC and Mercosur. That is, while all three are similar with regard to
this form of issue-specific hegemony, we see institutionalization in the
cases of the EC and Mercosur and a failure to so achieve institutionalization in the case of the proposed EAEG/EAEC.

Regional Variation in Europe, the Americas, and Asia: The Relative Disparity Shift Hypothesis

Functionalist and hegemonic leadership arguments help us understand in
some measure the variation that can be observed in regional economic
institutionalization in the three major components of the world economy.
Still, from the perspective of each of these two approaches the sharp differences in the trajectory of institutionalization in Western Europe and
East Asia remain puzzling. Indeed, the limitations of each perspective in
capturing these two extreme cases may help us recognize that something
very important is happening "out there" in regional political–economic
diplomacy. That is, in both regions there has been high and growing trade
encapsulation, which from a functionalist viewpoint should facilitate institutionalization in both areas. From a hegemonic leadership viewpoint
there should be either equally low levels of institutionalization in the two
regions (the issue-specific version), or there should be more favorable
prospects for the EAEG than for the EC (the overall capabilities version).
Yet, the actual track record of regional institutionalization in the two parts
of the world conform neither to functionalism nor to the two variants of
hegemonic leadership theory, and in fact there are rather sharp deviations
between functionalist and hegemonic leadership expectations about regionalism and observed outcomes in East Asia and Western Europe. We

also need to understand the intermediate cases more fully: why, in other words, do the prospects for ASEAN/AFTA and APEC seem to be rather modest when compared to Mercosur and NAFTA?

Based on previous work on the relative gains problem for international cooperation (Grieco 1990), it might be suggested that in addition to factors emphasized by functionalists and hegemonic leadership theorists, variation in contemporary regional institutionalization may be the result of the existence of differences in the amount of change taking place in the relative capabilities of partners in the different regions, and resulting differences in possible expectations of nations in those regions regarding the likely effects of enhanced regional institutionalization.[19]

More specifically, the following "relative disparity shift"[20] hypothesis may help us understand the variance in current regional institutionalization: when the relative disparities in capabilities within a region are shifting over time, disadvantaged states will become less attracted to institutionalization and the latter will become less likely to occur.

The rationale for this hypothesis begins with the proposal that states within a particular region may ascribe some connection between their relative economic (and therefore political and ultimately military) capabilities and their intraregional economic relationships. If the pattern of intraregional economic interactions in the recent past has been associated with (and perhaps contributed to) stability in relative economic capabilities, less powerful states within the region may be less fearful that their relative position will erode even further (and, if neoclassical trade theory is correct, their position might actually improve) as a result of closer economic ties with stronger partners that might be engendered by formal regional institutions.

In contrast, if less powerful countries in a region have experienced or are experiencing a significant deterioration in their relative capabilities, then they might be concerned that the enhancement of regional economic ties brought about by institutionalization could accentuate regional imbalances in capabilities even further in favor of the relatively stronger partners. From the viewpoint of the less powerful regional states, closer institutional ties and the thickening web of economic transactions they facilitate and foster might thereby yield a more domineering partner in the future. Concerned in this way about trends in relative capabilities and potential bargaining power, the relatively weaker partners might shy away from institutionalization of regional relationships with stronger partners in the area.

To investigate the possibility that a focus on shifts in relative disparities

Table 7.3

Changes in Economic Asymmetries
in Western Europe, East Asia, and the Americas, 1970–1990

Part A: Changes in Level of Overall Economic Capabilities

Country	Actual/Proposed Arrangement	Country GDP/Regional GDP (%)		
		1970	1980	1990
Germany	EC	26.2	27.1	25.4
U.S.	NAFTA	89.3	85.5	87.0
Brazil	Mercosur	56.3	75.3	80.9
Indonesia	ASEAN/AFTA	29.8	39.3	33.2
U.S.	APEC	66.6	57.1	51.6
Japan	EAEG/EAEC	54.0	67.2	72.3

Part B: Changes in Asymmetries in Distribution of Wealth

Actual/Proposed Arrangement	Ratio of GDP/capita of wealthier to poorer regional partners		
	1970	1980	1990
EC (1)	3.0	3.0	3.0
NAFTA (2)	7.1	5.9	8.8
Mercosur (3)	0.9	1.2	1.5
ASEAN (4)	1.6	4.3	6.3
APEC (5)	23.0	21.6	41.0
EAEG/EAEC (6)	8.5	12.4	29.4

Sources: For part A, see table 7.2 (A); for part B: see table 7.2 (B).

Notes: Country ratios of GDP/capita reported in part B follow:
(1) Average of Denmark, Germany, and France over Ireland, Greece, and Portugal.
(2) United States over Mexico.
(3) Average of Brazil and Uruguay over Argentina and Paraguay.
(4) Average of Malaysia and Singapore over Phillipines and Thailand.
(5) Average of Japan, U.S., and Canada over Phillipines, Indonesia, and People's Republic of China.
(6) Average of Japan, Hong Kong, and Singapore over Phillipines, Indonesia, and China.

in capabilities may help account for the variation in contemporary regionalism, table 7.3 presents data on changes in the degree to which the key states associated with the different arrangements in Western Europe, East Asia, and the Americas have enjoyed a predominance in relative capabilities during the past two decades.

As part A of table 7.3 indicates, Germany from 1970 to 1990 was the source of about one-fourth of Western European GDP. The United States was the source of a much greater percentage of North American GDP during the same period (well over 80 percent). Most interestingly, however, the level of German and American economic predominance in their respective regions remained notably stable over the twenty-year period. In contrast, Japan's economic hegemony in East Asia *increased* during those years, growing from 54 percent in 1970 to 72 percent in 1990. Thus, trends in relative economic capabilities correlate in the expected direction with, and possibly provide us with some explanatory leverage on, the two extreme cases of the accentuated regionalization in Europe and the failure of the EAEG/EAEC, and for the beginning of NAFTA. It is less helpful in accounting for the move to create Mercosur, for in fact we see in that group shifts in disparities in relative capabilities favoring Brazil that would seem to cut against expectations of success for that arrangement. Finally, according to this measure the United States and Indonesia have been losing their hegemonic positions in the Asia-Pacific and ASEAN regions, respectively, thus suggesting that if shifts in capability disparities favoring an existing hegemon may impede further institutionalization (but may not by itself abort the latter, as witnessed by the Brazil/Mercosur case), shifts that involve an erosion in the hegemon's position may not by itself facilitate such enhanced institutionalization.

Additional analysis of shifts in relative capabilities can be undertaken by reference to part B of the table, which presents data on changes over the past twenty years in the ratio of the per capita GDP of the wealthiest state or group of states within a region to the least well-off state or group of nations within the same region. As with changes in overall GDP, the data in part B of table 7.3 indicate remarkable stability over the past twenty years in the relative position of the wealthier and poorer countries of the European Community. They also highlight the vast increase in the gap that has developed over the same period in per capita income between the wealthy and poorer nations of the aborted EAEG/EAEC, and a marked increase in such a gap in the APEC region.

Hence, again, the relative disparity shift thesis seems to be able to help account for the differentiated outcomes of the two key cases of the EC and the EAEG/EAEC, and it may shed light on why APEC is achieving modest institutionalization to date. Moreover, Mercosur is closer to the EC than to the EAEC/EAEC or APEC in terms of disparities of per capita GDP and changes in such disparities, which would be in accord with the expectations of the hypothesis. In addition, while there has been a shift in the disparity in capabilities favoring the United States in the NAFTA region, the level of this shift has been much less than in the regions that would be covered by EAEG/EAEC or are covered by APEC. Finally, ASEAN/AFTA does not meet the expectations of the thesis using the measure reported in part B, for according to that measure ASEAN/AFTA has experienced no greater a shift in relative disparities than NAFTA, but while there are trade accords in both regions the prospects for NAFTA are more favorable than they are for AFTA.

It will be recalled from the previous section that functionalist and hegemonic leadership arguments have their greatest problems in accounting for the differences in institutionalization that obtain in Western Europe and East Asia. The relative disparity shift hypothesis may take us some distance in understanding that important paired comparison, for among the regions discussed above, the countries belonging to the EC and the countries that might have constituted the EAEG/EAEC have had extremely large differences in their respective trends in regional relative capabilities, with the former characterized by remarkable stability and the latter marked by tremendous change favoring the already hegemonic state in the region. The NAFTA and Mercosur countries have been experiencing trends in relative capabilities that fall between those that constitute the EC and those that would have constituted the EAEG/EAEC. This intermediate status of NAFTA and Mercosur with regard to regional power dynamics correlates with the intermediate status of institutionalization observed in those regions. With respect to changes in gaps in per capita wealth, the cases of APEC and ASEAN/AFTA also fall between the extremes of the EC and the EAEG/EAEC, but along this dimension as well as actual institutional performance both look more like EAEG/EAEC than the EC.

The factor of shifts in disparities in capabilities may then help account at least for the extreme cases of successful (the EC) and failed (the EAEG/EAEC) attempts by countries to undertake regional institutionalization. However, the view that the EC region has been characterized by relative stability in capabilities, and that this has served as (at least) a permissive condition for institutionalization, might be drawn into question by the reunification of Germany in 1990. On the one hand, it could be suggested that German reunification upset the balance of capabilities in Western Europe, and the fact that we have not seen a rollback in EC institutionalization would appear to lead to the conclusion that there is no relationship between shifts in national economic capabilities and regional preferences for institutionalization. Indeed, it could be suggested that German reunification has been acting since 1989 or 1990 as a spur to heightened cooperation among the EC countries, and in support of this one might cite the negotiation during 1991 of the Maastricht Treaty, and especially its construction of a path (now seriously off track) toward full Economic and Monetary Union (EMU). In this case one could suggest that the line of analysis suggested above is precisely wrong: rapid shifts in relative capabilities might catalyze rather than deter states from developing institutionalized arrangements in order to manage the growing power of a regional partner.

At least five points can be offered in response to this important line of criticism:

First, the move to construct a new and more robust EC monetary regime began in a serious way in June 1988 (with the formation of the Delors Committee, which issued in June 1989 an EC blueprint for EMU), well before German reunification was even on the European agenda.

Second, there is no question that France and other EC countries expressed doubts in 1990 about German reunification, but it appears that such expressions were largely a ploy to press Germany in the EMU negotiations.

Third, German reunification does not appear to have had a significant immediate impact on relative capabilities in Western Europe: while about 26 percent of the EC's GDP originated in Germany between 1988 and 1990, this rose to only 28 percent between 1991 and 1993 (OECD 1995:128–29). It would not appear to be the case that German reunification has had (at least to date) a significant impact on Western European relative capabilities, and if anything the massive costs associated with rehabilitating the economy of the former German Democratic Republic may be acting as a break on the current and near-term growth prospects of the Federal Republic.

Fourth, while Germany's overall economic capabilities may not make it a hegemon in Europe in the same way as Japan is in Asia or the United States is in the Americas, this does not mean that German power has not been considered a problem in European political-economic affairs, and especially in European monetary diplomacy. Students of EMU such as Sandholtz (1993) and Grieco (1995b, 1996a) have suggested that Germany's partners in the EMU negotiations were motivated at least in part to initiate and to pursue a path toward a more centralized form of European monetary cooperation as a way of dealing with Germany's particularly great influence in that issue area. Moreover, the monetary crises in Europe of 1992 and 1993—which led to the breakdown of the key component of the current European Monetary System, the Exchange Rate Mechanism— together with the almost complete domination by Germany of post-Maastricht European diplomacy relating to the timetable and terms for the movement toward EMU are raising serious doubts among Germany's EC partners as to whether EMU will in fact serve to constrain Germany's apparently growing power in the monetary domain.[21] Were this perception to persist and deepen, Germany's partners—and, in particular, France—may be faced with the difficult options of accepting continued German domination in monetary matters in a truncated EMS, going toward a slightly attenuated form of German domination in the framework of EMU, and, most problematic of all, reducing economic integration in Western Europe as a price for seeking (but not necessarily attaining) enhanced national autonomy in the monetary field.

Fifth, and finally, we need to address the question of why a country such as France might believe that it is the European Community's institutional framework that is associated with, and indeed might be facilitating, levels of economic performance that allow it to keep up with Germany. Again, part of the answer as to why France has not feared Germany in this way clearly rests at the domestic level of analysis (Bulmer and Paterson 1989). Yet, another part of the answer may be that France's actual trade performance both within and outside the European Community has perhaps persuaded French policy officials that their country is much better able to stand on more equal terms with Germany within rather than outside the framework of the Community.

Attention above focused on Germany's relative GDP. However, EC institutions do not have their greatest effect on the GDP of Community members (although they have a very large long-term indirect impact). Instead, they have their greatest immediate impact on the members' intra-Community trading opportunities. Table 7.4 thus presents data on French and German intra-EC export performance, as well as data on their extra-EC exports, from the 1960s through the 1980s.

Part A of the table indicates that Germany's share of the total exports of the twelve countries that belonged to the EC at the end of the 1980s (not all of these belonged to the Community throughout the period under review, but for the sake of consistency all are included in the numerical analysis) increased from an annual average level of about 26 percent during the early 1960s to about 30 percent during the late 1980s. However, this improved export performance was the result of better performance relative to its EC partners outside rather than inside the Community. That is, while Germany's share of EC extraregional exports increased from about 27 percent during the early 1960s to about 34 percent during the late 1980s (see part B of table 7.4), its share of intra-Community exports (see part C) increased only marginally—from 26.49 percent to 27.3 percent. France's share of exports was higher during the 1970s than in either

TABLE 7.4
German and French Export Performance, 1960–1989
(All figures are in percent)

Period	Part A French and German shares of total EC12 exports to the world			Part B French and German shares of EC12 extra-community shares			Part C French and German shares of EC12 intra-community exports		
	France	Germany	Difference =(G-F)	France	Germany	Difference =(G-F)	France	Germany	Difference =(G-F)
1960–64	15.39	26.65	11.26	15.56	26.81	11.25	15.15	26.49	11.33
1965–69	15.09	27.85	12.77	14.27	28.80	14.53	15.87	26.94	11.07
1970–74	16.11	29.44	13.33	14.85	31.89	17.04	17.16	27.42	10.26
1975–79	16.84	29.18	12.34	17.08	32.24	15.16	16.65	26.63	9.98
1980–84	16.20	28.11	11.91	17.28	30.47	13.19	15.28	26.12	10.84
1985–89	15.69	30.00	14.31	16.08	33.70	17.62	15.39	27.30	11.91

SOURCES: IMF Direction of Trade Series.
NOTE: Market shares are based on value of current-dollar exports.

the 1960s or the 1980s. Nevertheless, throughout the period as a whole France was able to maintain a relatively constant gap—of about eleven percentage points—between its share of intra-Community exports and that of Germany. In marked contrast, the gap between its share of EC extra-Community exports and Germany's widened in favor of the latter over the thirty-year period and reached seventeen percentage points by the late 1980s.

Hence, over a period of three decades France has been able to keep up with Germany in trade to a greater degree within rather than outside the Community. As a result, French national officials perhaps have developed a rather stable belief and expectation that the EC is a regional arrangement through which France can stand on more equal terms with Germany—*at least within Europe.* By consequence, French officials may be predisposed to attempting to develop new, stronger elements of the Community.

It is at least plausible that similar views are beginning to take hold among elites in Canada and Mexico with regard to the United States, and this might help account for their willingness to work with U.S. in the framework of NAFTA. At the same time, the remaining large gap in over-all economic capabilities between the United States and its partners in NAFTA compared to the gap between Germany and its EC partners may help explain why NAFTA remains focused on trade while the EC is expanding to new issue-areas. In addition, it is quite likely that such views about being able to work on more or less equal terms are *not* yet present in significant measure among East Asian elites in regard to Japan. As a result, then, of these differences in regional-level dynamics associated with relative economic capabilities, and the likely expectations that have perhaps developed around them among regional-level national governments, cooperation may be much more readily and easily attained in Western Europe than in East Asia, with the Americas occupying a position between these two extremes.

Three initial conclusions may be derived from the above discussion. First, there is likely to be continued variation in the character of regional economic institutionalization in the areas of the world examined in this paper. Although it doubtless will experience setbacks, European institutionalization under the auspices of the EC/EU is highly likely to continue. This is because it is, in the final analysis, the main path available to countries such as France, Italy, and Britain to work toward mutually desirable ends with, but not in the process become dominated by, a relatively stronger Germany. The current Union of Fifteen will likely expand to include between three and six countries from Eastern and Central Europe by 2005. There is likely also to be movement not just toward completion of the common market of that enlarged EC/EU, but also a continuation of efforts to deepen its institutional authority, including in the monetary domain.

Prospects for regionalism in the Americas look moderately favorable. However, notwithstanding such developments as the Miami Summit's statement regarding a hemispheric free trade area, the possible expansion of NAFTA to include Chile, and the talks between Mercosur and the United States and the Andean countries, the problems the Clinton administration encountered in securing passage of the NAFTA agreement in the U.S. Congress suggest that further efforts at institutionalization of economic relationships in the Americas are not likely to lead in the near term to a single locus of institutional activity. Instead, it is likely that we will observe the continuation of the current trend, the development of a number of trade pacts among groups of countries in the region, which might in time formulate limited linkages to one another.

In contrast to Western Europe and the Americas, the complete failure of EAEG/EAEC, the uncertain prospects for AFTA, and the very modest success of APEC to date must induce low expectations about the likelihood of enhanced regional economic institutionalization in Asia. Moreover, in the discussion above the source of regional capabilities turbulence that might be acting as a constraint on regional institutionalization in East Asia was found to be Japan. There is, however, another rising economic power in that part of the world. It is a country that may have the capacity to surpass Japan and perhaps even to approach the United States in world economic matters, and it also has domestic structural conditions and foreign policy goals and practices that are not likely to attract neighbors to closer, formalized relationships in the economic or political-military domains. That country, of course, is China.[22]

Second, the realist-oriented notion of intraregional shifts in relative capabilities may shed light on the differentiated course of regional economic institutionalization that we observe in Western Europe, East Asia, and the Americas. However, we must recognize that we are only at an early stage in formulating such a realist-based explanation for the differences and similarities in regional institutionalization. Still, the discussion above suggests that a realist-oriented focus on intraregional shifts in capabilities may be helpful in accounting for the differences in the level of regional institutionalization that exist between Europe and the Americas on the one hand, and Asia on the other, and perhaps as well the differences in institutionalization that obtain between Europe and the Americas.

However, and this is the third and final conclusion, even if the concept of relative disparity shifts allows neorealism to account in some measure for the variation in regional institutionalization that is discussed here, it must be said that it is unlikely that any purely systemic-level argument will be able to account fully for that variation. A focus on systemic-level forces must be complemented with attention to domestic factors. A combined approach, if properly constructed, might allow us to come closer to a full understanding of the new politics of regionalism in the world economy.

Acknowledgments: I thank the Wissenschaftszentrum Berlin for its generous support in the preparation of an earlier draft of this paper. I benefited greatly from the comments provided by participants at seminars at the Centro de Investigacion y Docencia Economicas in Mexico City, the University of California at Santa Barbara, the University of California at San Diego, Columbia University, Ohio State University, and Stanford University. For their detailed comments and suggestions I thank Arturo Borja, Scott Cooper, Thomas Cusack, Wolf-Dieter Eberwein, Guadalupe Gonzalez, Joanne Gowa, Torben Iversen, Edward Mansfield, Helen Milner, John Owen, Brian Portnoy, David Priess, Wayne Sandholz, Randall Schweller, and Dagmar Simon.

NOTES

1. For helpful analyses of contemporary economic regionalism, see Schott (1991); Hine (1992); Aggarwal (1995); Haggard (1995); and Kahler (1995).

2. For earlier comparative analyses of regional institutionalized integration, see Haas and Schmitter (1964); Haas (1966, 1967b); and Nye (1970). It should be noted that countries in Africa, the Gulf, and the Caribbean have also sought to establish regional institutions, but with limited success. The problems that developing countries encounter in pursuing regional economic arrangements are reviewed in Vaitsos (1978). The International Monetary Fund (1993) provides a helpful overview of recent regional integration efforts that includes the developing countries.

3. In an earlier draft (Grieco 1994) I sought to evaluate the impact of domestic political structures and economic conditions on the variance in regionalism that can be observed in Asia, Europe, and the Americas.

4. The European Community (EC) is now the European Union (EU), but the earlier term is retained as it was the term that was current for the time period under review here.

5. For reporting on these developments, see "Tariff Accord Hits a Snag" (1994); "Focus on Mercosur" (1994); "Customs Union Encounters Hitch" (1995); "Brazil to Enlarge Mercosur

Exempt List" (1995); "Common External Tariff Under Pressure" (1995); and "Growing Pains for Mercosur Block" (1995).

6. For these developments see "Group of Three Agrees Programme" (1993); Brooke (1993); and "G-3 Trade Agreement" (1994: 40051).

7. See "Chile Likely to Join NAFTA" (1995); and "Next Round of NAFTA Talks" (1995).

8. See Greenhouse (1994); "US Promises" (1994); and "Hemispheric Trade Zone Endorsed" (1995).

9. On these developments see Vatikiotis (1993); "Malaysia: List Threatens AFTA" (1995); and "ASEAN Differences" (1995).

10. On the rise and decline of the EAEG and EAEC proposals, see Hoon (1991); Kandiah (1991); Ihlwan (1992); Makabenta (1993); and Grieco (1995a, 1995c).

11. On these developments see Moravcsik (1991); Cameron (1992); Lange (1992); Sandholtz (1993); and Grieco (1995b, 1996b).

12. See "Asia Forum Cutting Political Teeth" (1991); and "APEC's Chief Denies Group Will Deal with Politics" (1993).

13. See "U.S. Seeks Japan's OK to Upgrade APEC" (1993); "Asian Reservations on U.S. Proposal" (1993); "Australia Applauds President Clinton's APEC Upgrading" (1993); and "Australia Seeks to Overcome China Obstacle" (1993).

14. I am indebted to Joanne Gowa for emphasizing the point that institutionalization is costly, and that one useful way of thinking about the problem of institutionalization is in terms of explaining why countries ever choose to take on those costs.

15. For the early functionalist argument about institutions, see Mitrany (1943/44). In the 1950s and 1960s this functional logic was adapted to the question of regionalism by such scholars as Ernst Haas (1958, 1967a, 1967b, 1968) and Philippe Schmitter (1969); in the 1980s it was applied to international regimes by such scholars as Robert Keohane (1984), Arthur Stein (1983), and Charles Lipson (1984).

16. Similarly, Yamazawa (1992:1523) finds that overall trade encapsulation—that is, exports and imports—increased from 35.2 percent in 1980 to 40 percent in 1990 in East Asia; from 31.5 percent to 37.3 percent in North America; and from 52.4 percent to 63.4 percent in the EC.

17. In making these points about the economic functions of a hegemon, neorealists drew from the historical and analytical work of Charles Kindleberger (1973). It should be noted that Stephen Krasner's work on hegemony and regional development banks (1981) suggests that we could expect the general hegemonic leadership model to be applicable to the question of variation in regional economic institutionalization.

18. The latter trend is due in large measure to the fact that the East Asian countries have had a major alternative to Japan as an export market—namely, the United States. See the study by the World Bank (1993b:48–49). It should be noted that the World Bank staff emphasizes that, in regard to foreign aid and foreign direct investment, Japan is becoming more, not less, important to the East Asian newly industrializing countries.

19. It might also be the case, as Randall Schweller has suggested to me, that differences in actual, operative political-military conflicts of interest in the three regions have induced differences in sensitivities to relative gains in partners in the regions in such a way as to cause the variation in levels and types of institutionalized economic cooperation that we see in the three parts of the world. This insight may help account for the relatively higher level of regional economic institutionalization one observes in Western Europe as opposed to East Asia. However, it is not clear that actual, existing conflicts of interests and thus sensitivities to gaps in capabilities and gaps in gains from cooperation have in recent decades been higher in the Americas than in Western Europe.

20. In an earlier draft (Grieco 1994) this line of analysis is referred to as the "capabilities-turbulence hypothesis." However, a helpful critique provided by David Priess highlighted the point that this terminology was unsatisfactory insofar as the main point of the hypothesis was that shifts in relative power and therefore position were at the core of the argument, and that this main point would be communicated more effectively through the term "relative disparity shift."

21. For commentary on Germany's near-total control over contemporary West European diplomacy surrounding EMU, see the commentary by Barber (1995), and the recent essay by the former Governor of the Bank of Denmark (Hoffmeyer 1996).

22. On the remarkable economic performance of China in recent years, see Lardy (1994: 14–25, 29–35). On the problems that East Asian countries and indeed the international system may encounter in accommodating growing Chinese power, see Betts (1993/94), Roy (1994), and Segal (1995).

EIGHT

The Political Economy of Major-Power Trade Flows

Edward D. Mansfield and Rachel Bronson

In recent years, considerable interest has been expressed in commercial regionalism. This interest has given rise to a wide variety of empirical analyses of the extent to which international trade is guided by preferential trading arrangements (PTAs). Many of these studies have concluded that PTAs have had a marked influence on patterns of trade and that the magnitude of their effect has risen in recent years. These conclusions have contributed to the widely held view that regionalism is becoming increasingly prevalent.

Extant analyses of this topic, however, have largely ignored the political-military context in which trade relations take place. Particularly important in this regard is the role that political-military alliances play in shaping trade flows. Alliances are likely to influence trade flows because commerce generates efficiency gains that augment the potential political-military power of states. A state has incentives to limit trade with actual or potential adversaries, since increases in their power threaten to undermine its security. A state also has incentives to liberalize trade with allies, since the gains from trade bolster the alliance's power, thereby enhancing its security.

Yet few empirical studies have analyzed the effects of alliances on trade, and virtually no effort has been made to compare their effects with those of PTAs. In this chapter, we examine the influence of alliances and PTAs on bilateral trade flows involving major powers during the period from 1960 to 1990. Our findings indicate that alliances have had a much larger impact than PTAs on commerce, but that differences exist among the major powers in the extent to which alliances have guided trade flows. Whereas the United States, the Soviet Union, China, and Great Britain conducted significantly more trade with their allies than with other countries, France conducted somewhat less trade with its allies than with other states. Further, China and the Soviet Union engaged in far less trade with nonallies than the United States, Great Britain, or France.

PREFERENTIAL TRADING ARRANGEMENTS AND TRADE

As already pointed out, much of the contemporary literature on regionalism centers on the effects of PTAs (e.g., Bhagwati 1993:22), which are arrangements stipulating that members impose lower levels of protection on each others' goods than on those of third parties. Among the most common types of PTAs are free trade areas, customs unions, common markets, and economic unions. Although obvious differences exist among these commercial arrangements, "the reciprocal nature of the preferential treatment which the participants accord to one another" is a feature they all share (Anderson and Blackhurst 1993:5).

Some observers argue that the recent proliferation of new PTAs and deepening commercial integration within some existing PTAs are placing considerable strains on the international trading system (e.g., Bhagwati 1991). Others, however, view these developments as having the potential to strengthen this system and promote commercial liberalization (e.g., Oye 1992). Neither PTAs nor interest in their effects is new. But deepening economic integration within Europe, the formation of the North American Free Trade Agreement, nascent commercial agreements among developing countries (such as the Association of Southeast Asian Nations and Mercosur), and the prospects of an East Asian trade bloc have revived interest in the extent to which PTAs guide trade flows.

It is clear that the degree to which a PTA facilitates trade among members is likely to depend on a variety of factors, including the factor endowments of members, the height and uniformity of the PTA's external trade barriers, and the extent to which internal trade barriers are eliminated. Equally clear, however, is the likelihood that preferential treatment will spur commerce among PTA members. Further, the trade-promoting effects of PTAs are not due solely to the reduction of trade barriers among members. For example, PTAs increase the predictability of members' access to markets and help to safeguard the integrity of their dedicated assets (Yarbrough and

Yarbrough 1992). They also may promote macroeconomic and monetary coordination among members, which is likely to contribute to economic growth and the expansion of trade (Genberg and De Simone 1993).

In the introduction to this book it was noted that PTAs may or may not involve geographically proximate states. In this sense, our analysis of regionalism differs from those conducted by many other contributors to this volume who focus on geographic regions. Further, as mentioned earlier, some studies of regionalism treat this phenomenon as a "natural" outgrowth of proximity, income and policy convergence, and other factors; whereas other studies consider it the product of government policies. Since PTAs and alliances are designed by governments, our analysis is consistent with the latter approach.

Interest in the influence of PTAs on trade has spawned a vast empirical literature. Existing studies have found that differences exist among PTAs regarding the extent to which they promote trade, but that members of such arrangements tend to conduct more commerce with each other than with other countries (e.g., Aitken 1973; Brada and Mendez 1983; Frankel 1993; Linnemann 1966; Pelzman 1977; Tinbergen 1962).

But these studies rarely take into account the political-military relationship between trade partners. We argue that this omission is important. Most of the empirical literature on the effects of PTAs focuses on the period since World War II and many PTA members during this period also have been political-military allies (Mansfield 1993). Moreover, there is substantial reason to expect that, in addition to PTAs, alliances guide trade flows. As a result, studies focusing on PTAs and ignoring alliances may overstate the effects of PTAs on trade flows.

ALLIANCES AND TRADE

The effects of alliances on commerce emanate from the efficiency gains from trade (Gowa 1994). These gains yield increases in national income that can be used to augment the political-military power of any state that engages in trade. As a result, trade relations are likely to influence power relations and, hence, to generate security externalities.[1] Since the anarchic nature of the international system places pressure on states to attend to the power of others (Waltz 1979), they cannot ignore these security externalities without bearing substantial risks.

States with sufficient market power to improve their terms of trade by imposing an optimal tariff (or equivalent trade barrier) have little incentive to liberalize trade with an adversary.[2] The tariff helps to redress the security diseconomy arising from trade by degrading an adversary's national income and thus its potential political-military power.[3] Liberalizing trade with an adversary therefore is likely to undermine such states' security.[4]

In contrast, states with sufficient market power to impose an optimal tariff do have an incentive to liberalize trade with allies (Gowa 1994). Unlike trade relations among adversaries, states realize political benefits from the commercial gains of their allies. Open trade among allies is likely to enhance the participants' security, since the gains from trade accrue to states with common security goals and bolster the aggregate political-military power of the alliance. Indeed, the failure to liberalize commerce will undermine the alliance's power by redistributing the gains from trade toward the state vested with market power while reducing them altogether for its allies. This suggests that trade should be more open and trade flows should be significantly greater among allies than among adversaries.[5]

The available evidence supports this argument. Rebecca Summary (1989) used the number of foreign agents registered by various countries in the United States as a proxy for the extent to which a political alliance exists between the United States and each country, and found that this number was directly related to bilateral trade flows involving the United States in 1978 and 1982. Joanne Gowa and Mansfield (1993; Gowa 1994) examined the effects of alliances on bilateral trade flows from 1905 to 1985, based on the Correlates of War (COW) Project's list of alliances. They focused on explaining trade flows between major powers, since these states are likely to possess some market power and, as noted earlier, alliances are likely to have a particularly pronounced influence on trade involving such states. Their results indicated that higher levels of trade have been conducted between allies than between potential or actual adversaries during the twentieth century, and that the magnitude of alliances' effects on trade has been greater during bipolar than multipolar periods.

This chapter extends the existing empirical work on alliances and trade in a number of ways. First, whereas Gowa and Mansfield analyzed trade flows between major powers, they pointed out that it also would be useful to analyze the effects of alliances on all trade flows involving major powers (i.e., those between major powers and nonmajor powers, as well as those between major powers) (1993:412). In the following analysis, we do so.

Second, existing studies of PTAs and trade have not addressed the effects of alliances, and existing studies of alliances and trade only have addressed the effects of PTAs in a preliminary manner. In this chapter, we conduct a more extensive comparison of alliances' and PTAs' influences on commerce. Third, in addition to examining the extent to which alliances guide trade flows involving major powers, it also is important to determine whether differences exist among the major powers in this regard. After presenting some initial results on the effects of alliances on trade, we take up this issue.

ALLIANCES, PTAS, AND TRADE—
A STATISTICAL MODEL

To test the effects of alliances and PTAs on bilateral trade flows, we begin with a gravity model, which includes the national income and population of both the importer and exporter, and the geographic distance between them (Anderson 1979; Deardorff 1984:503–4). This type of model has been used in many existing studies of PTAs (e.g., Aitken 1973; Frankel 1993; Linnemann 1966; Pelzman 1977; Tinbergen 1962), alliances (Gowa 1994; Gowa and Mansfield 1993; Summary 1989), and other political effects on trade (Pollins 1989). It is expected that national income will be directly related to trade and that population and distance will be inversely related to commerce.

In addition to these variables, we include in this model dummy variables pertaining to whether the trading partners are members of a political-military alliance or a PTA. We also control for the effects of three factors that might influence the relationship between alliances and PTAs, on the one hand, and trade, on the other. First, we analyze the effects of membership in the General Agreement on Tariffs and Trade (GATT), since previous studies have found that this is an important influence on bilateral trade flows (Pollins 1989). Second, we include a variable pertaining to whether the trading partners had a prior colonial relationship, since a number of studies have linked this factor to commercial patterns (Kleiman 1976; Srivastava and Green 1986). Third, we analyze whether pairs of states that both have command economies engage in more trade than other states. Many pairs of states with command economies also were allied during the post-World War II era. It is important to ensure that any observed effect of alliances on trade is not a product of the unusual extent to which states having command economics can direct trade toward allies and away from other countries.

Thus, the initial model we estimate is:

$$\log X_{ij(t)} = \log A + B_1\log(GDP)_{i(t-1)} + B_2\log(GDP)_{j(t-1)} +$$
$$B_3\log(POP)_{i(t-1)} + B_4\log(POP)_{j(t-1)} + B_5\log(DIST)_{ij(t-1)} +$$
$$B_6\log(ALLY)_{ij(t-1)} + B_7\log(PTA)_{ij(t-1)} + B_8\log(GATT)_{ij(t-1)} +$$
$$B_9\log(COL)_{ij(t-1)} + B_{10}\log(COM)_{ij(t-1)} + \log z_{ij(t)}. \quad (8.1)$$

The dependent variable is the natural logarithm of the nominal value of exports from state i to state j in year t.[6] Turning to the independent variables, $\log(GDP)_{i(t-1)}$ and $\log(GDP)_{j(t-1)}$ are the natural logarithms of the nominal gross domestic products (GDPs) of states i and j, respectively, in year t-1; $\log(POP)_{i(t-1)}$ and $\log(POP)_{j(t-1)}$ are the natural logarithms of the national populations of i and j, respectively, in year t-1;[7] and $\log(DIST)_{ij(t-1)}$ is the natural logarithm of the geographical distance between i and j in year t-1.[8] In addition, $\log(ALLY)_{ij(t-1)}$ is a dummy variable that equals one if i and j are engaged in an alliance in year t-1 and zero otherwise;[9] $\log(PTA)_{ij(t-1)}$ is a dummy variable that equals one if i and j are party to a common preferential trading arrangement in year t-1 and zero otherwise;[10] $\log(GATT)_{ij(t-1)}$ is a dummy variable that equals one if i and j are both parties to the GATT in year t-1 and zero otherwise;[11] $\log(COL)_{ij(t-1)}$ is a dummy variable that equals one if i and j had a colonial relationship ending in or before year t-1 (provided that the relationship ended after the onset of World War II) and zero otherwise;[12] and $\log(COM)_{ij(t-1)}$ is a dummy variable that equals one if i and j both have command economies in year t-1 and zero otherwise.[13] Finally, $\log z_{ij(t)}$ is a stochastic error term.

In the following analysis, we estimate the parameters in equation (8.1) for seven cross sections during the period from 1960 to 1990 by five-year intervals (where 1960, 1965, . . . ,1990 are years t-1).[14] While it would be desirable to examine earlier periods as well, data limitations preclude a reliable analysis of years prior to 1960.[15] Included in our sample are all pairs of states involving a major power for which complete data are available.[16] Following the COW Project (Singer and Small 1994; Small and Singer 1982), we define the major powers during this period as the United States, the Soviet Union, China, Great Britain, and France. These states are widely regarded as having been the preeminent political-military powers during the post-World War II era and focusing on them is appropriate in light of our emphasis on the effects of political-military relations on trade. Clearly, however, this list omits states—particularly Japan and West Germany— with less military power but substantial economic capacity; and we also will analyze the extent to which our results are sensitive to whether these states are considered major powers.

ESTIMATES OF THE PARAMETERS

Ordinary least squares (OLS) estimates of the parameters in equation (8.1) are shown in table 8.1. Because there is evidence of heteroskedasticity in each regression, the t-ratios reported in table 8.1 are computed using White heteroskedasticity-consistent standard errors (White 1980).

A Wald test of the joint significance of the coefficients in equation (8.1) is conducted for each regression (Greene 1993:391–92). The Wald statistic, which is referred to as χ^2 in table 8.1, is statistically significant in each case; and, on average, the model explains about 60 percent of the variation in trade flows. Further, the coefficients of GDP, population, and distance have the expected signs and are statistically significant in all but one case.

Particularly important for our purposes is the strong, direct effect of alliances on trade flows. The regression coefficient of $\log(ALLY)_{ij}$ is positive and statistically significant in each case. Moreover, the effects of alliances are quantitatively large: on average, allies conduct roughly 140 percent more trade than nonallies. Also noteworthy is the relatively consistent effect of alliances across time. The predicted flow of trade between allies is more than 100 percent greater than that between nonallies for each year shown in table 8.1, but does not exceed 185 percent for any year.

As expected, PTAs also promote trade among members. But their effect is neither as strong nor as large as that of alliances. The regression coefficient of $\log(PTA)_{ij}$ is positive in five cases, and positive and statistically significant in four. This coefficient, however, is negative in two cases; and, on average, members of a common PTA conduct only about 30 percent more trade than other states, a much smaller increase than that generated by alliances. In fact, the effect of PTAs on trade is considerably smaller than the corresponding effect of alliances for each year shown in table 8.1.

Besides alliances and PTAs, there also is evidence that GATT membership, former colonial ties, and the existence of command economies on the part of both trade partners heighten trade. The regression coefficients of $\log(GATT)_{ij}$, $\log(COL)_{ij}$, and $\log(COM)_{ij}$ are positive in each case, and they are statistically significant in six, seven, and four instances, respectively. On average, GATT members conduct about 75 percent more trade than other countries, the existence of a prior colonial relationship increases

TABLE 8.1.

Regression of Exports on GDP, Population, Distance, Alliances,
Preferential Trading Arrangements, GATT, Prior Colonial Ties,
and Command Economies, 1960–1990

	1960	1965	1970	1975
log A	−.73	−2.51	−3.97**	−5.96***
	(−.35)	(−1.25)	(−2.01)	(−2.73)
log$(GDP)_i$	.54***	.36***	.35***	.48***
	(5.98)	(3.83)	(3.98)	(5.10)
log$(GDP)_j$	1.01***	1.02***	1.10***	1.23***
	(10.30)	(11.16)	(13.17)	(15.38)
log$(POP)_i$	−.56***	−.23*	−.08	−.25**
	(−5.96)	(−1.95)	(−.78)	(−2.28)
log$(POP)_j$	−.43***	−.40***	−.48***	−.59***
	(−4.07)	(−4.12)	(−5.21)	(−6.61)
log$(DIST)_{ij}$	−.25***	−.30***	−.47***	−.45***
	(−4.00)	(−5.15)	(−8.09)	(−7.68)
log$(ALLY)_{ij}$	1.02***	.94***	.73***	.72***
	(6.10)	(6.71)	(6.16)	(5.98)
log$(PTA)_{ij}$	−.02	.46**	.51***	.20
	(−.10)	(2.24)	(2.61)	(1.19)
log$(GATT)_{ij}$	.30**	.21	.24*	.31**
	(2.11)	(1.61)	(1.76)	(2.34)
log$(COL)_{ij}$	2.55***	1.78***	1.59***	1.80***
	(12.04)	(8.10)	(6.07)	(8.03)
log$(COM)_{ij}$	2.36***	.63	2.10***	1.70***
	(6.10)	(.76)	(6.82)	(5.41)
χ^2	1043.92***	1031.99***	1279.95***	1380.66***
Adjusted R^2	.60	.56	.55	.57
N	512	556	645	654

(continued on next page)

the predicted volume of trade by almost 500 percent, and the existence of command economies on the part of both trading partners increases the predicted volume of trade by about 250 percent.[17]

The Effects of Omitted Variables

Before proceeding, a number of issues concerning the specification of equation (8.1) should be addressed. First, it is useful to determine whether trade flows between two major powers differ from those between a major

TABLE 8.1.
(continued)

	1980	1985	1990
log A	−6.08***	−8.13***	−9.54***
	(−2.72)	(−3.82)	(−4.76)
$\log(GDP)_i$	.53***	.54***	.55***
	(6.73)	(6.75)	(7.43)
$\log(GDP)_j$	1.14***	1.14***	1.23***
	(15.77)	(16.08)	(19.08)
$\log(POP)_i$	−.39***	−.40***	−.33***
	(−4.93)	(−4.94)	(−4.45)
$\log(POP)_j$	−.40***	−.36***	−.51***
	(−4.86)	(−4.43)	(−6.69)
$\log(DIST)_{ij}$	−.51***	−.44***	−.42***
	(−7.03)	(−6.78)	(−7.49)
$\log(ALLY)_{ij}$	.79***	.91***	1.04***
	(5.63)	(6.30)	(8.05)
$\log(PTA)_{ij}$	−.08	.40**	.29**
	(−.45)	(2.41)	(2.00)
$\log(GATT)_{ij}$	.74***	.95***	1.08***
	(4.98)	(6.99)	(8.66)
$\log(COL)_{ij}$	1.73***	1.49***	1.54***
	(7.51)	(7.05)	(7.37)
$\log(COM)_{ij}$	.24	1.11***	.52
	(.66)	(4.22)	(1.28)
χ^2	1577.10***	1858.63***	2488.39***
Adjusted R^2	.61	.64	.67
N	780	796	813

NOTE: Years shown are year t–1 in equation (8.1). Entries are unstandardized regression coefficients. Figures in parentheses are t–ratios, computed using White heteroskedasticity–consistent standard errors. *** $p \le .01$. Two-tailed tests are conducted for each regression coefficient.
** $p \le .05$. See note ***.
* $p \le .10$. See note ***.

power and a nonmajor power. To address this issue, we introduce a variable in equation (8.1) that equals one if both i and j are major powers and zero otherwise. Our results indicate that the coefficient of this variable is negative in each case and significant (at the .10 level) in three. Further, on average, major powers conduct about 35 percent less trade with each other than they do with nonmajor powers. Including this variable in the model, however, has virtually no effect on the signs, sizes, or significance levels of any of the estimates shown in table 8.1.

Second, the political influences on bilateral trade flows involving major powers may depend on whether the major power is the importer or the exporter. To determine whether this is the case, we define a variable that equals one if the major power in a given dyad is the importer, and zero if it is the exporter. Our findings indicate that the coefficient of this variable is negative in four cases and positive in three. Moreover, it is never significant and its average value is close to zero. Thus, bilateral trade flows involving a major power do not seem to depend on whether the major power is the importer or the exporter. It also is important to recognize that including this variable in our model has no bearing on the coefficients of the remaining variables in equation (8.1).

Third, the results in table 8.1 indicate that pairs of states having command economies conduct more trade than other pairs. Since command economies usually characterize Communist regimes, pairs of countries with similar regime types may, in general, trade more with one another than pairs with different regime types. Although it is beyond the scope of this chapter to address this issue in detail, one issue that we can treat in a very preliminary manner is whether democracies also tend to trade more with one another than with other countries. This topic has been raised in a number of previous studies (e.g., Doyle 1986; Gowa 1995), but has not been the subject of much empirical analysis.[18]

In order to analyze this issue, we identify pairs of states that are both democracies, based on Michael Doyle's (1986) data. Since these data do not extend beyond 1982, we only are able to estimate the effects of democracy on trade flows for the period from 1960 to 1980. Our results indicate that the coefficient of a dummy variable for joint democracy is positive in four out of five cases. But there is no case in which it is positive and significant, and there is one case in which it is negative and significant (at the .10 level). Moreover, on average, democracies conduct only about 5 percent more trade with other democracies than they do with nondemocracies. While the crudeness of this analysis is obvious, our results do not support the view that, in general, a common regime type promotes trade. And like the other analyses described in this section, including this variable has no influence on the remaining coefficients in our model.[19]

Definition of a Major Power

We mentioned earlier that our analysis of major powers is based on a definition that emphasizes political-military power. It is useful to determine whether the effects of alliances (and the other independent variables in our model) change if we expand the list of major powers to include states with substantial economic power but that lack sufficient military capabilities to meet the COW Project's criterion for a major power, which guided the above analysis. Japan and West Germany are the obvious examples of such states. We therefore estimate the parameters in equation (8.1) after adding all dyads including these countries (for which complete data are available) to the sample analyzed earlier.

Our results indicate that the effects of PTAs and the GATT tend to be very similar to those based on the findings in table 8.1, and that the effects of prior colonial relations and command economies tend to be marginally smaller than those based on our earlier findings. However, the effects of alliances on trade decline sharply when Japan and West Germany are included among the ranks of the major powers. Whereas our earlier results indicated that, on average, allies conduct about 140 percent more trade than nonallies, this value falls to about 95 percent. While the effects of alliances continue to be much larger than those of PTAs when these states are considered major powers, our results indicate that alliances exert a greater influence on trade flows involving political-military major powers than on trade flows involving other economic powers.

The Effects of Alliance Type on Trade

Another issue bearing on the effects of alliances on trade flows concerns whether bilateral alliances (i.e., those comprised of two states) promote trade to a greater degree than multilateral alliances (i.e., those comprised of more than two states). Recent research has found this to be the case when trade flows between major powers are analyzed (Gowa 1994; Gowa and Mansfield 1993);[20] and it is useful to determine whether this tendency persists when all bilateral flows involving major powers are considered.

To this end, we replace $\log(ALLY)_{ij(t-1)}$ in equation (8.1) with $\log(BALLY)_{ij(t-1)}$ and $\log(MALLY)_{ij(t-1)}$. The former variable equals one if states i and j are members of a bilateral alliances in year t-1 and zero otherwise; the latter variable equals one if i and j are members of a multilateral alliance in year t-1 and zero otherwise. The results of this analysis indicate that bilateral alliances generate more trade than multilateral alliances. The regression coefficients of both $\log(BALLY)_{ij}$ and $\log(MALLY)_{ij}$ are positive and significant in each year analyzed here, but the coefficient of $\log(BALLY)_{ij}$ always is larger than the corresponding coefficient of log(*MALLY*)$_{ij}$. On average, the predicted volume of trade between bilateral allies is about 220 percent greater than that between countries that are not bilateral allies, whereas the predicted volume of trade between multilateral allies is roughly 120 percent greater than that between states that are not multilateral allies.

But while bilateral alliances generate more trade than multilateral alliances, both types of alliances yield greater trade than PTAs. In fact, the coefficients of both log(*BALLY*)$_{ij}$ and log(*MALLY*)$_{ij}$ are larger than that of log(*PTA*)$_{ij}$ in every case.[21]

VARIATIONS AMONG MAJOR POWERS IN THE EFFECTS OF ALLIANCES ON TRADE

Thus far, we have treated the effects of alliances on trade flows as the same for the United States, the Soviet Union, China, Great Britain, and France. The extent to which this is the case, however, is an empirical matter that warrants attention. To analyze this issue, we extend equation (8.1) in the following way:

$$\log X_{ij(t)} = \log A + B_1\log(GDP)_{i(t-1)} + B_2\log(GDP)_{j(t-1)} +$$
$$B_3\log(POP)_{i(t-1)} + B_4\log(POP)_{j(t-1)} + B_5\log(DIST)_{ij(t-1)} + B_6\log(ALLY)_{ij(t-1)}$$
$$+ B_7\log(PTA)_{ij(t-1)} + B_8\log(GATT)_{ij(t-1)} + B_9\log(COL)_{ij(t-1)} +$$
$$B_{10}\log(COM)_{ij(t-1)} + B_{11}\log(US)_{ij(t-1)} + B_{12}[\log(US)_{ij(t-1)} \cdot \log(ALLY)_{ij(t-1)}]$$
$$+ B_{13}\log(USSR)_{ij(t-1)} + B_{14}[\log(USSR)_{ij(t-1)} \cdot \log(ALLY)_{ij(t-1)}] +$$
$$B_{15}\log(CHINA)_{ij(t-1)} + B_{16}[\log(CHINA)_{ij(t-1)} \cdot \log(ALLY)_{ij(t-1)}] +$$
$$B_{17}\log(FRANCE)_{ij(t-1)} + B_{18}[\log(FRANCE)_{ij(t-1)} \cdot \log(ALLY)_{ij(t-1)}] +$$
$$\log e_{ij(t)}. \quad (8.2)$$

In this model, log(*US*)$_{ij}$, log(*USSR*)$_{ij}$, log(*CHINA*)$_{ij}$, and log(*FRANCE*)$_{ij}$ are dummy variables that equal one if states i or j include the United States, the Soviet Union, China, or France, respectively, and zero otherwise. Further, log $e_{ij(t)}$ is a stochastic error term. Because Great Britain is arbitrarily defined as the omitted condition in this model, no dummy variable for pairs of countries involving it is included in equation (8.2). However, the effects of alliances on British trade flows can be assessed via the coefficient of log(*ALLY*)$_{ij}$ when log(*US*)$_{ij}$, log(*USSR*)$_{ij}$, log(*CHINA*)$_{ij}$, and log(*FRANCE*)$_{ij}$ all equal zero.

Estimates of the parameters in equation (8.2) are presented in table

8.2. As expected, the effects of GDP, population, distance, PTAs, the GATT, command economies, and prior colonial relations are much the same as those based on equation (8.1). But a number of minor variations exist in some of their effects. The quantitative effects of PTA membership are somewhat greater based on equation (8.2) than equation (8.1).[22] Further, the coefficient of $\log(PTA)_{ij}$ is positive in six out of seven cases and positive and statistically significant in five instances in table 8.2, whereas it is positive in five cases and positive and statistically significant in four instances in table 8.1. In addition, the quantitative effects of GATT membership are somewhat smaller based on equation (8.2) than equation (8.1).[23]

The results in table 8.2 also indicate that the effects of alliances on trade vary among the major powers. These findings should be interpreted with some caution, since, especially during the 1960s, trade data for the Soviet Union and China are much more limited than for the United States, France, and Great Britain. But they provide rather striking evidence that, during the period after World War II, the United States, the Soviet Union, China, and Great Britain each conducted considerably more trade with their allies than with other countries. In contrast, France engaged in more trade with nonallies than with its allies. Further, the Soviet Union and China conducted less trade with nonallies than the United States, France, and Great Britain.

These patterns are readily discernible in table 8.3, which presents the average effects of alliances on trade for each major power, holding constant the remaining variables in equation (8.2). Based on these average effects, the Soviet Union conducted more than five times as much trade with its allies as with other states; China conducted about four and a half times as much trade with its allies as with other countries; the United States engaged in more than two and a half times as much trade with its allies as with other states; and Great Britain conducted almost twice as much trade with its allies as with other countries. France, however, conducted roughly 10 percent less trade with its allies than with other states.

Further, the average predicted volume of trade between allies has been highest for China and the United States. The Soviet Union traded slightly (about 15 percent to 20 percent) less with its allies. Great Britain engaged in noticeably (about 20 percent to 35 percent) less trade with its allies than the United States, China, or the Soviet Union did with theirs, although considerably more trade than it did with nonallies. But these variations pale in comparison to those between France and the other four

TABLE 8.2.

Regression of Exports on GDP, Population, Distance, Alliances,
Preferential Trading Arrangements, GATT, Prior Colonial Ties, Command Economies,
and Country Dummy Variables, 1960–1990

	1960	1965	1970	1975
log A	−.26	−1.34	−4.12*	−5.25**
	(−.12)	(−.63)	(−1.94)	(−2.36)
log(GDP)$_i$	.43***	.37***	.38***	.44***
	(4.75)	(3.94)	(3.95)	(4.54)
log(GDP)$_j$	.88***	1.02***	1.10***	1.14***
	(10.03)	(12.02)	(13.56)	(15.88)
log(POP)$_i$	−.40***	−.26**	−.12	−.22**
	(−3.88)	(−2.24)	(−1.06)	(−1.96)
log(POP)$_j$	−.23**	−.40***	−.48***	−.45***
	(−2.49)	(−4.64)	(−5.34)	(−5.74)
log(DIST)$_{ij}$	−.30***	−.38***	−.46***	−.49***
	(−4.67)	(−6.06)	(−7.58)	(−7.56)
log(ALLY)$_{ij}$	.64***	.72***	.54***	.59***
	(2.77)	(3.46)	(2.58)	(2.90)
log(PTA)$_{ij}$	.20	.71***	.76***	.33*
	(.81)	(3.68)	(4.08)	(1.89)
log(GATT)$_{ij}$	.26*	.18	.30**	.20
	(1.82)	(1.42)	(2.01)	(1.33)
log(COL)$_{ij}$	2.44***	1.75***	1.49***	1.67***
	(10.67)	(7.84)	(5.62)	(7.28)
log(COM)$_{ij}$	2.14***	.57	1.87***	1.54***
	(8.93)	(.62)	(5.11)	(4.31)
log(US)$_{ij}$	−.21	.11	−.31	.12
	(−.74)	(.48)	(−1.24)	(.49)
(log US$_{ij}$•log ALLY$_{ij}$)	.43	.25	.63**	.26
	(1.24)	(.89)	(2.13)	(.86)
log(USSR)$_{ij}$	−.97***	−.73**	−.08	−.48*
	(−3.20)	(−2.14)	(−.28)	(−1.82)
(log USSR$_{ij}$•log ALLY$_{ij}$)	1.16***	1.43***	.52	.81**
	(3.60)	(2.70)	(1.22)	(2.31)
log(CHINA)$_{ij}$	−1.34***	−.04	−.27	−.59*
	(−4.17)	(−.10)	(−.76)	(−1.71)
(log CHINA$_{ij}$•log ALLY$_{ij}$)	3.96***	3.29***	−.05	−2.83***
	(3.64)	(7.27)	(−.10)	(−6.09)
log(FRANCE)$_{ij}$	−.65***	−.42***	−.38**	−.08
	(−3.63)	(−2.62)	(−2.32)	(−.47)
(log FRANCE$_{ij}$•log ALLY$_{ij}$)	−.43	−.67***	−.72***	−.69***
	(−1.57)	(−2.58)	(−2.79)	(−2.84)
χ^2	2102.14***	4448.97***	2609.23***	12768.22***
Adjusted R^2	.65	.58	.56	.58
N	512	556	645	654

(continued on next page)

TABLE 8.2
(continued)

	1980	1985	1990
log A	−4.83** (−2.12)	−7.14*** (−3.21)	−9.03*** (−4.47)
log(GDP)$_i$	.42*** (4.60)	.50*** (5.64)	.57*** (7.68)
log(GDP)$_j$	1,03*** (14.72)	1.09*** (15.76)	1.25*** (20.91)
log(POP)$_i$	−.24** (−2.41)	−.33*** (−3.50)	−.33*** (−4.03)
log(POP)$_j$	−.24*** (−2.97)	−.29*** (−3.60)	−.51*** (−7.21)
log($DIST$)$_{ij}$	−.59*** (−7.89)	−.52*** (−7.59)	−.57*** (−9.21)
log($ALLY$)$_{ij}$	.64*** (2.70)	.54** (2.45)	.68*** (2.96)
log(PTA)$_{ij}$	−.08 (−.40)	.44** (2.51)	.27* (1.65)
log($GATT$)$_{ij}$	.39** (2.42)	.74*** (4.62)	.61*** (3.98)
log(COL)$_{ij}$	1.47*** (6.21)	1.29*** (5.96)	1.39*** (6.52)
log(COM)$_{ij}$	.44 (1.26)	1.21*** (4.39)	.86** (2.00)
log(US)$_{ij}$	.15 (.62)	.03 (.10)	.33 (1.59)
(log US_{ij}•log $ALLY_{ij}$)	.19 (.60)	.53* (1.68)	.12 (.42)
log($USSR$)$_{ij}$	−1.14*** (−4.17)	−.83*** (−3.05)	−1.18*** (−4.48)
(log $USSR_{ij}$•log $ALLY_{ij}$)	.87 (1.20)	1.08* (1.84)	1.07*** (3.04)
log($CHINA$)$_{ij}$	−.72*** (−2.81)	−.32 (−1.22)	−.20 (−.77)
(log $CHINA_{ij}$•log $ALLY_{ij}$)	.31 (.95)	.44 (1.39)	1.22 (1.56)
log($FRANCE$)$_{ij}$	.26* (1.73)	.15 (1.08)	.29* (1.95)
(log $FRANCE_{ij}$•log $ALLY_{ij}$)	−.90*** (−3.74)	−.68*** (−3.16)	−.79*** (−3.25)
χ^2	1949.22***	2318.84***	2882.46***
Adjusted R^2	.63	.65	.69
N	780	796	813

NOTE: Years shown are year t–1 in equation (8.2). See also Note: table 8.1.
*** $p \le .01$. Two–tailed tests are conducted for each regression coefficient.
** $p \le .05$. See note ***.
* $p \le .10$. See note ***.

TABLE 8.3.
*Average Effects of Alliances on the Predicted Volume of Exports for the United States,
the Soviet Union, China, Great Britain, and France
(Based on Estimates in Table 8.2.)*

	Trade with:	
	Allies	Nonallies
United States	269	103
Soviet Union	232	46
China	280	61
Great Britain	186	100
France	82	89

NOTE: In computing these values, the predicted volume of exports between Great Britain and states it is not allied with is set equal to 100.

major powers. France conducted only about 30 percent to 45 percent as much trade with its allies as the remaining major powers did with theirs.

Another interesting source of variation in the commercial patterns of the major powers involves the extent to which they traded with nonallies. The predicted volume of trade with nonallies is roughly the same for the United States, Great Britain, and France. This predicted volume also is similar for China and the Soviet Union, but they conducted much less commerce with nonallied trade partners than the United States, Great Britain, and France.

DISCUSSION OF THE RESULTS

The results in this chapter provide considerable evidence that alliances shaped bilateral trade flows involving the major powers during the period after World War II and that the effects of alliances were larger and stronger than those of PTAs. However, the extent to which major powers engaged in trade with their allies was not uniform. Particularly striking is the tendency for France to conduct less commerce with its allies than with other countries, and the tendency for China and the Soviet Union to engage in less trade with nonallied trade partners than the United States, Great Britain, or France.

The latter finding may reflect the unusual extent to which Communist governments are able to direct trade flows. The absence of an independent private sector and the strong central control of the economy exercised by the Chinese and Soviet governments clearly enhanced their ability to limit trade with potential and actual adversaries. Of course, the U.S., British, and French governments also had some ability to use trade policy to influence trade flows and, as in the case of the Coordinating Committee for Multilateral Export Controls (COCOM) and other sanctions efforts, had some success doing so. But the capacity of these governments to limit trade with nonallies has been hampered by the influence of interest groups on trade policy and private agents that sometimes circumvented trade restrictions.

The other important difference in the effects of alliances on trade among the major powers is that France traded much less with its allies than the remaining major powers did with theirs. On average, France also conducted more trade with nonallies than with its allies. At first blush, French trade patterns might appear to reflect the extensive economic ties between France and those former colonies with which it was not allied. But more is at work here, since we controlled for the effects of prior colonial relations in our analysis.

We argued earlier that one reason why alliances are expected to have a particularly large effect on trade involving major powers is that these states are likely to be vested with the ability to influence their terms of trade. Our results are consistent with this explanation. But, as we have argued elsewhere (Mansfield and Bronson 1994), another reason why alliances involving major powers may have an especially large influence on trade stems from their tendency to be more stable and durable than alliances comprised solely of nonmajor powers. Major powers also tend to be more reliable allies and less likely to shift alliances than nonmajor powers. Hence, nonmajor powers are likely to discount less heavily the future benefits arising from trade, and therefore to liberalize trade to a greater extent, with major power allies than with other allies.

France, however, clearly was an unreliable ally within the North Atlantic Treaty Organization (NATO), which may help to explain why trade flows with its allies were relatively depressed. Even before the French decision to "partially withdraw" from NATO in 1966, it had taken actions to reduce its involvement in the alliance. Moreover, as Michael Harrison (1981:134) points out, de Gaulle's foreign policy "implied that a resolve to engage in hostilities along with the [NATO] allies should depend on a free decision reached by responsible civilian authorities at the time. There could thus be no binding prior commitments and no blind submission to the force of events, because of either military integration or the presence of foreign military installations in France." At the same time, de Gaulle was actively attempting to promote closer relations between France and the Soviet Union, and concluded an agreement, signed in October 1964, calling for the expansion of trade between these countries (Kolodziej 1974: 361). Although France remained a member of NATO even after its partial withdrawal, it seems unlikely that France was viewed as especially dependable by its allies during much of the period analyzed in this chapter.

In addition, both of the multilateral alliances (including NATO) to which France belonged during the period analyzed here included at least one other major power. Not only was France relatively unreliable, its nonmajor power allies therefore had other major powers on which they could depend to enhance their security. This may have led them to strengthen commercial ties with these other major powers and weaken such ties with France.

The purpose of this chapter has been to analyze the effects of alliances and PTAs on trade. Our results indicate that both factors tend to promote trade flows involving major powers, but that the effects of alliances are considerably larger and stronger than those of PTAs. These findings accord with the argument that the security externalities generated by commerce create political incentives for states to trade more freely with allies than with other countries. They also suggest that existing studies of PTAs, virtually all of which ignore the effects of alliances, are likely to overstate their effects on trade, since PTAs often comprise states that also are allies (Mansfield 1993).

In addition, our findings have some implications for contemporary discussions of economic regionalism. Many concerns voiced about commercial regionalism focus on the increasing tendency for PTAs to guide trade (e.g., Bhagwati 1993; Gilpin 1987). Yet others have expressed doubt that regionalism is on the rise (e.g., Milner 1991; Pomfret 1988). While our results only offer indirect evidence bearing on this issue, the effects of PTAs on trade flows involving major powers do not seem to have risen (or declined) during the period from 1960 to 1990 (see tables 8.1 and 8.2).

Nor is there much evidence of a change over time in the effects of alliances on trade flows involving major powers. Only during the détente of the 1970s was there any noticeable dip in the magnitude of this relationship. Further, while we analyzed only one year (1990) after the cold war's conclusion, it is interesting that the influence of alliances in this year was greater than in any earlier year analyzed here except 1960. But while the effects of alliances on trade do not seem to have changed much over time, alliance themselves have changed. Most notably, the Warsaw Pact has expired and changes in the membership of NATO soon may occur.[24] Based on our results, these changes are likely to have a significant influence on the direction of trade flows.

It is obvious that ours is a very limited comparison of the effects of alliances and PTAs on trade flows. For example, it would be useful to examine their effects on trade flows between nonmajor powers, as well as those involving major powers.[25] It also would be useful to analyze whether different types of alliances and PTAs influence trade to different degrees;[26] and to lengthen the time frame over which these relationships are examined.

But despite these limitations, our results provide considerable evidence that security relations have had a marked influence on trade relations during the post-World War II era. They also suggest that trade flows and any increased regional concentration of trade are likely to be shaped at least as much by the pursuit of power as by the pursuit of plenty.

Acknowledgments: We are grateful to Joanne Gowa, Miles Kahler, Walter Mattli, Helen Milner, two anonymous reviewers, and the participants at Columbia University's conference on The Political Economy of Regionalism and the University of Arizona's Department of Political Science Speaker Series for comments on this chapter. We also thank Gina Marie Finan for research assistance and Lynn Jacobsen, Salvatore Pitruzzello, and Susan Zayac for assistance with computer programming.

NOTES

1. Security externalities are uncompensated benefits or costs that influence the security of one actor due to the actions of another actor. For a more extensive discussion of this issue, see Gowa (1994).

2. For example, in addition to tariffs, embargoes or quotas designed to undermine the political-military capacity of an adversary are likely to serve a similar purpose.

3. Absent sufficient market power, the imposition of a tariff (or equivalent trade barrier) only will serve to degrade the national income of the intervening state, thereby undermining its political-military power.

4. It is clear that this state might have an incentive to liberalize trade with an adversary if its expected benefits from doing so exceeded those of its adversary. However, under these conditions, its adversary would have little incentive to engage in free trade with this state.

5. Our discussion has emphasized the incentives for states to impose trade barriers, and it is clear that these barriers need not move in tandem with trade flows. However, data on bilateral trade restrictions are not available for the sample of states analyzed here. Moreover, after controlling for other influences on trade, trade barriers are likely to be inversely related to trade flows. Thus, like a number of previous studies of the relationship between alliances and trade (Gowa 1994; Gowa and Mansfield 1993), we focus on explaining trade flows in the following analysis.

6. Data on exports are expressed in U.S. dollars and are taken from the International Monetary Fund's (IMF's) *Direction of Trade* (various years).

7. Data on GDP and population are taken from Summers and Heston (1991) and subsequent updates of these data, which are available from the National Bureau of Economic

Research. Data on GDP are expressed in nominal U.S. dollars. It should be noted that this data set does not include values of GDP and population for a variety of countries in 1990. However, it does include data for some of these countries in 1989, and we use them in our analyses of trade flows involving these states in 1990.

8. Consistent with previous studies using gravity models, we rely on the shortest distance between ports in states i and j, measured in nautical miles. In those cases in which at least one trading partner was land-locked, we rely on land distances (either road or rail) to measure the distance between them. Data on geographical distances are taken from the Defense Mapping Agency's *Distances Between Ports* (1985, 5th ed.); *The Times Atlas of the World* (1992, 9th ed.); and *The Times Concise Atlas of the World* (1972).

9. Data on alliances are taken from Small and Singer (1969) and the COW Project's preliminary updates of these data, dated March 1993. Consistent with previous studies of this topic (Gowa 1994; Gowa and Mansfield 1993), we also include as allies the United States and Japan. Although the Japanese-United States Security Treaty (1951–1960) and the Treaty of Mutual Cooperation and Security (1960 to present) are not included in Small and Singer's data set, they served much the same purpose as an alliance (Grenville 1974:270, 286–87).

10. Data on PTAs are taken from Belous and Hartley (1990:141–43), Schott (1989), and Hartland-Thunberg (1980). We also include the Council for Mutual Economic Assistance among our list of PTAs (Pomfret 1988).

11. Data on this variable are taken from *GATT: The Annecy Protocol of Terms of Accession and the Annecy Schedules of Tariff Concessions* (Washington, D.C.: Department of State, Publication 3664, Commercial Policy Series 121, 1949); and various issues of the GATT's *Basic Instruments and Selected Documents* (Geneva) and *International Trade* (Geneva).

12. Data on prior colonial relations are taken from Kurian (1992).

13. Data on command economies are taken from Kornai (1992:6–7) for the period from 1960 through 1985 and, for 1990, from Staar et al. (1991). It should be noted that alliances, PTAs, GATT membership, prior colonial relations, and command economies are coded based on the status of states i and j at the end of year t-1.

14. This cross-sectional design is consistent with many previous studies of the effects of PTAs and alliances on bilateral trade, including Aitken (1973), Eichengreen and Frankel (1994), Frankel (1993), Gowa and Mansfield (1993), Pollins (1989), and Summary (1989).

15. Data are not available for all of the variables included in equation (8.1) for years before World War II. For years subsequent to World War II and before 1960, trade data for China and the Soviet Union are too sketchy and incomplete to conduct an adequate analysis of their trade patterns.

16. Only those states listed by the COW Project as members of the international system are included in this analysis. The size of our samples ranges from 512 in 1960 to 813 in 1990. These differences occur primarily because the IMF does not report trade flows for all pairs of states in its *Direction of Trade*. It also does not distinguish between pairs of countries for which so little trade is conducted that this trade flow is reported as zero and pairs of countries for which data are not available. As such, we do not include either type of pairs in our analyses.

17. In addition to the cross-sectional design used in the preceding analysis, we estimated the parameters in equation (8.1) after pooling the data across the seven years analyzed here (and deflating the values of exports and GDP). Dummy variables for country-specific and year-specific fixed effects and an instrument for the lagged value of exports also were included in this analysis. The results indicate that, except for GATT membership, the estimate of each variable in equation (8.1) is statistically significant, and the quantitative effect of each variable is quite similar to its average effect based on the results in table 8.1. The estimate of $\log(GATT)_{ij}$ derived

using this pooled model, however, is not significant and is much smaller than the estimate of this variable for any year shown in table 8.1.

Further, we examined whether the results based on a pooled design were sensitive to the model's specification, by replacing $\log(GDP)_i$, $\log(GDP)_j$, $\log(POP)_i$, and $\log(POP)_j$ in equation (8.1) with $\log(GDP_i \cdot GDP_j)$ and $\log(POP_i \cdot POP_j)$. This specification of the gravity model is closely related to that used in a number of previous studies (e.g., Eichengreen and Irwin 1995; Frankel 1993). As expected, the estimate of $\log(GDP_i \cdot GDP_j)$ is positive, that of $\log(POP_i \cdot POP_j)$ is negative, and both are statistically significant. Moreover, virtually no variation exists in the signs, sizes, or significance levels of the remaining variables in the model. For an analysis of the effects of alliances and PTAs on trade flows based on a pooled design, see Mansfield and Bronson (1994).

18. See Dixon and Moon (1993) for one exception. They analyze the effects of democracy on trade flows involving the United States from 1966 to 1983, and find that the United States conducted more trade with democratic than with nondemocratic trade partners.

19. Other studies have also analyzed the effects of war on international trade (Gowa 1994; Gowa and Mansfield 1993; Mansfield 1994; Pollins 1989). However, no wars took place between the pairs of states for which we have complete data during the years analyzed here, based on Small and Singer's (1982; Singer and Small 1994) list of wars.

20. These studies attribute this finding to the fact that while the aggregate trade among a set of states is likely to be greater when they are allied than when they are not, it need not be the case that all bilateral trade flows among them will be greater under these conditions. Indeed, trade flows between any given pair of states within a multilateral alliance may be relatively unaffected by the alliance, although this should be offset by trade flows between other pairs within the alliance. In contrast, for any given pair of states, the flow of trade between them always is expected to be greater when they are engaged in a bilateral alliance than when they are not, since commerce between them constitutes the entire flow for the alliance. See Gowa (1994:62) and Gowa and Mansfield (1993:412).

21. As noted earlier (see note 9), we include the United States and Japan as allies during the period analyzed here. This is our only deviation from the COW Project's list of alliances, and while we believe it is appropriate to include it in our sample of alliances, it is important to note that doing so has little bearing on our results. The estimates of $\log(ALLY)_{ij}$ when this alliance is excluded are virtually identical to those in table 8.1. Further, the estimates of $\log(BALLY)_{ij}$ also are much the same regardless of whether or not this alliance is included.

22. On average, the predicted volume of trade between PTA members is about 45 percent greater than between states that do not share a PTA based on the results in table 8.2, whereas the corresponding increase is about 30 percent based on the results in table 8.1.

23. On average, parties to the GATT conduct roughly 45 percent more trade than other countries based on the results in table 8.2, whereas they conduct roughly 75 percent more trade than other countries based on the results in table 8.1. Further, the average predicted volume of trade between states that had a prior colonial relationship is about 420 percent greater than between other states based on the results in table 8.2, whereas this volume is almost 500 percent greater based on the results in table 8.1.

24. For an analysis of security relations in the post-cold war era and the future of NATO, see Charles Kupchan's chapter in this book.

25. See Mansfield and Bronson (1994) for an analysis of this issue.

26. For analyses that address some causes and effects of institutional variations across regional economic unions, see the chapters in this book by Joseph Grieco, Stephan Haggard, Helen Milner, and Beth Yarbrough and Robert Yarbrough.

NINE

Regionalizing Europe's Security: The Case for a New Mitteleuropa

Charles A. Kupchan

How to promote peace and stability in post-cold war Europe is one of the most important challenges facing the community of established democracies. With the Continent in the midst of profound change, choices made today about the composition and nature of new security institutions will help shape—and will not simply follow from—a new strategic landscape in Europe. If new lines are drawn, where they fall will have a major influence on how new power centers are defined in Europe, on the nature of relations among these power centers, and on the character of regimes governing major European states. Unless unforeseen political or ideological cleavages emerge in the meantime, the alignments and alliances deliberately crafted by Europe's main powers will be important determinants of the structure of post-cold war Europe. Opportunities to fashion international structure, as opposed to react to it, are historical rarities. It is important to take advantage of this opportunity—and to get it right.

NATO has launched the Partnership for Peace (PFP) as its main initiative for building new security arrangements in Europe. The Partnership provides a vehicle for concrete military cooperation between NATO and the new democracies of Europe's east as well as a pathway toward full NATO membership for states that successfully consolidate market-oriented democracy and acquire the capabilities needed to operate with NATO forces. Although NATO has not yet specified who will be eligible for membership or indicated a timetable for admitting new members, the outlines of a strategic vision are clear: the enlargement of NATO will serve as the principal vehicle for building a new security order in post-cold war Europe.

I argue in this chapter that NATO members are making a fundamental strategic error by proceeding down the pathway of enlargement. Far from building cooperation and peace across today's Europe, NATO's eastward expansion would have two markedly adverse effects on Europe's strategic landscape. First, because of the logic of power balancing, NATO enlargement would precipitate the redivision of Europe into two competing blocs. Second, because the geopolitical interests of Europe's major powers are contracting in the absence of a dominant external threat, the expansion of the Alliance would saddle member states with unwanted and unsustainable commitments, ultimately undermining NATO.

As an alternative to NATO expansion, I propose that new security arrangements for Europe be based upon the notion of institutionalized regional subgroups within a pan-European architecture.[1] Security cooperation and political consultation would take place on a pan-European basis, but security guarantees would be extended via three regional defense organizations—one encompassing Western Europe, one encompassing Central Europe, and one encompassing Eastern Europe.[2] Through the designation of Germany and Ukraine as pivot states—states that would be members of two regional groupings—these bodies would be interlocking.

This approach to regionalizing Europe's security is consistent with the logic of power balancing: it would create a rough equilibrium among three centers of power. It is also consistent with current and prospective changes in the geopolitical interests of Europe's major powers. In the post-cold war era, Europe's security *is* divisible; without a common, pervasive threat, the strategic interests of states will grow more limited and become increasingly defined by proximity. To enlarge an alliance that is a legacy of the cold war and to assume that Europe's major powers will continue to have expansive interests is to violate the geopolitical trends that are inevitably emerging as a result of the Soviet Union's demise. Furthermore, my proposal offers an innovative means of dealing with the unique security predicaments faced by Germany and Ukraine—states that for geopolitical and historic reasons will be most stable if provided a means of straddling between two regions.

In the following section, I discuss the relationship between my analysis and the broader theoretical issues raised in this volume. I then spell out the analytic suppositions that inform my examination of the policy options. In doing so, I show why institutional decisions will have a profound effect on the strategic landscape. I next show that the eastward expansion of NATO creates more problems than it solves. In the final section of the essay, I argue that building regional subgroups within a pan-European structure provides the best alternative for constructing a new European security order. I develop the logic behind regional subgroups and pivot states and then anticipate potential objections to my proposal.

THEORETICAL FOUNDATIONS

This essay builds on and contributes to three aspects of the theoretical debate about regionalism. First, it offers a new perspective on the causes and effects of regionalism. Most analyses of when and why regional bodies form focus on the material incentives motivating participating states. Functionalists and realists alike look to the prospect of increases in security and/or prosperity as the driving force behind regional groupings. Other variables—proximity, common language, shared culture—help these regional groupings cohere and deepen. In general, agency is located in the states that ultimately comprise the regional grouping. Once in place, the effects of regional institutions are usually measured in terms of their ability to facilitate economic exchange and to promote collective action against common threats.[3] Structure changes the payoffs facing individual agents so that they have more incentive to cooperate with each other than before.

My analysis reverses the causal connection between agent and structure; my argument rests on the assertion that conceiving of a certain group of states as a region can be a necessary precondition for inducing them to behave as if they belong to that region and thus enabling them to share in the associated benefits. Structure shapes agency. States will adopt a sense of communal identity only after being defined by their own elites and publics as well as those of outside states as part of a unique region. The states constituting this imagined region will then come to appreciate the material incentives and exhibit the behavior conventionally viewed as necessary preconditions for regionalism.[4] Ideational change precedes, and does not follow from, changes in behavior. A region is conceived of, then it comes to exist.[5]

More concretely, I propose in the following pages that the geographic area between NATO and the former Soviet Union be designated a distinct regional grouping (Central Europe, for want of a better name) and that this grouping be institutionalized. At present, the states that would belong to this region have little or no interest in forming a Central European grouping and are not pursuing policies in either the economic realm or the security realm that give rise to a functional need for new regional institutions. In this sense, my argument diverges from the conventional narrative about the causes of regionalism. It rests instead on the supposition that designating a group of states as a specific region will have the normative value of encouraging those states to behave as if they comprise that region. They will cooperate more with each other than otherwise. Outside states will view the region as an independent center of power and commerce; perceptions of the continental balance of power will be shaped accordingly. Central Europe becomes a region and reaps the associated benefits because it comes to be conceived as a region by participating states and outside powers alike.

The second theoretical issue that informs my analysis concerns the extent to which the body of theory that has evolved in the study of economic regionalism can be applied readily to security matters. The end of the cold war has promoted a significant degree of convergence between economic and security regimes, increasing analytic overlap between the two issue-areas. Writing in 1984, Charles Lipson argued that one of the key differences between the two issues-areas is that cooperation is more difficult to attain in the security realm than in the economic realm. Except among allies who band together to resist a common threat, states tend to pass up opportunities for joint gains in security because of the "costs of betrayal, the difficulties of monitoring, and the tendency to comprehend security issues as strictly competitive struggles" (Lipson 1984:18). The disappearance of the endemic competition that accompanied the East–West struggle and the increases in transparency afforded by technological change are eliminating these basic differences between economic and security regimes. Security bodies will look more like economic ones, promoting incremental increases in cooperation among states seeking joint gains, deepening norms and rules, and monitoring day-to-day developments.

For these reasons, a mounting number of insights from the political economy literature can be transferred to the security realm with no loss of analytic power. The trade-offs between the scope of regional arrangements and the ability of member-states to win domestic support for participation in those arrangements apply equally in both realms. A more comprehensive and intrusive trade regime will generally be harder to sell to electorates just as participation in a security organization will be harder to sustain as the commitments and sacrifices entailed become more onerous.[6] So too does Jacob Viner's dictum that trading zones are beneficial to their members as long as the trade created outweighs the trade diverted have its security counterpart (Viner 1950). The peace-causing effects of including certain states in a security grouping should outweigh the potentially destabilizing effects of excluding others.

The literature on institutional design and performance also applies across subfields. Both security and economic groupings face a potential decline in performance as the number of members increases. Large membership complicates policy coordination and increases opportunities for free riding.[7] In addition, degree of institutionalization generally correlates with degree of integration. The European Union and NATO are both the most institutionalized and the most integrated groupings in their respective issue-areas. Finally, economic and security groupings promote cooperation through many of the same processes. They lower transaction costs, increase transparency, and strengthen enforcement mechanisms.

In two critical analytic respects, however, economic and security groupings part company. First, the output of regional economic groupings— whether focused on reducing trade barriers, coordinating currencies, or both—vary along one principal dimension: their ability to enhance economic efficiency. Different types of arrangements produce more or less liberalization of trade, or more or less coordination of currencies.

Security groupings do not share this simplicity. Different institutional arrangements produce different goods, not just more or less of the same good. All security institutions seek to enhance their members' security. But variation in institutional design leads to radical variation in core functions, not just more or less security. A collective defense organization, for example, aggregates military power against a specific threat emanating from a nonmember. A collective security organization, on the other hand, seeks to preserve peace among its members. The two types of bodies operate according to different logics and have fundamentally different strategic implications for both members and nonmembers. Economic groupings vary as to the degree of efficiency they produce. Security groupings vary as to the core functions they fulfill. This difference has important analytic and normative implications.

The second key difference between economic and security groupings concerns whether the goods they produce can be considered excludable public goods.[8] The core body of literature on regional economic institutions is predicated on the assumption that free trade does qualify. It is excludable in that only members enjoy its benefits. It is a public good in that it is joint—members benefit from it without limiting its availability to other members.

The good produced by security institutions is an excludable public good only under a narrow set of circumstances. During the cold war, the deterrence provided by NATO was an excludable public good inasmuch as membership was limited and all members benefited from the security provided without diminishing the deterrent effect available to others.[9] NATO continues to provide a stabilizing effect from which all members benefit simultaneously. But the publicness of the good provided by NATO has declined dramatically since the demise of the Soviet Union. Because most threats to NATO members are now both isolated and contained, the good produced by NATO is far more private in nature. Individual members have security interests that are not shared by other members. Germany, for example, will have far more direct interests in stopping a minor war in Central Europe than will most other NATO countries. NATO engaged so reluctantly in the war in Bosnia because members disagreed about whether common interests were at stake and about whether they would enjoy joint gains from deeper military involvement. These differences in the publicness of the goods produced by economic and security bodies have important implications for analyzing the effects of geopolitical change on the design, performance, and political desirability of regional institutions.

The final theoretical debate that bears on the analysis in this essay follows logically; it concerns linkages between regional economic groupings and regional security groupings. During the bipolarity of the cold war, economic and security groupings were largely congruent. Most commerce was intrabloc; allies traded mainly with each other, not with their adversaries. Mansfield and Bronson (1994) have shown through a statistical analysis that this congruence had consequential effects: alliances deepened the trade-enhancing effects of preferential trading arrangements. Trade areas comprised of states that were also allies enjoyed far greater trade flows than economic groupings of nonallied states.

The boundaries of economic and security groupings are now becoming increasingly incongruent. Indeed, the two types of groupings are experiencing contradictory trends. Regional trade groups are expanding in number, geographic reach, and the scope of measures pursued to liberalize and coordinate commerce. In contrast, security groupings are shrinking in scope; the tightly knit structures associated with alliance are either dissolving altogether or becoming looser configurations. These opposing trends reflect the public nature of free trade as compared with the increasingly private nature of security. Several important questions follow.

First, will regional trade areas continue to provide efficiency gains even as they part company with their security counterparts? The security-enhancing effects of joint economic gains appear to have helped trade groups thrive when their members were allies. In the absence of alliances and a clear sense of who is friend and who is foe, increasing concern about relative gains may ultimately come to hamper efforts to further liberalize trade. Alternatively, elected officials, because they can no longer use strategic necessity as an argument for making domestic economic sacrifices, may have difficulty selling free trade to their electorates.

Second, in light of the fact that economic and security groupings appear to have been working in unison to deepen transnational linkages and interdependence, will economic ties alone be sufficient to hold together extant international communities and pick up the slack left behind by the diminishing strength of strategic bonds? More specifically, will the deepening and further institutionalization of economic relations between North America and Europe help preserve the strategic dimensions of the transatlantic relationship? It is at least plausible that just as alliance has enhanced the efficiency effects of trade areas, trade ties might help maintain strategic ties that would otherwise wither. In the same manner that elected officials used strategic arguments to sell economic sacrifice, they might now resort to economic arguments to sell strategic sacrifice. If strategic linkages do not at least to some extent piggyback on economic ones, economic and security groupings are likely to become increasingly incongruent.

Third, what types of tensions could potentially emerge from such incongruities? If, for example, some of Europe's new democracies join both NATO and the European Union and others only join the European Union, will new fault lines emerge? Extending the European Union far further east than NATO could plausibly provide a needed means of attaching to the West those countries likely to end up on the wrong side of NATO's eventual frontier. On the other hand, growing divergence between the memberships of NATO and the European Union could both leave much of Central Europe dissatisfied and erode the sense of common purpose that undergirds the transatlantic community. The long-term effects of messiness—the proliferation of economic and security groupings some of which overlap and some of which do not—remains uncertain.

I do not intend in this essay to provide definitive answers to these questions. Rather these are the general theoretical concerns that inform my analysis. In addition, the more policy-oriented discussion that follows will illuminate and advance thinking about these broader issues.

ANALYTIC SUPPOSITIONS

Contending views of how to adapt Europe's security institutions to the Continent's new landscape ultimately rest on differing assessments of the causes of war and of the value of institutions in preventing war. I therefore begin by making plain the assumptions that inform my analysis.

The Nature of the Security Problem and the Causes of Great Power Conflict

Central Europe lies at the core of the current debate about European security. The region is in strategic limbo, effectively free from Russia's sphere of influence to its east, but not yet formally a part of the transatlantic security community to its west. That Central Europe was the starting point for this century's two world wars underscores the need to address the region's security. So too does the war in Bosnia make amply clear that Central Europe is still one of the Continent's flashpoints.

Many analysts contend that there is now a dangerous security vacuum in Central Europe, that filling this vacuum is essential to European stability, and that incorporating the states of the region into Western structures should therefore be the top priority of a new security architecture.[10] Proponents of this view make two principal arguments. First, isolated pockets of instability and conflict in the region will ultimately spread, eventually turning into regionwide crises that directly threaten the interests of outside powers. It is better to act preventively than to allow small crises to escalate until outside powers have no choice but to become engaged. Second, even isolated instability and conflict in Central Europe will tempt the major powers bordering the region—Germany and Russia—to compete for dominance in the lands between them. As frontier states, neither power will be able to tolerate the uncertainties and potential threats associated with regional turmoil. Both of these arguments rest on the claim that developments inside Central Europe will be key determinants of both the Continent's well-being and relations between Germany and Russia.

Although addressing Central Europe's security needs represents a principal and urgent challenge, my analysis is informed by a different assessment of the region's security problem. Rather than viewing developments inside Central Europe as being the key determinant of relations between Germany and Russia, I view relations between Germany and Russia as being the key determinant of security in Central Europe. World Wars I and

II started in Central Europe not because little wars in the region spread into big ones as a matter of course, but because the region was the location of geopolitical rivalry among Europe's great powers. Isolated pockets of instability or conflict should by no means be ignored, but addressing them should not be given priority over managing relations among the great powers. Central Europe's welfare will follow from, and not be determinative of, relations among the Continent's major states.

What, then, are the causes of great power rivalry and how should a new security architecture be constructed so as to avoid it? Scholars of international relations remain deeply divided over this question. Structural realists contend that great power rivalry is inevitable; it emerges from the anarchic, competitive nature of the international system. Rivalry escalates into conflict when one or more great powers see war as the best way to enhance their security (Mearsheimer 1994). From this perspective, Germany started two world wars this century to deal with the vulnerability stemming from its location in the center of Europe. Similarly, the Cold War resulted from two garden-variety great powers—the United States and the Soviet Union—vying for primacy. Institutions, if they matter at all, matter only at the margins. All great powers are created equal, and great-power relations are solely a function of the distribution of power; in the end, institutional commitments will be overridden by the dictates of power balancing. Rather than seeking institutional solutions to great power war, policy makers should focus on creating a stable balance of power among national units.[11]

Two very different suppositions about the causes of great power war inform the analysis in this essay. First, institutions have important effects on the behavior of great powers. They do so by helping to shape the distribution of power and by mitigating the competitiveness of the international system through promoting shared norms and common identities and by increasing transparency. Second, all great powers are not the same, with each continuously challenging the other for primacy, ultimately triggering war through unintended spirals of hostility. On the contrary, the chief cause of major war is aggressor states—states that for reasons of domestic structure and ideology seek to overturn the status quo through force. Power balancing and the security dilemma do trigger moderate levels of competition even among like-minded, status quo states. And such competition can contribute to the emergence of aggressor states. But great powers infected with domestic pathologies, not endemic rivalry associated with the international system, are the main causes of major war.

It is therefore conceptually vital to distinguish between benign, democratic great powers and malign, autocratic ones.[12] The former use their power constructively and are providers of international security and stability. The latter use their power destructively and are the principal threat to international security and stability. The most appropriate strategy for dealing with any individual great power depends on the motivation driving that state's foreign behavior, which in turn depends on its domestic structure and phase of democratic development. Democratic great powers, because they are likely to pursue benign, status quo policies, should be reassured and encouraged to assume international responsibilities. To adopt deterrent strategies with such states is likely to lead to unnecessary spirals of hostility. Autocratic aggressor states, because they are likely to pursue malign, predatory policies, should be confronted with deterrent strategies and the prospect of countervailing force. To accommodate such states is to invite aggression. Hedge strategies are appropriate for states in the midst of transition to democracy. Strategies of reassurance and accommodation should be pursued to help facilitate democratic transition. But precisely because democratizing states are war-prone, status quo powers should be on guard and prepared to reverse course if and when necessary.[13]

This analysis has the following implications for Germany and Russia—the two key states that are at the core of debate about how to forge a new European order and deal with security challenges in Central Europe. As a stable, democratic country, Germany does not need to acquire nuclear weapons, be bound and gagged by multilateral institutions, or otherwise be treated exceptionally if its international ambition is to be kept in check. On the contrary, new security arrangements in Europe should take advantage of Germany's emergence as a benign, status quo power. Germany for historical reasons is an under-provider of security; it therefore needs to be encouraged to come on line as a "normal" great power and to take on new responsibilities in Europe commensurate with its size and resources.

Russia's future is far less certain; it may edge haltingly toward stable democracy or experience new bouts of authoritarian rule. The nature of its foreign policy will vary accordingly. During this period of transition, hedge strategies are appropriate. The guiding rule of thumb for policy makers should be to include Russia as a democratic partner and provider of security if possible, and to exclude Russia as an autocratic challenger and threat to security only if necessary. At least for now, Russia is a weak, quasi-democratic state that has neither the capability nor the intent to reconstitute a political union among the former Soviet republics or to invade and occupy all or even a portion of Central Europe. Nor is there any historical basis to support the claim that Russia, because of geopolitics or culture, has a congenital imperial impulse. Each of Europe's major powers has experienced a phase of imperialism coincident with domestic political turmoil. With the exception of Russia, each has later been democratized and its foreign behavior domesticated. There is no reason to believe that Russia will not follow suit as markets and democracy continue to spread eastward.

Why Security Institutions Matter

European states are redefining their national interests and new power balances are taking shape on the Continent. The international roles and geopolitical orientations of a newly unified Germany and a quasi-democratic Russia are up for grabs. The future of America's military engagement in Europe is unclear. Ukraine is struggling to maintain itself as an intact nation-state as well as to recover and redefine its nationhood.

Such pervasive uncertainty and fluidity magnify the importance of institutional choices. Security institutions have consequential effects on the strategic landscape through three principal mechanisms. First, security institutions are instruments that enable states to define and manipulate international concentrations of power. Institutions define centers of power by including some states and excluding others. They allow for manipulation of these power centers by providing mechanisms for states to marshal their resources against common threats. Institutions thus facilitate deterring and defending against aggressors and reassuring and accommodating partners.

Second, security institutions deepen cooperation among their members, thereby mitigating the competitiveness of the international system. Like other types of international institutions, security institutions promote cooperation by establishing widely recognized rules and norms, by increasing the punitive costs to states that violate these rules and norms, by decreasing transaction costs, and by increasing transparency and trust (Keohane 1984). Routinized consultation helps build personal contacts among policy makers, which can contribute to shared understandings, mutual trust, and expectations of reciprocity.

Third, security institutions affect domestic politics in individual states. Inasmuch as they represent groupings of like-minded states, security institutions are political communities, not just forums for military cooperation. Participation in these communities, as well as exclusion from them, helps shape national self-images and encourages polities to identify with a certain grouping or region. Especially among states in the midst of transition, these identities and self-images play a role in guiding state behavior and determining what range of policies is politically acceptable and sustainable.[14] Because they shape the international environment in which states operate, security institutions also affect domestic perceptions of vulnerability, which in turn affect political stability and the allocation of resources.[15] Finally, regional security bodies affect domestic politics by formalizing, sometimes by treaty, a set of international commitments. These commitments communicate to publics the nature and location of their state's external interests. This link between domestic politics and international institutions can also work in reverse. Domestic constraints can limit the demands institutions can place on their members. If institutions demand too much of their members, those institutions will founder as states back away from unwanted and unsustainable commitments.

The strength of these effects varies according to institutional design. There are three main types of security organizations: collective defense institutions, collective security institutions, and cooperative security institutions. Collective defense institutions—more commonly called military alliances—have the strongest effects. Because they entail binding guarantees to come to the aid of allies, alliances provide the most effective deterrence and the deepest military cooperation, but are also the most demanding in political terms. Even if pledges to collective action do not come due, treaty-based security guarantees usually require broad-based political support. The automaticity and cohesiveness that make alliances such effective security institutions also make them more difficult to sustain politically.

A collective security institution focuses on managing relations and preventing conflict among its members, not on aggregating military capability against a specified external enemy.[16] Its effects are generally more muted than those of collective defense. Collective security institutions may provide for less effective deterrence against aggressors than collective defense, but because they are focused on preserving peace among their members and not on external threats, they do not trigger responsive balancing by excluded states in the same way alliances do. Collective security's domestic effects follow logically. On the one hand, the flexible, nonbinding nature of collective security commitments reduces their credibility and their ability to shape public attitudes. On the other hand, it is just this flexibility that would make such commitments more politically sustainable should the formal territorial guarantees associated with alliances prove to be unacceptable.

Cooperative security institutions, such as the Partnership for Peace and Organization for Security and Cooperation in Europe, are the least formalized type of security organization. They provide a forum for political consultation and military cooperation, but do not entail either explicit or implicit commitments to defend members against attack by other members or by third parties. Cooperative security institutions fulfill the same generic functions as other types of security bodies, but in watered-down form. They provide the least effective deterrence against aggression, although members do engage in concrete military cooperation and reap the associated benefits. Because cooperative security entails no commitments to undertake collective action against aggression, it has less pronounced domestic effects—but is also the option requiring least expenditure of political capital to implement. Accordingly, cooperative security offers an attractive alternative when domestic politics may make collective defense or collective security commitments impossible to sustain.

THE EXPANSION OF NATO

The Partnership for Peace (PFP) is only the beginning of a long-term process of building a new security order in Europe. The Central Europeans continue to argue vociferously that a cooperative security institution does not go far enough to meet their security needs and alleviate their anxieties. The key issue looming on the horizon is that of security guarantees. As long as NATO extends Article V guarantees to its current members, many of Europe's other democracies will argue that they need them and are entitled to them. The solution to this problem, according to NATO members, is to expand the alliance eastward.

Before making the case against expansion, it is important to acknowledge that enlarging NATO would have some benefits.[17] Extending NATO membership to the countries of Central Europe would offer NATO strategic depth and increase the military and industrial resources at its disposal. Should the western and eastern halves of Europe again become estranged, the western half would be significantly enlarged in terms of manpower, territory, and industrial capability. Inclusion of the new democracies in NATO would enhance their domestic stability. Membership would win popular support for democratic reformers in the region, most of whom are strong proponents of entry into NATO. NATO guarantees would also help moderate perceived vulnerabilities and fill what is viewed in the region as a security vacuum, building domestic confidence and consolidating democratic governance (Dunay 1994). Finally, NATO enlargement would help keep Germany embedded in the West. Because of its location in the center of Europe and its steadily increasing level of trade with and investment in Central Europe, Germany wants to push the boundaries of the West's defense community considerably east of its own borders. NATO enlargement offers one alternative for meeting Germany's security needs while guarding against unilateral German efforts to address its strategic concerns in Central Europe.

The Case Against

The case against the expansion of NATO rests on four main points.[18] First, because NATO is still a military alliance whose purpose is to concentrate power against an outside threat, its enlargement is likely to precipitate the redivision of Europe into two competing blocs. Unless the age-old dictates of power balancing fail to operate, Russia cannot but take steps to redress the adverse shift in the constellation of power associated with Central Europe's inclusion in NATO. Furthermore, even though extending NATO security guarantees to Central Europe would warn Russia to steer clear of Poland and its neighbors, it would also indicate the outer boundaries of NATO's new security perimeter, inviting the reassertion of Russian control of its "near-abroad." Russian leaders across the political spectrum have made clear that they oppose NATO expansion. As Sergei Karaganov, a leading Russian analyst and adviser to President Yeltsin wrote, if "NATO expands eastward, Russia under any government will become a revisionist power striving to undermine the already fragile European order (Blackwill and Karaganov 1994:21).

Second, the expansion of NATO into Central Europe would have adverse effects on domestic politics in the states of the former Soviet Union. In Russia, the enlargement of NATO would make it more difficult for democratic reformers to counter the claim of conservative nationalists that the country's security and status as a great power are at risk. President Yeltsin faced vociferous criticism from domestic opponents for allowing NATO to become the dominant external actor in the former Yugoslavia (Kaplan 1994). In other former Soviet republics, NATO expansion into Central Europe would similarly undermine pro-Western elites. It would also strengthen those calling for closer relations with Russia and the resurrection of some form of political and security union.

Third, it makes much more sense to expand NATO when necessary—should Russia again pose a military threat to Central Europe—than to act in anticipation of that threat. To act now might give Poles and their neighbors a welcome psychological boost, but by triggering responsive balancing on the part of Russia and undercutting reformers, such behavior risks setting in motion a self-fulfilling prophecy. There simply is no need to take that risk when Central European countries do not now face a serious external threat and when NATO can always expand later, if and when Russia exhibits imperial intent.

Fourth, it is by no means certain that electorates in current NATO countries will be willing to take on the new responsibilities associated with expansion. Declining internationalism associated with the cold war's end makes it hard to imagine that all sixteen NATO legislatures would approve the extension of Article V security guarantees to Central European states. Germany's strategic location provides a ready rationale for the eastward expansion of NATO's borders. But public opinion polls show that Germans are reluctant to take on new defense commitments in Central Europe.[19] It would be even harder to convince Americans, Britains, Spaniards, or Portuguese that they should be prepared to defend countries many of which they could surely not locate on a map.[20] NATO governments should not embark on the process of expansion if the support of their electorates is in serious doubt. NATO itself, not just prospective members, will be dealt a serious blow if expansion is rejected by national legislatures.

For these reasons, NATO expansion does not provide the solution to Europe's new security dilemma. That NATO continues to exist as a military alliance in the absence of the threat that led to its creation is itself surprising. To expand the institution eastward would run contrary to the essential logic of power balancing and risk redividing Europe into competing blocs. Expanding cold war institutions would also broaden the foreign commitments of member states when, in the absence of an external threat, political willingness to support foreign commitments is shrinking. Accordingly, efforts to enlarge NATO are likely to lead to its demise—even as its expansion alienates Russia and triggers responsive balancing.

These problems stem in large part from the fact that NATO is still a collective defense institution. As an alliance, it provides too much definition to the strategic landscape and is too demanding politically. Precisely because Europe itself is in a state of transition, the Continent's security institutions must retain more ambiguity and flexibility. It is simply unnecessary and unwise to force a decision on where Europe's new boundary should be drawn, to leave Germany with the choice of being wedged into a broader NATO or left as a frontier state in a Central Europe in limbo, and to confront NATO with the task of choosing who is in the West and who is out. These are false choices resulting from the effort to erect security institutions ill-suited to the new strategic landscape.

REGIONAL SUBGROUPS IN A PAN-EUROPEAN ARCHITECTURE

Conceptual Foundations

Eliminating these false choices means moving away from the formality and rigor of alliances to security institutions that contribute to stability without delineating by design or default opposing power centers and that require less explicit and less binding commitments on behalf of their members. In practical terms, these conceptual requirements mean that collective defense institutions must give way to either collective security or cooperative security institutions. The challenge is to find a formula that both contributes to stability on the Continent and entails commitments in keeping with the changing interests of Europe's major powers.

A pan-European collective security system offers an attractive endpoint for Europe. A collective security system guided by a concert of major powers provides a way of promoting cooperative relations among all European states in a manner consistent with power realities.[21] But it will take years, if not decades, of state-building and institution-building before conditions will be conducive to successful operation of a pan-European collective security body.[22] Pan-European collective security will become more feasible and more effective as Europe itself evolves and becomes composed of like-minded states that share similar values and purposes. In the meantime, pan-European forums such as the Partnership for Peace and the Organization for Cooperation and Security in Europe are likely to be limited to cooperative security. The key question is how to get from here to there—how to build a transitional security order that will preserve a democratic anchor in the west, promote stability and peace in the east, and set the stage for a pan-European collective security system.

The above discussion indicates that this interim middle road should be constructed of the following conceptual components. First, collective security provides the appropriate compromise between the formality and rigor of collective defense and the inadequacies of cooperative security. Collective security avoids the pitfalls associated with alliances while preserving the peace-causing effects lost by cooperative security.

Second, to the extent a new security architecture helps define and delineate new power centers, those centers should represent a stable balance of power over the long term. One of the key problems with NATO expansion is that it confronts Russia with a preponderant coalition to its west. The groupings created by a new security architecture should produce a rough equilibrium of power, not a striking imbalance. Opposing preponderance is desirable when dealing with aggressor states, but counterproductive when dealing with potential partners.

Third, new security arrangements must reflect the fact that the geopolitical interests and priorities of NATO's major powers are in the midst of dramatic change. Because states base their external commitments on assessments of threats that take into consideration intentions and not just capabilities, the absence of a threatening power in Europe means that the strategic commitments of status quo powers will continue to retract from their cold war boundaries.[23] Although the United States, for example, may well keep a small military presence in Europe for years to come, it is unlikely (unless a new threat emerges) that several decades from now the United States will be a member of a defensive military alliance that extends security guarantees to all West European countries, not to mention to the states of Central Europe.

Power position and geographic location will be the key factors determining how European states adjust their commitments during this period of transformation. Those states with predominant economic and military power will continue to exercise most influence and their interests will have the most expansive reach. But proximity will matter much more than during the cold war. The United States will continue to focus on the major industrial powers close to the Atlantic littoral and on Russia. France will focus on Germany and North Africa, and Germany on Central Europe. Russia will be preoccupied with its "near-abroad."

In short, new geopolitical interests will evolve primarily along regional lines. Security commitments and the institutions that embody them should channel these naturally evolving interests, not seek to extend them in ways that contradict geopolitical logic. Institutions can go only so far in turning private, national interests into public, multinational ones. Relying on interests and obligations that devolve from proximity is far more likely to produce robust institutions and enforcement mechanisms than relying on agreements or institutions whose multilateral aspirations are simply too ambitious—and therefore prone to failure.

Fourth, a new security architecture should provide a clear pathway to a specified endpoint—a pan-European collective security system guided by a concert of benign, democratic great powers. Accordingly, it should seek to facilitate the emergence of stable democracy in Russia and to encourage all the Continent's major states to exercise their power responsibly in their respective spheres of influence. It is also important, however, that these spheres be interlocked, for if a pan-European collective security system is to emerge, it must be based on joint, cooperative management.

Institutional Design

These conceptual components point to the following institutional design. Three regional collective security bodies should be created in Europe: a West European Security Organization (WESO), a Central European Security Organization (CESO), and an East European Security Organization (EESO). WESO would essentially be a renamed NATO and consist of current NATO members; CESO would consist of Germany, Austria, non-NATO Scandinavian countries, Central Europe's new democracies, and Ukraine; and EESO would consist of Russia and its former Soviet republics minus the Baltics. Germany and Ukraine would be pivot states—each would belong to two groups (Germany to WESO and CESO, Ukraine to CESO and EESO). Consultation, exercises, and when possible military operations would continue on a pan-European basis through the PFP and OSCE, but these regional subgroups would take responsibility for extending security guarantees and deepening regional cooperation.

The security guarantees in all three groups should be cast as commitments to collective security rather than to collective defense.[24] The three groups would operate not as alliances against each other, but as regional groupings aimed at preserving peace among the members of that grouping. Unless strategic circumstances change, there would be no need for fixed frontier defenses between the groupings. The activities in each group would range from dispute resolution, to joint training and maneuvers, to the deployment of troops for peacekeeping or peace enforcement. Ideally, all three groupings would work toward the adoption of common doctrine and standardized equipment to facilitate interoperability and pan-European exercises and operations. At least at the outset, NATO members would assist CESO and, perhaps, EESO in building up their institutional and military infrastructure.

The PFP and OSCE would continue to serve as pan-European forums for addressing security matters and coordinating joint action—such as the involvement of NATO troops in exercises or operations in Central Europe and vice versa. But initial responsibility for managing security relations in a region would fall to the states of that region. Building security in Europe's east entails promoting trust and cooperation among the states of the former Soviet bloc, not erecting new walls between them or encouraging them to believe that outside powers will provide the answer to their security needs.

This design fulfills the conceptual criteria specified above. Collective security offers inclusivity for states in search of community without conveying the directed exclusivity associated with collective defense. And it will be more sustainable politically among countries facing no immediate threats. The creation of three regional groupings is also consistent with a stable balance of power over the long term. CESO, which would effectively recreate an expanded *mitteleuropa* of Germany, Austria, non-NATO Scandinavian countries, and the post-communist states of Central Europe, would create a ballast of stability in the center of Europe and a rough equilibrium among three centers of power. German participation would, at least to some extent, provide the reassurance the new democracies of Central Europe are seeking. CESO alone would not be able to cope with a Russian threat to the region. But, as I explain below, Germany's participation in both WESO and CESO would ensure WESO engagement in Central Europe in the event of a Russian threat to the region. In the meantime, however, because a collective security grouping in Central Europe would be distinct from NATO and focused more on internal security than on an external threat, it would not trigger Russian attempts to marshal a countervailing coalition. The creation of CESO would thus be consistent with the logic of power balancing: it would reverse Yalta by symbolizing and codifying Central Europe's exit from a Russian sphere of influence without confronting Moscow with a preponderant coalition to its west.[25]

In addition, the regionalization of European security provides the flexibility needed to deal with potential changes in threat perceptions and the strategic orientations of different areas of the Continent. Although EESO would initially be concerned primarily about internal security and focus on becoming part of a pan-European security community, it could eventually build links with regional security organizations in Asia. Although WESO would initially inherit NATO's primary concern with extending stability eastward, it may well find itself in the coming decade more preoccupied with developments in North Africa than in Europe's east. Smaller bodies of geographically proximate members will be better able to balance European and extra-European responsibilities than larger bodies whose members do not share similar regional orientations.

Regional subgroups would also be consistent with the shrinking scope of geopolitical interest among major European states. Because threats are more minor and largely proximate in nature, new interests and commitments are evolving primarily along regional lines. As a result, security institutions that are regional in scope are more in keeping with the interests of key actors—and thus more likely to be robust. Regional security organizations work because they match responsibilities with interests. They will also tap into and strengthen reemerging regional identities and affiliations. A named, defined geographic area constitutes a region not just because of proximity and the interdependence that it breeds.[26] Countries that are part of a given region often share similar cultures, languages, religions, and histories. These commonalities contribute to the formation of collective regional identities and thereby strengthen the case for regionally based security arrangements. As the artificial boundaries of the cold war continue to fade, culture, language, and history will play a more important role in shaping the strategic landscape.

Finally, my proposal lays the foundation, in a cautious, deliberate way, for the establishment of a pan-European collective security system guided by a great power concert. As CESO and EESO mature, their members will develop the habits of cooperation and the shared norms that underpin collective security. Trust and mutual confidence would gradually replace residual hostility and suspicion. If and when appropriate, WESO would merge with security communities already enjoying a significant level of stability and cooperation.

Regional subgroups would also encourage the Continent's major powers to assume primary responsibility in their respective geographic zones. Central European countries now feel in strategic limbo in part because Germany is an under-provider of security. CESO would provide a multilateral vehicle for both Germany and Germany's neighbors to become more comfortable with a larger German role in the region. CESO would take advantage of German resources and interests—assets that might otherwise be wasted because of lingering ambivalence inside and outside Germany about the country's international role. So too would EESO provide a forum for influencing Russia's behavior in its periphery. Unlike Germany, Russia is already heavily engaged in shaping the strategic environment in its neighboring areas. At least for now, the risk is not that Russia will do too little, but that it will do too much. Russia has on its own attempted to erect a collective security system among the former Soviet republics under the guise of the Commonwealth of Independent States (CIS). Because it embeds in a pan-European framework Russian efforts to erect a collective security structure in Eastern Europe, EESO offers a far more attractive vehicle than the CIS and is more likely to encourage Russia to abide by the same norms of behavior as other European powers.

Because the three regional groupings I propose would be interlocking, they would also contribute to the enterprise of building a *pan-European* security community. The groupings would be made interlocking through the designation of two pivot states: Germany would be a member of both WESO and CESO, Ukraine of both CESO and EESO. Because the notion of pivot states is novel and plays an important role in my proposal, I will address it in some detail.

Pivot States

The logic of pivot states is threefold. First, whereas regional groupings reflect a recognition that distance limits interests, pivot states reflect a recognition that interdependence among regions can at times expand interests. Some developments in Central Europe will threaten Western Europe, just as some developments in Eastern Europe will threaten Central Europe. Pivot states capture such interdependence; they trigger the involvement of a neighboring region when, and only when, developments are significant enough to warrant it.

For example, Germany will be far more interested in settling minor disputes in Central Europe than most other WESO members. But should developments in the region come to threaten German security, the involvement of the United States and Germany's West European neighbors would be both needed and likely. Their security guarantees to Germany would thus draw WESO members into Central Europe when, and only when, they are needed and warranted: in the event of major conflict in Central Europe. In this sense, the establishment of Germany as a pivot state effectively sneaks a Western security guarantee to Central Europe. If Russia were to pose a military threat to the region, Germany, and by association Germany's NATO allies, would likely take steps to counter that threat. When a given conflict is more minor and localized in nature, principal responsibility for responding would fall to the countries of Central Europe, obviating the need for the involvement of West European countries, most of whom would be reluctant to be involved in any case. This arrangement extends a Western guarantee to Central Europe in a meaningful and realistic way because it engages NATO members out of interest, not obligation.

Second, pivot states provide a vehicle for more regular consultation and cooperation between separate regional groupings. Although ongoing contact on a pan-European basis would continue through the PFP and OSCE, some issues would be addressed primarily within the regional subgroups. Pivot states could serve as conduits of information. Overlapping membership would ensure that each group is aware of discussions taking place in the others. It would also allow one group to voice directly its concerns in another group. CESO members, for example, would be able to influence EESO, and vice versa, via their common member, Ukraine.

Third, the notion of pivoting is extremely useful for dealing with states that, for geopolitical reasons, need to be both empowered and restrained. These are states that, because of their size and historical experience, will most effectively contribute to stability if poised between two regions. Pivot states are empowered because they wield influence in two separate groupings and because they enjoy security guarantees from two mutually exclusive bodies. They are restrained because they must answer to two separate regional groupings and pursue policies that meet with the approval of both.

Germany: Pivoting between West and Center. Designating Germany as the pivot between WESO and CESO provides a solution to one of the most intractable problems on the horizon: how to balance Germany's deepening engagement in Central Europe with the need to keep Germany embedded in Western Europe. Because Germany's economic and strategic interests are already shifting eastward, foregoing NATO expansion will leave Germany feeling insecure and unsatisfied with security arrangements in Central Europe.[27] But expanding NATO will saddle Germany's allies with unwanted commitments and alienate Russia. How, then, to proceed?

Keeping NATO intact while sanctioning German security guarantees to its Central European neighbors provides the solution. For better or for worse, the security concerns of West European countries are no longer congruent. Germany has security interests in Central Europe that Spain does not. Spain cares far more about developments in North Africa than does

Germany. Unnaturally forcing NATO eastward will only weaken those bodies as the diverging security interests of member states surface and sharpen. Enabling Germany to pivot between WESO and CESO is to get the best of both worlds: Germany remains embedded in Western Europe's security institutions while being able to address its legitimate security concerns to its east.

In this scenario Germany would continue to enjoy NATO membership, while NATO members would reap the benefits of increased German responsibility in Central Europe. Germany would be encouraged to take on this responsibility, helping the country gain confidence about playing a broader international role. Because of continuing American guarantees and the presence of U.S. troops, Germany would likely not seek to acquire nuclear weapons or pursue a major conventional buildup; its neighbors would be accordingly relieved.[28] Germany would also remain anchored in Western Europe through its engagement in NATO and then WESO, the EU, and other multilateral institutions.

Ukraine: Pivoting between Center and East. A viable, independent Ukraine will act as a hedge against the reassertion of Russian control over the former Soviet republics and reassure Central and West Europeans alike about Russia's willingness to be a cooperative partner.[29] But Ukraine is in an unenviable geostrategic position. It is too far from Western Europe to be of immediate strategic interest to NATO members. If NATO were to expand eastward, Ukraine would enter well after most Central European states, if at all. At the same time, it is too close to Russia—both geographically and historically— to stand on its own outside Russia's sphere of influence. Because of Russia's size and proximity and its long history of domination over Ukraine, Kiev cannot but fall under Moscow's shadow.

Giving Ukraine a formal perch in Central Europe provides the solution to this dilemma. Participation in and security guarantees from CESO would give Ukraine the confidence and leeway it needs to resist subordination and chart an independent course. Although Ukraine would also be a member of EESO, its foothold in Central Europe would act as a brake on Russian efforts to use EESO to exercise control over its former republics. If Ukraine were to be attacked by Russia, CESO would likely need to rely on WESO's manpower and military capability to mount a defense. Furthermore, it is entirely plausible that WESO and CESO would choose not to defend Ukraine in such circumstances. Instead, they might choose to draw a new defense line elsewhere in Central Europe, effectively expanding NATO in response to Russian aggression against Ukraine. Even if this proved to be the case, Ukraine's participation in CESO would provide a clear deterrent against Russian aggression, help Ukraine develop a more independent foreign policy, and encourage Kiev to uphold its commitment to denuclearization.

Membership in CESO would also provide Ukraine domestic benefits. Because of the political power of Ukraine's russified eastern half, the proponents of a more western orientation need firm prospects on which to build their political program. Without such prospects, Russia might reabsorb Ukraine because of Kiev's default, not Moscow's design. In the years after independence, supporters of a westward-oriented foreign policy suffered because Americans, West Europeans, and Central Europeans alike reacted sluggishly to Ukraine's repeated requests for deeper cooperation and security assistance. Giving Ukraine a foothold in Central Europe and helping it pivot between Europe's center and east is a key step toward building a stable security order in post-Soviet Europe.

Anticipating Objections

Sanctioning Spheres of Influence. My proposal for the establishment of regional subgroups admittedly sanctions the return to Europe of great power spheres of influence. The United States, Great Britain, France, and Germany would dominate WESO, just as they have dominated NATO. Germany would be the preponderant power in the center. And Russia would dominate EESO. Needless to say, the prospect of German and Russian zones of influence evokes historical memories that are quite sobering.

But to assume that a return to German and Russian spheres of influence would again inflict upon Europe's center and east subjugation, repression, and hostile jockeying for competitive advantage is to fail to recognize the important distinction between benign and malign great powers discussed above.[30] References to Germany's or Russia's sphere of influence provoke revile because their last attempts at hegemony were both malign—that is, colored by totalitarian repression and aggression. But it is quite possible that the reconstituted zones of influence that these two countries will build (and they *will* build zones of influence) will be benign—that is, guided by democratic principles, the rule of law, and respect for the sovereignty of other states. Indeed, a Europe in which Germany and Russia exercise a moderating, restraining influence in their respective peripheries is a far more stable and peaceful Europe than one in which both countries turn inward. Assuming that the emergence of both Germany and Russia as benign, democratic great powers is a desirable endpoint, that my proposal would facilitate the reemergence of spheres of influence is one of its key strengths, not one of its weaknesses.

Abandoning Central Europe. To create a separate Central European security organization is to disappoint the new democracies of Central Europe, most of whom have made clear their desire to enter NATO. Some analysts contend that a decision against NATO expansion would constitute an outright rejection of the bid of Central European countries to enter the West, having negative repercussions on the course of reform and on the conduct of their foreign policies (Dunay 1994; Longworth 1994).

But this argument is overstated. The countries of Central Europe are not struggling to decide whether to orient their economies and foreign policies to the east or west. Even if NATO makes clear that it will not expand, these countries will continue to look west and are not about to ask Moscow to reintegrate them into a Russian sphere of influence. NATO is only one of many vehicles through which the integration of Europe can proceed. Central European leaders have done themselves a disservice by fixating on NATO membership as the talisman of entry into the West. Access to the EU's markets and institutions will do far more to consolidate democratic reform than a NATO security guarantee. Elites in Central Europe should inform their electorates accordingly and begin to wean them from expectations of imminent NATO membership. In the meantime, the EU should quicken the pace of its eastward enlargement.[31]

Theory

This essay has contributed to three elements of the theoretical debate about the causes and effects of regionalism. First, I have made a case for the normative value of a constructivist approach to regionalism. My analysis suggests that constructing regions that would not come about of their own accord can enhance the welfare of states both within and outside the proposed grouping. Especially because the cold war's end has left the strategic landscape malleable and susceptible to conscious efforts to reshape it, identifying and helping to encourage the formation of new regional groupings may have valuable payoffs.

Imagining and then constructing Central Europe offers a means of promoting a stable balance of power on the Continent. A Central European security zone provides reassurance to states that want, but are unlikely to get, a collective defense guarantee from NATO. And it provides states seeking to distance themselves from Russia the political space needed to nurture independent national identities. A constructivist approach to regionalism could have similar benefits in other areas.

Second, my analysis underscores the importance of distinguishing carefully between different forms of regionalism. Especially in the policy community, economic and security bodies tend to get lumped together; joining the "West" means joining the EU and NATO. But economic and security groupings operate according to different logics and have dramatically different effects. So too do different types of security institutions vary widely as to how they promote cooperation and enhance the welfare of their members. In terms of both strategic effects and political feasibility, collective defense, collective security, and cooperative security provide alternative organizing principles for regional security bodies. Getting regionalism right depends on identifying not only the appropriate grouping but also the appropriate institutional design.

Third, this essay has illuminated the complexities stemming from growing incongruities in the respective memberships of economic and security groupings. Expansive economic interests are leading to an expansion in the number, size, and scope of regional trade zones. In contrast, more proximate strategic interests mean that regional security zones may shrink in geographic reach and that more relaxed configurations will replace the tight alliance structures of the cold war.

The resultant tension between economic forces of expansion and strategic forces of contraction is inevitable. My analysis suggests, however, that this tension can be put to good use. Economic linkages provide a desirable second-best option when more formal strategic linkages are not available. Membership in the EU will provide reassurance even to those countries that would prefer NATO membership. Moreover, institutional messiness may well offer the appropriate response to a strategic landscape that promises to remain fluid for the foreseeable future. My notion of pivot states and interlocking regional groupings is admittedly complicated and leaves somewhat ambiguous the ultimate disposition of Europe's economic and security institutions. But that ambiguity is desirable in light of the uncertainty that continues to characterize the trajectory of states in Europe's east. And it is consistent with a setting in which the centrifugal forces associated with broader and more ambitious economic groupings need to be balanced with the centripetal forces associated with smaller and looser security groupings.

Policy

Embarking down the pathway of erecting regional subgroups in Europe would be to prepare for either of two possible endpoints. Should Russia's experiment with democracy falter and EESO prove to be nothing more than a vehicle for the reassertion of malign Russian domination, Europe's west and center would form a new anti-Russian coalition. The merging of WESO and CESO would constitute effective NATO expansion, although such expansion would occur in response to a Russian threat, not in anticipation of that threat. Furthermore, through the evolution of CESO, the new democracies of Central Europe would have built their own security community, making the region more of a strategic asset than a strategic liability to the established democracies in the West.

Should Russia emerge as a benign, democratic great power, regional subgroups would serve equally well to facilitate transition to a concert-based collective security system. This collective security system would be pan-European in scope and guided by Europe's major powers. Because the proposal in this article calls for the development of the PFP and the OSCE as pan-European forums for security cooperation, it would lay the groundwork for such a collective security body. At the same time, the evolution of regional subgroups would routinize and institutionalize cooperation and an appropriate division of labor among Europe's major powers—a necessary condition for the success of a concert-based system.

NATO members now face decisions of historic geopolitical consequence. Should they proceed with the expansion of the Alliance, they will be making a major, perhaps irreparable, strategic mistake. NATO still has a major role to play in making Europe secure, but as one of three interlocking regional organizations, not as an enlarged alliance in search of an enemy.

NOTES

1. For a broader discussion of how to adapt Europe's security and economic institutions to the post-cold war landscape, see Kupchan and Kupchan (1991); and Kupchan (1996). This essay is an exploratory one which examines in detail one particular option for building toward the pan-European institutions outlined in these two other essays. My proposal for separate regional subgroups is not intended to be an alternative to a concert-based Atlantic Union, but a potential pathway for attaining that endpoint.

2. I use geographic terms as follows. Western Europe refers to current NATO members; Central Europe refers to Austria, Sweden, Finland, Germany, the Baltic states, the former

Yugoslavia, and former Warsaw Pact members that were not part of the Soviet Union; Eastern Europe refers to the former Soviet republics.

3. For synthetic overviews of this literature, see Bhagwati (1991); Gilpin (1987); and Mansfield and Milner (this volume).

4. My argument is consistent with a constructivist perspective in that I am claiming that state identity is socially and politically structured, malleable, and central to policy choice. At the same time, my argument stands recent constructivist literature on its head by positing that structure shapes agency, not vice versa. Rather than structure emerging from what states make of it, I am suggesting that a region is conceived, that the identity and behavior of relevant states adjusts accordingly, and that that region then comes to exist (with existence measured in terms of the flows and shared attributes commonly associated with regionalism). For a clear presentation of the constructivist position, see Wendt (1992:391–425).

5. The constructivist argument can only be taken so far. To assert that, say, Bali and Burkina Faso constitute a region obviously makes no sense in light of the fact that they have very little, if anything, in common. In this sense, some minimum level of geographic proximity, interaction, or shared attributes is needed to make the conception of a particular region credible and meaningful.

6. On the linkages between trade regimes and domestic politics, see Haggard (this volume).

7. On the relationship between regime performance and size of membership, see Haggard (this volume); Padoan (this volume); and Snidal (1985:580–614).

8. For discussion of the applicability of the concept of public goods to economic and security regimes, see Snidal (1985).

9. See Kupchan (1988).

10. See, for example, Holbrooke (1995:38–51); Kissinger (1994).

11. John Mearsheimer, for example, argues that Europe will be more stable if Germany acquires nuclear weapons. Otherwise, the vulnerability stemming from Germany's geostrategic location will again cause it to seek security through unilateral, and perhaps aggressive, means. See Mearsheimer (1990:5–56).

12. See Russett (1993); Doyle (1986); Owen (1994).

13. On the connection between democratization and war-proneness, see Mansfield and Snyder (1995:79–97).

14. Consider the situation in Europe's east. Virtually all the states of the former Soviet bloc are in the midst of profound domestic change that is affecting national identities and geopolitical orientations. Reformist elites throughout the new democracies of Central Europe have staked their political fortunes on entry into the West's markets and security institutions. In its symbolism as much as in its direct economic and strategic benefits, formally joining Europe's community of established democracies will consolidate the westward orientation of these polities and reward reformers. In Russia, Ukraine, and other former Soviet republics, elites and masses alike remain undecided as to whether they are European or Euro-Asian states and as to whether they should look east or west to secure their well-being and their sense of nationhood. Their decisions will in large part depend on their options. And their options will in large part depend on decisions made about the evolution of Europe's security architecture.

15. Perceptions of external vulnerability can impair democratic reform by strengthening the hands of conservative nationalists and diverting resources to the military, while perceptions of security undercut nationalists and extremists and enable elites to devote resources to the domestic economy. On the effect of the international system on domestic regimes, see Snyder (1990); Kupchan (1994b:ch. 2).

16. The attributes of collective security differ from those of collective defense in two key respects. First, collective security is based on the principle of all against one—that members will

band together to resist an aggressor should one emerge. Directed balancing against a specific state occurs only when that state exhibits aggressive intent. In the absence of an aggressor state, stability emerges through cooperation and institutionalized, regulated behavior among member states. Under collective defense, directed balancing against an opposing power center occurs continuously. Stability emerges through competition and unregulated balancing between power centers. Second, unlike alliance commitments to territorial defense, which are generally seen as automatic and binding, commitments to joint action made under the rubric of collective security are viewed as being more informal and less binding. Indeed, collective security organizations, such as the Concert of Europe, the League of Nations, and the United Nations are often criticized because they lack the formality and credibility of alliances. For further discussion of the difference between collective security and collective defense see Wolfers (1962); Claude (1962). For different interpretations of the nature of commitments to joint action under collective security, see Mearsheimer (1994); Kupchan and Kupchan (1995:52–61).

17. Articles arguing in favor of expansion include Asmus, Kugler, and Larrabee (1993); Brzezinski (1994); Kissinger (1993); Kissinger (1994); Holbrooke (1995); Talbott (1995:27–30).

18. Articles arguing against expansion include Kupchan (1994a); Brown (1995:34–52); Ikle (1995); Mandelbaum (1995:9–13); Kupchan (1995).

19. See Koecher (1995).

20. During 1994 and 1995, the U.S. Senate and House both approved by wide margins motions calling for the rapid inclusion of the Visegrad states into NATO. These motions were, however, largely symbolic in nature. In neither the Senate nor the House did debate focus on the financial costs associated with defending these states, nor did legislators consider whether Americans would and should be prepared to die in their defense. A similar gap exists in public opinion. Some forty-two percent of the U.S. public supports extending NATO membership to Poland, but only thirty-two percent support using U.S. troops to defend Poland should it be invaded by Russia. See Rielly (1995:35–36).

21. See Kupchan and Kupchan (1991).

22. For discussion of the conditions conducive to collective security, see Claude (1971); Bennett and Lepgold (1993); Kupchan and Kupchan (1991).

23. On states balancing against threats rather than against capabilities alone, see Walt (1987).

24. The treaties forming these bodies should be identical in form and substance, making clear that they are part of a common, pan-European framework. Although the language in the North Atlantic Treaty will have to be revised, NATO and its successor, WESO, should retain the capability to mount collective defense of its territory until Russia has emerged as a stable, democratic power. Even so, it should continue to reorient its core missions and focus primarily on crisis management and power projection, not territorial defense.

25. Critics might charge that Russia would be more threatened by a German-dominated security grouping in Central Europe than by the region's integration into NATO. Admittedly, for historical reasons, Moscow is not likely to respond favorably to calls for a new *mitteleuropa*, at least at the outset. But proposals for a new security architecture in Europe must be evaluated on the basis of their contribution to stability over the long run, not on their short-term emotional appeal. And over the long run, NATO's eastward expansion, simply because of the logic of power balancing, is far more likely to trigger Russian efforts to reconstitute an opposing coalition than the establishment of a regional security organization in Central Europe. Not only will three power centers lead to a more equitable distribution than two, but this approach also avoids the sense of political exclusion that would accompany NATO expansion.

26. For an excellent discussion of how to define the notion of a region, see Lake (1997).

27. In 1988, Germany's exports to the Visegrad four amounted to 1.4 percent of its total

exports. By 1993, this figure had risen to 3.9 percent. The figure for imports rose from 1.7 percent to 3.8 percent. From 1990 to 1991, German foreign direct investment in Czechoslovakia rose from $1 million to $500 million. See OECD Department of Economics and Statistics, January 1995 and previous; and *Außen Wirtschaft*, September 1992.

28. To take on additional responsibilities in Central Europe, Germany would have to expand its conventional capabilities. But because military operations in the region would entail primarily peacekeeping and monitoring missions, the German army would need to acquire mainly lift and light, mobile troops, not significant firepower or the heavy armor that would raise concerns about German intentions. Furthermore, the Germans would still be able to draw on American, NATO, and WEU assets to carry out missions in Central Europe.

29. See Vydrin (1994); Brezezinski (1994); Lewis (1994); Asmus, Kugler, and Larrabee (1993).

30. Compare, for example, how Europe's major powers have reacted to the recent breakup of Yugoslavia with their behavior during periods of Balkan instability earlier this century. Far from competing for advantage and influence, the major powers have approached military involvement with great reluctance and have effectively chosen to stay out of the conflict. Germany has been criticized for *not* sending troops to the region, not for being overbearing or seeking to gain national advantage.

31. Because of space constraints, I have not dealt with the Western European Union (WEU) in this essay. The WEU should not expand eastward in step with the EU for two main reasons. First, the EU is not ready either institutionally or politically to manage security affairs in Central Europe. Asking it to do so will impair its ability to proceed with the region's economic integration. Second, if Central European states were to become WEU members, all European members of NATO (except Iceland, Norway, and Denmark) would provide security guarantees to states in Central Europe that would have no security arrangements with the United States. Symbolically and actually, American and West European security commitments in Europe would no longer be congruent and the principles of solidarity and common interest that undergird NATO would be jeopardized, leading to a significant downgrading, if not the dissolution of the transatlantic security community.

Bibliography

Aggarwal, Vinod K. 1985. *Liberal Protectionism: The International Politics of Organized Textile Trade.* Berkeley: University of California Press.

Aggarwal, Vinod K. 1992. "The Political Economy of Service Sector Negotiations in the Uruguay Round." *Fletcher Forum* (Winter): 34–54.

Aggarwal, Vinod K. 1994. "Comparing Regional Cooperation Efforts in the Asia-Pacific and North America." In Andrew Mack and John Ravenhill, eds., *Pacific Cooperation: Building Economic and Security Regimes in the Asia-Pacific Region.* St. Leonards, Australia: Allen and Unwin.

Aglietta, Michel and Pierre Deusy-Fournier. 1994. "Internationalisation des monnaies et organisation du systeme monetaire." *Economie Internationale* 59:71–106.

Aho, C. Michael and Sylvia Ostry. 1990. "Regional Trading Blocs: Pragmatic or Problematic Policy?" In William E. Crock and Robert Hormats, eds., *The Global Economy: America's Role in the Decade Ahead.* New York: Norton.

Aitken, Norman D. 1973. "The Effect of the EEC and EFTA on European Trade: A Temporal and Cross-Section Analysis." *American Economic Review* 63:881–92.

Alesina, Alberto and Vittorio Grilli. 1993. "On the Feasibility of a One-Speed or Multi-Speed European Monetary Union." *Economics and Politics* 5:145–65.

Anderson, James E. 1979. "A Theoretical Foundation for the Gravity Equation." *American Economic Review* 69:106–16.

Anderson, Kym and Richard Blackhurst. 1993. "Introduction and Summary." In Kym Anderson and Richard Blackhurst, eds., *Regional Integration and the Global Trading System.* London: Harvester Wheatsheaf.

Andrews, A. Piatt. 1904. "The End of the Mexican Dollar." *Quarterly Journal of Economics* 18:321–56.

Andrews, David M. 1994. "Capital Mobility and State Autonomy: Toward a Structural Theory of International Monetary Relations." *International Studies Quarterly* 38:193–218.

"APEC's Chief Denies Group will Deal With Politics." 1993. *Kyodo Economic Newswire*, April 19, Nexus.

"ASEAN Differences Over Tariff Cuts For Raw Farm Products May Drag On." 1995. *BNA International Trade Daily*, May 5, Nexus.

"Asia Forum Cutting Political Teeth: APEC Meeting Lays Groundwork for Broader Scope of Cooperation." 1991. *The Nikkei Weekly*, November 23, Nexus.

"Asian Reservations on U.S. Proposal to Upgrade APEC as Forum." 1993. *Kyodo News Service Tokyo*, BBC Summary of World Broadcasts, May 20, Nexus.

Asia-Pacific Economic Cooperation. 1993. *A Vision for APEC: Towards an Asia Pacific Economic Community: Report of the Eminent Persons Group to APEC Ministers*. Singapore: Asia-Pacific Economic Cooperation.

Asia-Pacific Economic Cooperation. 1994. *Achieving the APEC Vision: Free and Open Trade in the Asia Pacific: Second Report of the Eminent Persons Group*. Singapore: Asia-Pacific Economic Cooperation.

Asia-Pacific Economic Cooperation. 1995. "The Osaka Action Agenda: Implementation of the Bogor Declaration." MM-008, Nov. 16, 1995.

Asmus, Ronald, Richard Kugler, and F. Stephen Larrabee. 1993. "Building a New NATO." *Foreign Affairs* 72:28–40.

"Australia Applauds President Clinton's APEC Upgrading." 1993. *United Press International*, July 7, Nexus.

"Australia Seeks to Overcome China Obstacle to APEC Summit." 1993. *Reuters Business Report*, July 11, Nexus.

Axelrod, Robert. 1984. *The Evolution of Cooperation*. New York: Basic Books.

Axelrod, Robert. 1986. "An Evolutionary Approach to Norms." *American Political Science Review* 80:1095–1111.

Axelrod, Robert and Robert O. Keohane. 1986. "Achieving Cooperation Under Anarchy: Strategies and Institutions." In Kenneth A. Oye, ed., *Cooperation Under Anarchy*. Princeton: Princeton University Press.

Baldwin, David A., ed. 1993. *Neorealism and Neoliberalism*. New York: Columbia University Press.

Baldwin, J. and Paul Gorecki. 1983. *Trade, Tariffs, and Relative Plant Size in Canadian Manufacturing Industries*. Economic Council of Canada discussion paper.

Baldwin, Richard. 1993. "A Domino Theory of Regionalism." Cambridge, Mass.: National Bureau of Economic Research Working Paper no. 4465.

Baldwin, Richard. 1996. *Towards an Integrated Europe*. London: Center for Economic Policy Research.

Baldwin, Richard and Anthony Venables. 1994. "Regional Economic Integration." In Gene Grossman and Kenneth Rogoff, eds., *Handbook of International Economics*, vol. 3. Amsterdam: North-Holland.

Baldwin, Robert E. 1985. *The Political Economy of U.S. Import Policy*. Cambridge: MIT Press.

Baldwin, Robert E. 1987. "Politically Realistic Objective Functions and Trade Policy." *Economic Letters* 24:287–90.

Bannister, Geoffrey and Patrick Low. 1992. "Textiles and Apparel in NAFTA: A Case of Constrained Liberalization." Washington D.C.: World Bank Policy Research Working Papers WPS 994 (October).

Barber, Lionel. 1995. "Bonn Sets Agenda for Monetary Union." *Financial Times*, October 2:2.

Bayoumi, Tamil. 1994. "A Formal Model of Optimum Currency Areas." Center for Economic Policy Research Discussion Paper no. 968.

Belous, Richard S. and Rebecca S. Hartley, eds. 1990. *The Growth of Regional Trading Blocs in the Global Economy*. Washington, D.C.: National Planning Association.

Ben, David. 1993. "Equalizing Exchange. Trade Liberalization and Income Convergence." *Quarterly Journal of Economics* 108:653–80.

Bennett, Andrew and Joseph Lepgold. 1993. "Reinventing Collective Security After the Cold War and Gulf Conflict." *Political Science Quarterly* 108:213–37.

Bernholz, Peter. 1989. "Currency Competition, Inflation, Gresham's Law, and Exchange Rate." *Journal of Institutional and Theoretical Economics* 145:465–88.

Betts, Richard K. 1993/94. "Wealth, Power, and Instability: East Asia and the United States After the Cold War." *International Security* 18:34–77.

Bhagwati, Jagdish. 1971. "The Generalized Theory of Distortions and Welfare." In Jagdish Bhagwati, ed., *Trade, Balance of Payments and Wealth*. Amsterdam: North-Holland.

Bhagwati, Jagdish. 1991. *The World Trading System at Risk*. Princeton: Princeton University Press.

Bhagwati, Jagdish. 1993. "Regionalism and Multilateralism: An Overview." In Jaime de Melo and Arvind Panagariya, eds., *New Dimensions in Regional Integration*. New York: Cambridge University Press.

Bhagwati, Jagdish and Hugh Patrick, eds. 1990. *Aggressive Unilateralism: America's 301 Trade Policy and the World Trading System*. Ann Arbor: University of Michigan Press.

Bilson, John F. O. 1983. "The Choice of an Invoice Currency in International Transactions." In Jagdeep S. Bhandari and Bluford H. Putnam, eds., *Economic Interdependence and Flexible Exchange Rates*. Cambridge: MIT Press.

Black, Stanley W. 1991. "Transactions Costs and Vehicle Currencies." *Journal of International Money and Finance* 10:512–26.

Black, Stanley W. 1993. "The International Use of Currencies." In Dilip K. Das, ed., *International Finance*. London: Routledge.

Blackwill, Robert and Sergei A. Karaganov, eds. 1994. *Damage Limitation or Crisis? Russia and the Outside World*. Washington, D.C.: Brassey.

Boughton, James M. 1993. "The Economics of the CFA Franc Zone." In Paul R. Masson and Mark P. Taylor, eds., *Policy Issues in the Operation of Currency Unions*. Cambridge and New York: Cambridge University Press.

Bouzas, Roberto and Jaime Ros, eds. 1994. *Economic Integration in the Western Hemisphere*. Notre Dame: University of Notre Dame Press.

Brada, Josef C. and Jose A. Mendez. 1983. "Regional Economic Integration and the Volume of Intra-Regional Trade: A Comparison of Developed and Developing Country Experience." *Kyklos* 36:589–603.

Brand, Diana. 1993. *Currency Substitution in Developing Countries: Theory and Empirical Analysis for Latin America and Eastern Europe*. Munich and London: Weltforum Verlag.

Brand, Ronald A. 1993. "Competing Philosophies of GATT Dispute Resolution in the Oilseeds Case and the Draft Understanding on Dispute Settlement." *Journal of World Trade* 27:117–44.

Brander, James A. and Barbara J. Spencer. 1984. "Tariff Protection and Imperfect Competition." In H. Kierzkowski, ed., *Monopolistic Competition and International Trade*. Oxford: Oxford University Press.

Brander, James A. and Barbara J. Spencer. 1985. "Export Subsidies and International Market Share Rivalry." *Journal of International Economics* 18:83–100.

Branson, William. 1990. "Financial Market Integration, Macroeconomic Policy and the EMS." In Christopher Bliss and Jaime De Macedo, eds., *Unity with Diversity in the European Economy*. Cambridge: Cambridge University Press.

"Brazil to Enlarge Mercosur Exempt Products List to Meet Economic Crisis." 1995. *International Trade Reporter*, May 3, Nexus.

Brezezinski, Ian. 1994. "Missing the Boat on NATO and Kyev." *Washington Times*, December 30.

Brooke, James. 1993. "With a View of One Hemisphere, Latin America is Freeing Its Own Trade." *New York Times*, December 29, Nexus.

Brown, Michael. 1995. "The Flawed Logic of NATO Expansion." *Survival* 37:34–52.

Brzezinski, Zbigniew. 1994. "The Premature Partnership." *Foreign Affairs* 73:67–82.

Buchanan, James. 1965. "The Economic Theory of Clubs." *Economica* 37:1–14.

Bulmer, Simon and William Paterson. 1989. "West Germany's Role in Europe: 'Man Mountain' or 'Semi-Gulliver.'" *Journal of Common Market Studies* 28:95–117.

Burley, Anne-Marie and Walter Mattli. 1993. "Europe Before the Court: A Political Theory of Legal Integration." *International Organization* 47:41–76.

Busch, Marc and Helen V. Milner. 1994. "The Future of the International Trading System: International Firms, Regionalism, and Domestic Politics." In Richard Stubbs and Geoffrey Underhill, eds., *Political Economy and the Changing Global Order*. London: Macmillan.

Caballero, Riccardo and Richard Lyons. 1990. "Internal vs External Economies in European Industry." *European Economic Review* 34:805–30.

Caballero, Riccardo and Richard Lyons. 1991. "External Effects and Europe's Integration." In L. A. Winters and A. Venables, eds., *European Integration: Trade and Industry*. New York: Cambridge University Press.

Calvo, Guillermo A. 1989. "Incredible Reforms." In Guillermo Calvo et al., *Debt, Stabilization, and Development*. London: Blackwell.

Calvo, Guillermo A. and Carlos A. Vegh, eds. 1992. "Convertibility and Currency Substitution." *Revista de Analisis Economico* 7.

Calvo, Guillermo A. and Carlos A. Vegh. 1993. "Currency Substitution in High Inflation Countries." *Finance and Development* 30:34–37.

Cameron, David R. 1990. "Sovereign States in the Single Market: Integration and Intergovernmentalism in the European Community." Paper presented at the annual meeting of the American Political Science Association, San Francisco, August 30–September 1.

Cameron, David R. 1992. "The 1992 Initiative: Causes and Consequences." In Alberta M. Sbragia, ed., *Euro-Politics: Institutions and Policymaking in the "New" European Community*. Washington, D.C.: Brookings Institution.

Carse, Stephen, John Williamson, and Geoffrey E. Wood. 1980. *The Financing Procedures of British Foreign Trade*. Cambridge: Cambridge University Press.

Casella, Alessandra. 1992. "Participation in a Currency Union." *American Economic Review* 82:847–63.

Casella, Alessandra. 1995. "Large Countries, Small Countries, and the Enlargement of Trade Blocs." Typescript, Columbia University.

Casella, Alessandra and James Feinstein. 1990. "Public Goods in Trade: on the Formation of Markets and Political Jurisdictions." National Bureau of Economic Research Working Paper no. 3554.

Caves, Richard. 1976. "Economic Models of Political Choice: Canada's Tariff Structure." *Canadian Journal of Economics* 9:278–300.

Center for Economic Policy Research. 1992. "Is Bigger Better?" Monitoring European Integration no. 3.

Center for Economic Policy Research. 1995. "Flexible Integration." Monitoring European Integration no. 6.

Chamberlin, Edward. 1962. *The Theory of Monopolistic Competition*. Cambridge: Harvard University Press.

Cheit, Earl. 1992. "A Declaration on Open Regionalism in the Pacific," *California Management Review* 35:116–30.

"Chile Likely to Join NAFTA." 1995. *Associated Press*, June 30, Clarinet.

"Chile Wants Free Trade with Mercosur, Not Membership for Now."1995. *Agence France Presse*. June 16, Lexus.

Claude, Inis. 1962. *Power and International Relations*. New York: Random House.

Claude, Inis. 1971. *Swords Into Plowshares*. 4th ed. New York: Random House.

Cohen, Benjamin J. 1963. "The Euro-Dollar, the Common Market, and Currency Unification." *Journal of Finance* 18:605–21.

Cohen, Benjamin J. 1971. *The Future of Sterling as an International Currency*. London: Macmillan.

Cohen, Benjamin J. 1992. "Sterling Area." In Peter Newman, Murray Milgate, and John Eatwell, eds., *The New Palgrave Dictionary of Money and Finance*. London: Macmillan Press.

Cohen, Benjamin J. 1993. "Beyond EMU: The Problem of Sustainability." *Economics and Politics* 5:187–203.

Cohen, Benjamin J. 1994. "The Geography of Money: Currency Relations Among Sovereign States." OFCE Working Paper no. 94–07. Paris, France: Observatoire Francais des Conjonctures Economiques.

Cohen, Benjamin J. 1996. "Phoenix Risen: The Resurrection of Global Finance." *World Politics* 48:268–96.

Collier, Paul. 1979. "The Welfare Effects of Customs Unions: An Anatomy." *Economic Journal* 89:84–95.

Collins, Susan and Dani Rodrik. 1991. *Eastern Europe and the Soviet Union in the World Economy*. Washington, D.C.: Institute for International Economics.

Commission of the European Communities. 1990. "One Market, One Money." *European Economy* 44.

Commission of the European Communities. 1991. *The Regions in the 1990s*. Luxembourg: Office for Official Publications of the European Communities.

"Common External Tariff Under Pressure." 1995. *Latin America Regional Reports: Southern Cone*, June 1, Nexus.

Conybeare, John A. C. 1986. "Trade Wars: A Comparative Study of Anglo-Hanse, Franco-Italian, and Hawley-Smoot Conflicts." In Kenneth Oye, ed., *Cooperation Under Anarchy*. Princeton: Princeton University Press.

Conybeare, John A. C. 1987. *Trade Wars: The Theory and Practice of International Commercial Rivalry*. New York: Columbia University Press.

Corden, W. M. 1972. "Economies of Scale and Customs Union Theory." *Journal of Political Economy* 80:465–75.

Corden, W. M. 1974. *Trade Policy and Economic Welfare*. Oxford: Oxford University Press.

Corden, W. M. 1984. "The Normative Theory of International Trade." In Ronald W. Jones and Peter B. Kenen, eds., *Handbook of International Economics*, vol. 1. Amsterdam: North-Holland.

Cornes, James and Todd Sandler. 1985. *The Theory of Externalities, Public Goods, and Club Goods*. Cambridge: Cambridge University Press.

Correia, Dora. 1994. "The Origins and the Scope of the Cohesion Fund in the European Union." Master's thesis, College of Europe, Bruges.

Cowhey, Peter. 1994. "Pacific Trade." Typescript, University of California, San Diego.

Crone, Donald. 1993. "Does Hegemony Matter? The Reorganization of the Pacific Political Economy." *World Politics* 45:501–25.

"Customs Union Encounters First Hitch." 1995. *Latin America Regional Reports: Southern Cone*. April 20, Nexus.

Dandeker, Rebecca. 1992. "The Rose Garden Agreement: Is Mercosur the Next Step to a Hemispheric Free Trade Agreement?" *Law and Policy in International Business* 24:157–80.

De Benedictis, Luca and Pier Carlo Padoan. 1993. "The Integration of Eastern Europe into the EC: A Club Theory Interest Group Approach." In Siro Lombardini and Pier Carlo Padoan, eds., *Europe Between East and South*. Dordrecht: Kluwer Academic Press.

De Grauwe, Paul. 1992. *European Monetary Integration*. Oxford: Oxford University Press.

De Grauwe, Paul. 1994. "European Monetary Union Without the European Monetary System." *Economic Policy* no. 19.

de Melo, Jaime and Andit Panagariya, eds. 1993. *New Dimensions in Regional Integration*. New York: Cambridge University Press.

Destler, I. M., John Odell, and Kimberly Ann Elliott. 1987. *Anti-Protection: Changing Forces in United States Trade Politics*. Washington D.C.: Institute for International Economics.

Deutsch, Karl W. et al. 1957. *Political Community and the North Atlantic Area: International Organization in the Light of Historical Experience*. Princeton: Princeton University Press.

Dick, A. 1994. "Does Import Protection act as Export Promotion?" *Oxford Economic Papers* 46:83–101.

Dixit, Avinash. 1984. "International Trade Policy for Oligopolistic Industries." *Economic Journal*, supplement:1–16.

Dixit, Avinash and Joseph Stiglitz. 1977. "Monopolistic Competition and Optimum Product Diversity." *American Economic Review* 67:297–308.

Dixon, William and Bruce Moon. 1993. "Political Similarity and American Foreign Trade Patterns." *Political Research Quarterly* 46:5–25.

Doner, Richard. 1993. "Japanese Foreign Direct Investment and the Creation of a Pacific Asian Region." In Jeffrey A. Frankel and Miles Kahler, eds., *Regionalism and Rivalry: Japan and the United States in Pacific Asia*. Chicago: University of Chicago Press.

Dowd, Kevin, and David Greenaway. 1993. "Currency Competition, Network Externalities and Switching Costs: Towards an Alternative View of Optimum Currency Areas." *Economic Journal* 103:1180–89.

Doyle, Michael. 1986. "Liberalism and World Politics." *American Political Science Review* 80:1151–69.

Drysdale, Peter and Ross Garnaut. 1993. "The Pacific: An Application of a General Theory of Economic Integration." In C. Fred Bergsten and Marcus Noland, eds., *Pacific Dynamism and the International Economic System*. Washington D.C.: Institute for International Economics.

Dunay, Pal. 1994. "NATO and the West: A Sea of Mysteries." *World Policy Journal* 11:123–27.

Eaton, Jonathan and Gene Grossman. 1986. "Optimal Trade and Industrial Policy Under Oligopoly." *Quarterly Journal of Economics* 101:383–406.

EC (European Community) Commission. 1985. *Report on the Costs of Non-Europe*. Brussels: EC Commission.

"Economists Demonstrate that Neighbors, Not Wardens, Hold Keys to Cutting Crime." 1994. *Wall Street Journal*, December 7: B1.

Edwards, Sebastian. 1993. "Latin American Economic Integration: A New Perspective on an Old Dream." *World Economy* 16:317–38.

Eichengreen, Barry. 1990. *Elusive Stability: Essays in the History of International Finance, 1919–1939*. New York: Cambridge University Press.

Eichengreen, Barry. 1994. *International Monetary Arrangements for the 21st Century*. Washington D.C.: Brookings Institution.

Eichengreen, Barry and Douglas A. Irwin. 1995. "The Role of History in Bilateral Trade Flows."

Paper presented at the National Bureau of Economic Research conference on Regionalization of the World Economy, Woodstock, Vermont.

Eichengreen, Barry and Jeffrey A. Frankel. 1994. "Economic Regionalism: Evidence from Two 20th Century Episodes." Typescript, University of California, Berkeley.

Elek, Andrew. 1991. "The Challenge of Asian-Pacific Economic Cooperation." *The Pacific Review* 4:322–32.

Erzan, Refik and Alexander Yeats. 1992. "U.S.-Latin America Free Trade Areas: Some Empirical Evidence." In Sylvia Saborio et al., eds., *The Premise and the Promise: Free Trade in the Americas*. Washington D.C.: Overseas Development Council.

Fischer, Stanley. 1982. "Seigniorage and the Case for National Money." *Journal of Political Economy* 90:295–313.

Fishlow, Albert and Stephan Haggard. 1992. *The United States and the Regionalization of the World Economy*. Paris: OECD Development Center Research Project on Globalization and Regionalization.

"Focus on Mercosur: A Rocky Road." 1994. *Latin America Weekly Report*, January 20, Nexus.

"Fortress Asia?" 1992. *Economist*, October 24, Nexus.

Frankel, Jeffrey A. 1993. "Is Japan Creating a Yen Bloc in East Asia and the Pacific?" In Jeffrey A. Frankel and Miles Kahler, eds., *Regionalism and Rivalry: Japan and the United States in Pacific Asia*. Chicago: University of Chicago Press.

Frankel, Jeffrey A. and Shang-Jin Wei. 1994. "Yen Bloc or Dollar Bloc? Exchange Rate Policies of the East Asian Economies." In Takatoshi Ito and Anne O. Krueger, eds., *Macroeconomic Linkage: Savings, Exchange Rates, and Capital Flows*. Chicago: University of Chicago Press.

Frankel, Jeffrey A., Ernesto Stein, and Shang-jin Wei. 1995. "Trading Blocs and the Americas: the Natural, the Unnatural and the Super-Natural." *Journal of Development Economics* 47:61–95.

Fratianni, Michele and John Pattison. 1982. "The Economics of International Organizations." *Kyklos* 35:244–62.

Fratianni, Michele. 1992. "Dominant and Dependent Currencies." In Peter Newman, Murray Milgate, and John Eatwell, eds., *The New Palgrave Dictionary of Money and Finance*. London: Macmillan.

Fratianni, Michele. 1995. "Variable Integration in the European Union." Typescript, Indiana University.

Frey, Bruno. 1984. *International Political Economics*. New York: Basil Blackwell.

Friedberg, Aaron L. 1993/94. "Ripe for Rivalry: Prospects for Peace in a Multipolar Asia." *International Security* 18:5–33.

Frieden, Jeffry A. 1988. "Sectoral Conflict and U.S. Foreign Economic Policy." *International Organization* 42:59–90.

Frieden, Jeffry A. 1991. "Invested Interests: The Politics of National Economic Policies in a World of Global Finance." *International Organization* 45:425–51.

Frieden, Jeffry A. 1993a. "The Dynamics of International Monetary Systems: International and Domestic Factors in the Rise, Reign, and Demise of the Classical Gold Standard." In Jack Snyder and Robert Jervis, eds., *Coping with Complexity in the International System*. Boulder: Westview.

Frieden, Jeffry A. 1993b. "Economic and Monetary Union: What Happened? Exploring the Political Dimension of Optimum Currency Areas—Discussion." In G. de la Dehesa et al., eds., *The Monetary Future of Europe*. London: Centre for Economic Policy Research.

Frieden, Jeffry A. 1994. "Exchange Rate Politics: Contemporary Lessons from American History." *Review of International Political Economy* 1:81–103.

Friedman, Thomas L. 1994. "Never Mind Yen: Greenbacks are the New Gold Standard." *New York Times*, Section 4 (July 3): E5.

Froot, Kenneth A. and David B. Yoffie. 1991. "Strategic Trade Policies in a Tripolar World." *International Spectator* 26:3–28.

Froot, Kenneth A. and David B. Yoffie. 1993. "Trading Blocs and the Incentives to Protect: Implications for Japan and East Asia." In Jeffrey A. Frankel and Miles Kahler, *Regionalism and Rivalry: Japan and the United States in Pacific Asia*. Chicago: University of Chicago Press.

Funabashi, Yoichi. 1995. *Asia Pacific Fusion: Japan's Role in APEC*. Washington D.C.: Institute for International Economics.

"G-3 Trade Agreement." 1994. *Keesing's Record of World Events*, June: 40051.

Garrett, Geoffrey. 1992. "International Cooperation and Institutional Choice: The European Community's Internal Market." *International Organization* 46:533–60.

Garrett, Geoffrey. 1993 "The Politics of Maastricht." *Economics and Politics* 5:105–23.

Garrett, Geoffrey. 1995. "The Politics of Legal Integration in the European Union." *International Organization* 49:171–81.

Garrett, Geoffrey and Barry R. Weingast. 1993. "Ideas, Interests, and Institutions: Constructing the European Community's Internal Market." In Judith Goldstein and Robert O. Keohane, eds., *Ideas and Foreign Policy*. Ithaca: Cornell University Press.

Garten, Jeffrey E. 1992. *A Cold Peace: America, Germany, and the Struggle for Supremacy*. New York: Times Books.

Genberg, Hans and Francisco Nadal De Simone. 1993. "Regional Integration and Macroeconomic Discipline." In Kym Anderson and Richard Blackhurst, eds., *Regional Integration and the Global Trading System*. London: Harvester Wheatsheaf.

Gilpin, Robert. 1972. "The Politics of Transnational Economic Relations." In Joseph S. Nye, Jr. and Robert O. Keohane, eds., *Transnational Relations and World Politics*. Cambridge: Harvard University Press.

Gilpin, Robert. 1975. *U.S. Power and the Multinational Corporation: The Political Economy of Foreign Direct Investment*. New York: Basic Books.

Gilpin, Robert. 1987. *The Political Economy of International Relations*. Princeton: Princeton University Press.

Giovannini, Alberto and Bart Turtelboom. 1992. "Currency Substitution." National Bureau of Economic Research Working Paper no. 4232.

Giovannini, Alberto. 1993. "Economic and Monetary Union: What Happened? Exploring the Political Dimension of Optimum Currency Areas." In G. de la Dehesa et al., eds., *The Monetary Future of Europe*. London: Centre for Economic Policy Research.

Goodhart, Charles. 1995. "The Political Economy of Monetary Union." In Peter B. Kenen, ed., *Understanding Interdependence: The Macroeconomics of the Open Economy*. Princeton: Princeton University Press.

Gourevitch, Peter. 1986. *Politics in Hard Times: Comparative Responses to International Economic Crises*. Ithaca: Cornell University Press.

Gowa, Joanne. 1989. "Rational Hegemons, Excludable Goods, and Small Groups: An Epitaph for Hegemonic Stability Theory?" *World Politics* 41:307–24.

Gowa, Joanne. 1994. *Allies, Adversaries, and International Trade*. Princeton: Princeton University Press.

Gowa, Joanne. 1995. "Democratic States and International Disputes." *International Organization* 49:511–22.

Gowa, Joanne and Edward D. Mansfield. 1993. "Power Politics and International Trade." *American Political Science Review* 87:408–20.

Grassman, Sven. 1973. "A Fundamental Symmetry in International Payment Patterns." *Journal of International Economics* 3:105–16.

Greene, William H. 1993. *Econometric Analysis.* 2d ed. New York: Macmillan.

Greenhouse, Steven. 1994. "U.S. Plans Expanded Trade Zone." *New York Times*, February 4, Nexus.

Greif, Avner. 1992. "Institutions and International Trade: Lessons from the Commercial Revolution." *American Economic Review Papers and Proceedings* 82:128–33.

Greif, Avner, Paul Milgrom, and Barry R. Weingast. 1994. "Coordination, Commitment and Enforcement: The Case of the Merchant Guild." *Journal of Political Economy* 102:745–76.

Grenville, J. A. S. 1974. *The Major International Treaties 1914–1973.* London: Methuen.

Grieco, Joseph M. 1988. "Anarchy and the Limits of Cooperation: A Realist Critique of the Newest Liberal Institutionalism." *International Organization* 42:485–507.

Grieco, Joseph M. 1990. *Cooperation Among Nations: Europe, America, and Non-Tariff Barriers to Trade.* Ithaca: Cornell University Press.

Grieco, Joseph M. 1994. "Variation in Regional Economic Institutions in Western Europe, East Asia, and the Americas: Magnitude and Systemic Sources." Berlin: Wissenschaftszentrum Discussion Paper no. P94–006.

Grieco, Joseph M. 1995a. "American Power, German and Japanese Preferences for Regional Economic Institutions, and the Future of the Multilateral Trade Order." Prepared for Michael Leebron, ed., *The Multilateral Trade Regime in the Twenty-First Century: Structural Issues* (forthcoming), and delivered at a conference at Columbia University Law School, November 3–4.

Grieco, Joseph M. 1995b. "The Maastricht Treaty, Economic and Monetary Union, and the Neorealist Research Programme." *Review of International Studies* 21:21–40.

Grieco, Joseph M. 1995c. "Realism and Regionalism: American Power and German and Japanese Institutional Strategies During and After the Cold War." Prepared for Ethan Kapstein and Michael Mastanduno, eds., *Realism and International Relations After the Cold War* (forthcoming).

Grieco, Joseph M. 1996a. "Political-Military Dynamics and the Nesting of Regimes: An Analysis of APEC, the WTO, and Prospects for Cooperation in the Asia-Pacific." Delivered at the Conference on APEC and Regime Creation in Asia and the Pacific, the East-West Center, Honolulu, Hawaii, January 11–13.

Grieco, Joseph M. 1996b. "State Interests and International Rule Trajectories: A Neorealist Interpretation of the Maastricht Treaty and European Economic and Monetary Union." *Security Studies* 5:176–222.

Grossman, Gene M. and Elhanan Halpman. 1993. "Trade Wars and Trade Talks." Center for Economic Policy Research Discussion Paper no. 806.

Grossman, Gene M. and Elhanan Helpman. 1994. "Protection for Sale." *American Economic Review* 84:833–51.

Grossman, Gene M. and Elhanan Helpman. 1995. "The Politics of Free-Trade Agreements." *American Economic Review* 85:667–90.

"Group of Three Agrees Programme." 1993. *Latin America Weekly Report*, December 16, Nexus.

"Growing Pains for South America's Mercosur Block." 1995. *Reuters Money Report*, June 12, Nexus.

Grubel, Herbert and Peter Lloyd. 1975. *Intra-Industry Trade.* London: MacMillan.

Guerrieri, Paolo. 1995. "Globalism, Regionalism, and the Middle East." Typescript, IAI, Rome.

Guerrieri, Paolo and Cristina Mastropasqua. 1992. "Competitivita', Specializzazione, e Prospettive di Integrazione Commerciale dei Paesi dell'Est Europeo." In Andrea Bollino and Pier Carlo Padoan, eds., *Il Circolo Virtuoso Trilaterale.* Bologna: Il Mulino.

Guerrieri, Paolo and Pier Carlo Padoan. 1988. "International Cooperation and the Role of Macroeconomic Regimes." In Paolo Guerrieri and Pier Carlo Padoan, eds., *The Political Economy of International Cooperation*. London: Croom Helm.

Guidotti, Pablo E. and Carlos A. Rodriguez. 1992. "Dollarization in Latin America: Gresham's Law in Reverse?" *International Monetary Fund Staff Papers* 39:518–44.

Gunter, Frank R. 1989. "Customs Union Theory: Retrospect and Prospect." In David Greenaway, Thomas Hyclak, and Robert J. Thornton, eds., *Economic Aspects of Regional Trading Arrangements*. New York: New York University Press.

Haas, Ernst B. 1958. *The Uniting of Europe: Political, Social, and Economic Forces, 1950–1957*. Stanford: Stanford University Press.

Haas, Ernst B. 1964. *Beyond the Nation-State*. Stanford: Stanford University Press.

Haas, Ernst B. 1966. "International Integration: The European and the Universal Process." In *International Political Communities: An Anthology*. Garden City, N.Y.: Anchor Books.

Haas, Ernst B. 1967a. "International Integration." *Encyclopedia of the Social Sciences* 7:522–28.

Haas, Ernst B. 1967b. "The Uniting of Europe and the Uniting of Latin America." *Journal of Common Market Studies* 5:315–43.

Haas, Ernst B. 1968. "Technology, Pluralism, and the New Europe." In Joseph S. Nye, Jr., ed., *International Regionalism*. Boston: Little, Brown.

Haas, Ernst B. and Philippe C. Schmitter. 1964. "Economics and Differential Patterns of Political Integration: Projections About Unity in Latin America." *International Organization* 18:705–37.

Haggard, Stephan. 1990. *Pathways from the Periphery: The Politics of Growth in the Newly Industrializing Countries*. Ithaca: Cornell University Press.

Haggard, Stephan. 1994. "Thinking About Regionalism: The Politics of Minilateralism in Asia and the Americas." Paper presented at the annual meeting of the American Political Science Association, New York, September 1–4.

Haggard, Stephan. 1995. *The Developing Nations and the Politics of Global Integration*. Washington D.C.: Brookings Institution.

Haggard, Stephan. 1996. "The Political Economy of Regionalism in the Western Hemisphere." Typescript, University of California, San Diego.

Hall, Robert. 1988a. "Increasing Returns: Theory and Measurement with Industry Data." Typescript, Stanford University.

Hall, Robert. 1988b. "The Relation Between Price and Marginal Cost in US Industry." *Journal of Political Economy* 96:921–47.

Hardin, Russell. 1982. *Collective Action*. Baltimore: Johns Hopkins University Press.

Harrison, Michael. 1981. *The Reluctant Ally: France and Atlantic Security*. Baltimore: Johns Hopkins University Press.

Hartland-Thunberg, Penelope. 1980. *Trading Blocs, U.S. Exports, and World Trade*. Boulder: Westview.

Hartmann, P. 1994. "Vehicle Currencies in the Foreign Exchange Market." *Document de travail du seminaire*. Delta no. 94–13. Paris: Ecole Normale Superieure.

Helpman, Elhanan. 1984. "Increasing Returns, Imperfect Markets, and Trade Theory." In Ronald Jones and P. Kenen, eds., *Handbook of International Economics*, vol. 1. Amsterdam: North-Holland.

Helpman, Elhanan and Paul Krugman. 1985. *Increasing Returns, Imperfect Competition, and International Trade*. Cambridge: MIT Press.

"Hemispheric Trade Zone Endorsed." 1995. *Associated Press*, July 2, Clarinet.

Higgott, Richard A. 1994. "APEC: A Skeptical View." In Andrew Mack and John Ravenhill, eds., *Pacific Cooperation: Building Economic and Security Regimes in the Asia-Pacific Region.* St. Leonards, Australia: Allen and Unwin.

Higgott, Richard A., Andrew Fenton Cooper, and Jenelle Bonnor. 1990. "Asia-Pacific Economic Cooperation: An Evolving Case Study in Leadership and Cooperation Building." *International Journal* 45:823–66.

Higgott, Richard A., Richard Leaver, and John Ravenhill, eds. 1993. *Pacific Economic Relations in the 1990s.* Boulder: Lynne Rienner.

Higgott, Richard and Richard Stubbs. 1995. "Competing Conceptions of Economic Regionalism: APEC versus EAEC in the Asia Pacific." *Review of International Political Economy* 2:516–35.

Hinchberger, B. 1993. "Mercosur on the March." *Institutional Investor* 27:107–12.

Hine, Robert C. 1992. "Regionalism and the Integration of the World Economy." *Journal of Common Market Studies* 30:115–22.

Hirschman, Albert. 1981. "Three Uses of Political Economy in Analyzing European Integration." In Albert Hirschman, *Essays in Trespassing: Economics to Politics and Beyond.* Cambridge: Cambridge University Press.

Hoekman, Bernard and Simeon Djankov. 1995. "Catching up with Eastern Europe? The European Union's Mediterranean Free Trade Initiative." Center for Economic Policy Research Discussion Paper no. 1300.

Hoffmeyer, Erik. 1996. "Bystanders at the Infighting: The Real Debate on Monetary Union is About the Relative Power of France and Germany." *Financial Times*, February 9: 22.

Hojman, David E. 1981. "The Andean Pact: Failure of a Model of Economic Integration." *Journal of Common Market Studies* 20:139–60.

Holbrooke, Richard. 1995. "America, a European Power." *Foreign Affairs* 74:38–51.

Hoon, Lim Siong. 1991. "Hills Says Asian Trade Bloc Is Now Less Likely." *Financial Times*, October 11, Nexus.

Horlick, Gary N. and Amanda DeBusk. 1993. "Dispute Resolution Under NAFTA." *Journal of World Trade* 27:21–41.

Horstmann, Ignatius and James Markusen. 1986. "Up the Average Cost Curve: Inefficient Entry and the New Protectionism." *Journal of International Economics* 20:225–47.

Hudec, Robert E. 1990. "Dispute Settlement." In Jeffrey J. Schott, ed., *Completing the Uruguay Round.* Washington, D.C.: Institute for International Economics.

Hufbauer, Gary and Jeffrey Schott. 1992. *North American Free Trade: Issues and Recommendations.* Washington, D.C.: Institute for International Economics.

Hufbauer, Gary and Jeffrey Schott. 1993. *NAFTA: An Assessment.* Washington, D.C.: Institute for International Economics.

Hufbauer, Gary and Jeffrey Schott. 1994. *Western Hemisphere Economic Integration.* Washington D.C.: Institute for International Economics.

Hufbauer, Gary and Jeffrey Schott. 1995. "Toward Free Trade and Investment in the Asia-Pacific." *The Washington Quarterly* 18:37–45.

Hughes, Helen. 1991. "Does APEC Make Sense?" *ASEAN Economic Bulletin* 8:125–36.

Ihlwan, Moon. 1992. "ASEAN Moves Towards Free Trade, Political Impasse." *Reuters Library Report*, January 23, Nexus.

Ikle, Fred. 1995. "How to Ruin NATO." *New York Times*, January 11.

Ingram, James C. 1959. "State and Regional Payments Mechanisms." *Quarterly Journal of Economics* 73:619–32.

"Integration: Venezuela to Join Mercosur in 1996." 1995. *Inter Press Service*, May 17, Nexus.

International Monetary Fund. 1993. "Regional Trading Arrangements." Annex to *World Economic Outlook, May 1993*. Washington, D.C.: International Monetary Fund.

Jackson, John H. 1989. *The World Trading System*. Cambridge: MIT Press.

Jackson, John H. 1990. *Restructuring the GATT System*. New York: Council on Foreign Relations Press.

Jackson, John H. 1992. "Status of Treaties in Domestic Legal Systems: A Policy Analysis." *American Journal of International Law* 86:310–40.

Jackson, John H. 1994. "The World Trade Organization, Dispute Settlement, and Codes of Conduct." In Susan M. Collins and Barry M. Bosworth, eds., *The New GATT*. Washington, D.C.: Brookings Institution.

Jovanovic, Miroslav N. 1992. *International Economic Integration*. London and New York: Routledge.

Kahler, Miles A. 1992. "Multilateralism with Small and Large Numbers." *International Organization* 46:681–708.

Kahler, Miles A. 1994. "Institution-Building in the Pacific." In Andrew Mack and John Ravenhill, eds., *Pacific Cooperation: Building Economic and Security Regimes in the Asia-Pacific Region*. St. Leonards, Australia: Allen and Unwin.

Kahler, Miles A. 1995. "A World of Blocs: Facts and Factoids." *World Policy Journal* 12:19–27.

Kandiah, Peter. 1991. "ASEAN Agrees to Create Economic Cooperation Forum." *The Nikkei Weekly*, October 19, Nexus.

Kaplan, Fred. 1994. "Yelstin Decries Lack of Consultation on Bosnia Air Strikes." *The Boston Globe*, April 12.

Katzenstein, Peter J., ed. 1978. *Between Power and Plenty: Foreign Economic Policies of Advanced Industrial States*. Madison: University of Wisconsin Press.

Kaufman, Robert R., Carlos Bazdresch, and Blanca Herredia. 1994. "Mexico: Radical Reform in a Dominant Party System." In Stephan Haggard and Steven B. Webb, eds., *Voting for Reform*. New York: Oxford University Press.

Kemp, Murray C. and Henry Y. Wan, Jr. 1976. "An Elementary Proposition Concerning the Formation of Customs Unions." *Journal of International Economics* 6:95–97.

Keohane, Robert O. 1980. "The Theory of Hegemonic Stability and Changes in International Economic Regimes." In Ole R. Holsti, Randolph M. Siverson, and Alexander George, eds., *Change in the International System*. Boulder: Westview.

Keohane, Robert O. 1984. *After Hegemony: Cooperation and Discord in the World Political Economy*. Princeton: Princeton University Press.

Keohane, Robert O. and Joseph S. Nye, Jr. 1977. *Power and Interdependence: World Politics in Transition*. Boston: Little, Brown.

Kiewit, D. Roderick and Mathew McCubbins. 1991. *The Logic of Delegation*. Chicago: University of Chicago Press.

Kim, Han Soo and Ann Weston. 1993. "A North American Free Trade Agreement and East Asian Developing Countries." *ASEAN Economic Bulletin* 9:287–300

Kindleberger, Charles P. 1973. *The World in Depression, 1929–1939*. Berkeley: University of California Press.

Kirshner, Jonathan. 1995. *Currency and Coercion: The Political Economy of International Monetary Power*. Princeton: Princeton University Press.

Kissinger, Henry. 1993. "Not This Partnership." *Washington Post*, November 24.

Kissinger, Henry. 1994. "Expand NATO Now." *Washington Post*, December 19.

Kleiman, Ephraim. 1976. "Trade and the Decline of Colonialism." *Economic Journal* 86:459–80.

Klein, Lawrence R. 1993. "Some Second Thoughts on the European Monetary System." *Greek Economic Review* 15:1–9.

Koecher, Renate. 1995. "Unerwartete Wende." *Frankfurter Allgemeine Zeitung*, June 14.

Kolodziej, Edward A. 1974. *French International Policy Under de Gaulle and Pompidou: The Politics of Grandeur.* Ithaca: Cornell University Press.

Kornai, Janos. 1992. *The Socialist System: The Political Economy of Communism.* Princeton: Princeton University Press.

Kovenoch, Dan and Marie Thursby. 1992. "GATT, Dispute Settlement and Cooperation." *Economics and Politics* 4:151–70.

Krasner, Stephen D. 1976. "State Power and the Structure of International Trade." *World Politics* 28:317–47.

Krasner, Stephen D. 1978. *Defending the National Interest: Raw Materials Investments and U.S. Foreign Policy.* Princeton: Princeton University Press.

Krasner, Stephen D. 1981. "Power Structures and Regional Development Banks." *International Organization* 35:303–28.

Krasner, Stephen D. 1985. *Structural Conflict: The Third World Against Global Liberalism.* Berkeley: University of California Press.

Krasner, Stephen D. 1991. "Global Communications and National Power: Life on the Pareto Frontier." *World Politics* 43:336–66.

Krauss, M. B. 1972. "Recent Developments in Customs Union Theory: An Interpretive Essay." *Journal of Economic Literature* 10:413–36.

Krebhiel, Keith. 1991. *Information and Legislative Organization.* Ann Arbor: University of Michigan Press.

Krishna, Pravin. 1993. "Regionalism and Multilateralism: A Political Economy Approach." Typescript, Columbia University.

Krueger, Anne O. 1995. "Free Trade Agreements versus Customs Unions." National Bureau of Economic Research Working Paper no. 5084.

Krugman, Paul. 1979. "Increasing Returns, Monopolistic Competition and International Trade." *Journal of International Economics* 9:469–79.

Krugman, Paul. 1984. "Import Competition as Export Promotion." In H. Kierzkowski, ed., *Monopolistic Competition and International Trade.* Oxford: Oxford University Press.

Krugman, Paul, ed. 1986. *Strategic Trade Policy and the New International Economics.* Cambridge: MIT Press.

Krugman, Paul. 1990a. *Rethinking International Trade.* Cambridge: MIT Press.

Krugman, Paul. 1990b. "Macroeconomic Adjustment and Entry into the EC: A Note." In Christopher Bliss and Jaime De Macedo, eds., *Unity with Diversity in the European Economy.* Cambridge: Cambridge University Press.

Krugman, Paul. 1991. "Is Bilateralism Bad?" In Elhanan Helpman and Assaf Razin, eds., *International Trade and Trade Policy.* Cambridge: MIT Press.

Krugman, Paul. 1992a. *Currencies and Crises.* Cambridge: MIT Press.

Krugman, Paul. 1992b. "Integration, Specialization and Regional Growth: Notes on 1992, EMU and Stabilization." Typescript, Massachusetts Institute of Technology.

Krugman, Paul. 1993a. "Regionalism versus Multilateralism: Analytical Notes." In Jaime de Melo and Arvind Panagariya, eds., *New Dimensions in Regional Integration.* New York: Cambridge University Press.

Krugman, Paul. 1993b. *What Do We Need to Know about the International Monetary System?* Essays in International Finance no. 190. Princeton: International Finance Section.

Krugman, Paul. 1995. "Economic Conflicts among Nations: Perceptions and Reality." Paper presented at the annual meeting of the American Economic Association, Washington, D.C.

Krugman, Paul and Anthony Venables. 1993. "Integration, Specialization and Adjustment." Center for Economic Policy Research Discussion Paper no. 886.

Kupchan, Charles. 1988. "NATO and the Persian Gulf: Examining Intra-Alliance Behavior." *International Organization* 42:317–46.

Kupchan, Charles. 1994a. "Expand NATO—and Split Europe." *New York Times*, November 27.

Kupchan, Charles. 1994b. *The Vulnerability of Empire.* Ithaca: Cornell University Press.

Kupchan, Charles. 1995. "It's a Long Way to Bratislava: The Dangerous Fantasy of NATO Expansion." *Washington Post*, May 14.

Kupchan, Charles. 1996. "Reviving the West." *Foreign Affairs* 75:92–104.

Kupchan, Charles and Clifford Kupchan. 1991. "Concerts, Collective Security, and the Future of Europe." *International Security* 16:114–61.

Kupchan, Charles and Clifford Kupchan. 1995. "The Promise of Collective Security." *International Security* 20:52–61.

Kurian, George Thomas. 1992. *Encyclopedia of the Third World.* New York: Facts on File (rev. ed.), vols. 1–3.

Kurus, Bilson. 1993. "Agreeing to Disagree: The Political Reality of Asean Economic Cooperation." *Asian Affairs* 20:28–41.

Kwan, C. H. 1994. *Economic Interdependence in the Asia-Pacific Region: Towards a Yen Bloc.* London and New York: Routledge.

Lake, David A. 1988. *Power, Protectionism, and Free Trade.* Ithaca: Cornell University Press.

Lake, David A. 1997. "Regional Relations: A Systems Approach." In David A. Lake and Patrick Morgan, eds., *Regional Orders: Building Security in a New World.* College Park: Pennsylvania State University Press.

Lande, Stephen and Nellis Crigler. 1993. "The Caribbean and NAFTA: Opportunities and Challenges." Washington D.C.: Interamerican Development Bank-Economic Commission on Latin America Working Papers on Trade in the Western Hemisphere no. 51.

Lange, Peter. 1992. "The Politics of the Social Dimension." In Alberta M. Sbragia, ed., *Europolitics: Institutions and Policymaking in the "New" European Community.* Washington, D.C.: Brookings Institution.

Langhammer, Rolf J. 1991. "ASEAN Economic Co-operation: A Stock-Taking." *ASEAN Economic Bulletin* 8:137–50.

Lardy, Nicholas R. 1994. *China in the World Economy.* Washington, D.C.: Institute for International Economics.

Lavergne, Real. 1983. *The Political Economy of U.S. Tariffs.* New York: Academic Press.

Lawrence, Robert L. 1996. *Regionalism, Multilateralism, and Deeper Integration.* Washington D.C.: Brookings Institution.

Leidy, Martin and Bernard Hoekman. 1993. "What to Expect from Regional and Multilateral Trade Negotiations: a Public Choice Perspective." In Kym Anderson and Richard Blackhurst, eds., *Regional Integration and the Global Trading System.* London: Harvester Wheatsheaf.

Lewis, Flora. 1994. "Ukraine Between Russia and Western Comforts." *International Herald Tribune*, December 20.

Lincoln, Edward J. 1993. *Japan's New Global Role.* Washington D.C.: Brookings Institution.

Lindberg, Leon N. and Stuart A. Scheingold. 1970. *Europe's Would-Be Polity: Patterns of Change in the European Community*. Englewood Cliffs, N.J.: Prentice-Hall.

Linnemann, Hans. 1966. *An Econometric Study of International Trade Flows*. Amsterdam: North-Holland.

Lipsey, Richard G. 1960. "The Theory of Customs Unions: A General Survey." *Economic Journal* 70:496–513.

Lipson, Charles. 1984. "International Cooperation in Economic and Security Affairs." *World Politics* 37:1–23.

Lipson, Charles. 1991. "Why Are Some International Agreements Informal?" *International Organization* 45:495–538.

Long, William R. 1994. "Trade Winds Are Blowing Across Americas." *Los Angeles Times*, January 1, Nexus.

Longworth, R. C. 1994. "Time for NATO to Admit Trio from E. Europe." *Chicago Tribune*, October 16.

Lopez, Robert S. 1951. "The Dollar of the Middle Ages." *Journal of Economic History* 11:209–34.

Low, Linda. 1991. "The East Asian Economic Grouping." *The Pacific Review* 4:375–82.

Lustig, Nora. 1992. *Mexico: the Remaking of an Economy*. Washington, D.C.: Brookings Institution.

MacIntyre, Andrew, ed. 1994. *Business and Government in Industrializing East and Southeast Asia*. Ithaca: Cornell University Press.

Magee, Stephen P., William A. Brock, and Leslie Young. 1989. *Black Hole Tariffs and Endogenous Policy Theory: Political Economy in General Equilibrium*. New York: Cambridge University Press.

Makabenta, Leah. 1993. "Asia-Pacific: Clinton's Summit Call Raises Suspicions." *Inter Press Service*, July 16, Nexus.

"Malaysia: List Threatens AFTA." 1995. *Business Times* (Malaysia), April 29, Nexus.

Mancini, G. Federico. 1991. "The Making of a Constitution for Europe." In Robert O. Keohane and Stanley Hoffmann, eds., *The New European Community*. Boulder: Westview.

Mandelbaum, Michael. 1995. "The Case Against NATO Expansion." *Foreign Affairs* 74:9–13.

Mansfield, Edward D. 1993. "Effects of International Politics on International Trade." In Kym Anderson and Richard Blackhurst, eds., *Regional Integration and the Global Trading System*. London: Harvester Wheatsheaf.

Mansfield, Edward D. 1994. *Power, Trade, and War*. Princeton: Princeton University Press.

Mansfield, Edward D. and Rachel Bronson. 1994. "Alliances, Preferential Trading Arrangements, and International Trade." Paper presented at the annual meeting of the American Political Science Association, New York. Revised July 1996.

Mansfield, Edward D. and Marc L. Busch. 1995. "The Political Economy of Nontariff Barriers: A Cross-National Analysis." *International Organization* 49:723–49.

Mansfield, Edward D. and Jack Snyder. 1995. "Democratization and War." *Foreign Affairs* 74:79–97.

Manzetti, Luigi. 1992. "Economic Integration in the Southern Cone." *North-South Focus*. Miami: North-South Center, University of Miami.

Martin, Lisa L. 1993. "International and Domestic Institutions in the EMU Project." *Economics and Politics* 5:125–44.

Martin, Lisa L. 1993. "The Rational State Choice of Multilateralism." In John Gerard Ruggie, ed., *Multilateralism Matters: The Theory and Praxis of an Institutional Form*. New York: Columbia University Press.

Masson, Paul R. and Mark P. Taylor. 1993. "Currency Unions: A Survey of the Issues." In Paul R. Masson and Mark P. Taylor eds., *Policy Issues in the Operation of Currency Unions.* Cambridge and New York: Cambridge University Press.

Matsuyama, Kiminori, Nobuhiro Kiyotaki, and Akihiko Matsui. 1993. "Toward a Theory of International Currency." *Review of Economic Studies* 60:283–307.

Mattli, Walter and Anne-Marie Slaughter. 1995. "Law and Politics in the European Union: A Reply to Garrett." *International Organization* 49:183–90.

McGee, John. 1974. "Efficiency and Economies of Size." In Harvey Goldschmid, H. M. Mann, and J. F. Weston, eds., *Industrial Concentration: The New Learning.* Boston: Little, Brown.

McKeown, Timothy J. 1991. "A Liberal Trading Order? The Long-Run Pattern of Imports to the Advanced Capitalist States." *International Studies Quarterly* 35:151–72.

McKinnon, Ronald and K. Fung. 1993. "Floating Exchange Rates and the New Interbloc Protectionism: Tariffs vs Quotas." In Dominick Salvatore, ed., *Protectionism and World Welfare.* New York: Cambridge University Press.

McMillan, John. 1990. "Strategic Bargaining and Section 301." In Jagdish Bhagwati and Hugh T. Patrick, eds., *Aggressive Unilaterlism: America's 301 Trade Policy and the World Trading System.* Ann Arbor: University of Michigan Press.

Meade, James E. 1955. *The Theory of Customs Unions.* Amsterdam: North-Holland.

Mearsheimer, John. 1990. "Back to the Future: Instability in Europe after the Cold War." *International Security* 15:5–56.

Mearsheimer, John. 1994. "The False Promise of International Institutions." *International Security* 19:5–49.

Meigs, A. James. 1993. "Eurodollars: A Transition Currency." *Cato Journal* 12:711–27.

Melvin, Michael. 1988. "The Dollarization of Latin America as a Market-Enforced Monetary Reform: Evidence and Implications." *Economic Development and Cultural Change* 36:543–58.

Micossi, Stefano and Gianfranco Viesti. 1992. "Japanese Direct Manufacturing Investment in Europe." In L. Alan Winters and Anthony Venables, eds., *European Integration, Trade, and Industry.* Cambridge: Cambridge University Press.

Middlebrook, Kevin J. 1978. "Regional Organizations and Andean Economic Integration, 1969–75." *Journal of Common Market Studies* 17:62–82.

Milensky, Edward S. 1973. *The Politics of Regional Organization in Latin America.* New York: Praeger.

Milensky, Edward S. 1977. "Latin America's Multilateral Diplomacy: Integration, Disintegration, and Interdependence." *International Affairs* 53:73–96.

Milgrom, Paul, Douglass C. North, and Barry R. Weingast. 1990. "The Role of Institutions in the Revival of Trade: The Medieval Law Merchant, Private Judges, and the Champagne Fairs." *Economics and Politics* 2:1–23.

Milner, Helen V. 1988. *Resisting Protectionism: Global Industries and the Politics of International Trade.* Princeton: Princeton University Press.

Milner, Helen V. 1991a. "The Assumption of Anarchy in International Relations Theory: A Critique." *Review of International Studies* 17:67–85.

Milner, Helen V. 1991b. "The Evolution of the International Trade Regime: A Three Bloc Trading System?" Paper presented at the XVth World Congress of the International Political Science Association, Buenos Aires.

Milner, Helen V. and Neeraja Sivaramayya. 1996. "Increasing Returns to Scale and Regional Trade Blocs." Typescript, Columbia University.

Mitrany, David. 1943/44. *A Working Peace System: An Argument for the Functional Development of International Organization.* London: Oxford University Press for the Royal Institute of International Affairs.

Mizen, Paul and Eric Pentecost, eds. Forthcoming. *Currency Substitution and the International Use of Money.* London: Edward Elgar.

Moe, Terry. 1984."The New Economics of Organization." *American Journal of Political Science* 28:739–77.

Molot, Maureen Appel. 1993. *Driving Continentally: National Policies and the North American Auto Industry.* Ottawa: Carelton University Press.

Moravcsik, Andrew. l991. "Negotiating the Single European Act: National Interests and Conventional Statecraft in the European Community." *International Organization* 45:19–56.

Mundell, Robert A. 1961. "A Theory of Optimum Currency Areas." *American Economic Review* 51:657–65.

Nelson, Douglas. 1988. "Endogenous Tariff Theory: A Critical Survey." *American Journal of Political Science* 32:796–837.

"Next Round of NAFTA Talks Fixed for July 25." 1995. *Reuters,* July 3, Clarinet.

Nye, Joseph S., Jr. 1970. "Comparing Common Markets: A Revised Neo-Functionalist Model." *International Organization* 24:192–231.

Nye, Joseph S., Jr. 1971. *Peace in Parts: Integration and Conflict in Regional Organization.* Boston: Little, Brown

OECD Department of Economics and Statistics. 1995. *Monthly Statistics of Foreign Trade.* Paris: OECD Department of Economics and Statistics, January.

O'Keefe, Thomas Andrew. 1995. "The Prospects for Mercosur's Inclusion into the North American Free Trade Agreement." *International Law Practicum* 8:5–13.

Olson, Mancur. 1965. *The Logic of Collective Action: Public Goods and the Theory of Groups.* Cambridge: Harvard University Press.

Orléan, André. 1989. "Mimetic Contagion and Speculative Bubbles." *Theory and Decision* 27:63–92.

Owen, John. 1994. "How Liberalism Produces Democratic Peace." *International Security* 19:87–125.

Oye, Kenneth A. 1986. "Explaining Cooperation under Anarchy: Hypotheses and Strategies." In Kenneth A. Oye, ed., *Cooperation under Anarchy.* Princeton: Princeton University Press.

Oye, Kenneth A. 1992. *Economic Discrimination and Political Exchange: World Political Economy in the 1930s and 1980s.* Princeton: Princeton University Press.

Padoan, Pier Carlo and Marcello Pericoli. 1993. "The Single Market and Eastern Europe." *Economic Systems* 35:315–43.

Pastor, Manuel and Carol Wise. 1994. "The Origins and Sustainability of Mexico's Free Trade Policy." *International Organization* 48:459–89.

Pastor, Robert. 1990. "Salinas Takes a Gamble." *The New Republic,* September 10 and 17:27–32.

Pavitt, Keith. 1984. "Sectoral Patterns of Technical Change: Towards a Taxonomy and a Theory." *Research Policy* 13:343–73.

Pearson, Scott and William Ingram. 1980. "Economies of Scale, Domestic Divergences and Potential Gains from Economic Integration in Ghana and the Ivory Coast." *Journal of Political Economy* 88:994–1008.

Pelzman, Joseph. 1977. "Trade Creation and Trade Diversion in the Council of Mutual Economic Assistance: 1954–1970." *American Economic Review* 67:713–22.

Pena, Felix. 1995. "New Approaches to Economic Integration in the Southern Cone." *The Washington Quarterly* 18:113–22.

Perroni, Claudio and John Whalley. 1994. "The New Regionalism: Trade Liberalization or Insurance?" National Bureau of Economic Research Working Paper no. 4626.

Perroux, François. 1950. "Economic Space: Theory and Applications." *Quarterly Journal of Economics* 64:89–104.

Pescatore, Pierre. 1993. "The GATT Dispute Settlement Mechanism." *Journal of World Trade* 27:5–20.

Pincus, Jonathan. 1977. *Pressure Groups and Politics in Antebellum Tariffs.* New York: Columbia University Press.

Pollins, Brian M. 1989. "Conflict, Cooperation, and Commerce: The Effects of International Political Interactions on Bilateral Trade Flows." *American Journal of Political Science* 33:737–61.

Pomfret, Richard. 1988. *Unequal Trade: The Economics of Discriminatory International Trade Policies.* Oxford: Basil Blackwell.

Pomfret, Richard. 1989. "The Theory of Preferential Trading Arrangements." In A. Jacquemin and A. Sapir, eds., *The European Internal Market.* New York: Oxford University Press.

Powell, Robert. 1994. "Anarchy in International Relations Theory: The Neorealist-Neoliberal Debate." *International Organization* 31:313–44.

Ravenhill, John. 1995. Competing Logics of Regionalism in the Asia-Pacific." *Journal of European Integration* 18:179–99.

Ray, Edward. 1981. "The Determinants of Tariff and NonTariff Barriers in the US." *Journal of Political Economy* 89:105–21.

Rielly, John E. 1995. *American Public Opinion and U.S. Foreign Policy 1995.* Chicago: Chicago Council on Foreign Relations.

Rodrik, Dani. 1989. "Promises, Promises: Credible Policy Reform via Signalling." *Economic Journal* 99:756–72.

Rogowski, Ronald. 1989. *Commerce and Coalitions: How Trade Affects Domestic Political Alignments.* Princeton: Princeton University Press.

Roy, Denny. 1994. "Hegemon on the Horizon? China's Threat to East Asian Security." *International Security* 19:149–68.

Ruggie, John Gerard. 1993. "Territoriality and Beyond: Problematizing Modernity in International Relations." *International Organization* 47:139–74.

Russett, Bruce. 1967. *International Regions and the International System.* Chicago: Rand-McNally.

Russett, Bruce. 1993. *Grasping the Democratic Peace: Principles for a Post-Cold War World.* Princeton: Princeton University Press.

Saborio, Sylvia. 1992. *The Premise and the Promise: Free Trade in the Americas.* New Brunswick, N.J.: Transaction Books.

Sandholtz, Wayne. 1993. "Choosing Union: Monetary Politics and Maastricht." *International Organization* 47:1–40.

Sandholtz, Wayne and John Zysman. 1989. "1992: Recasting the European Bargain." *World Politics* 42:95–28.

Sandler, Todd and James Tschirhart. 1980. "The Economic Theory of Clubs: An Evaluative Survey." *Journal of Economic Literature* 18:1481–1521.

Santos, Paulo. 1993. "The Spatial Implications of Economic and Monetary Union." *European Economy* no. 54.

Schelling, Thomas. 1960. *The Strategy of Conflict.* Cambridge: Harvard University Press.

Scherer, F. M. 1974. "Economies of Scale and Industrial Concentration." In Harvey Goldschmid, H. M. Mann, and J. F. Weston, eds., *Industrial Concentration: The New Learning.* Boston: Little, Brown.

Schmitter, Philippe. 1969. "Three Neo-Functional Hypotheses About International Integration." *International Organization* 13:161–66.

Schott, Jeffrey J. 1989. "More Free Trade Areas?" In Jeffrey J. Schott, ed., *Free Trade Areas and U.S. Trade Policy*. Washington D.C.: Institute for International Economics.

Schott, Jeffrey J. 1991. "Trading Blocs and the World Trading System." *The World Economy* 14:1–18.

Schott, Jeffrey J. 1994. *The Uruguay Round: An Assessment*. Washington, D.C.: Institute for International Economics.

Schott, Jeffrey J., ed. 1989. *Free Trade Areas and U.S. Trade Policy*. Washington, D.C.: Institute for International Economics.

Scitovsky, Tibor. 1958. *Economic Theory and Western European Integration*. Stanford: Stanford University Press.

Segal, Gerald. 1995. "Tying China into the International System." *Survival* 37:60–73.

Shelburne, Robert. 1994. "The Staging Pattern of US Tariff Reductions Under NAFTA." *1994 Papers and Proceedings of the International Trade and Finance Association*.

Shepsle, Kenneth. 1989. "Studying Institutions: Some Lessons from the Rational Choice Approach." *Journal of Theoretical Politics* 1:131–47.

Simpson, John P. 1994. "North American Free Trade Agreement: Rules of Origin." *Journal of World Trade Law* 28:33–41.

Singer, J. David and Melvin Small. 1994. *Correlates of War Project: International and Civil War Data, 1816–1992*. Ann Arbor: ICPSR, no. 9905.

Small, Melvin and J. David Singer. 1969. "Formal Alliances, 1816–1965: An Extension of the Basic Data." *Journal of Peace Research* 6:257–82.

Small, Melvin and J. David Singer. 1982. *Resort to Arms: International and Civil Wars, 1816–1980*. Beverly Hills: Sage.

Smith, Alasdair and Anthony Venables. 1988. "Completing the Internal Market in the European Community." *European Economic Review* 32:1501–25.

Smith, Alisdair and Loukas Tsoukalis. 1996. "Report on Economic and Social Cohesion." Typescript, College of Europe, Bruges.

Snidal, Duncan. 1985. "The Limits of Hegemonic Stability Theory." *International Organization* 39:580–614.

Snyder, Jack. 1990. "Averting Anarchy in the New Europe." *International Security* 14:5–41.

Srivastava, Rajendra K. and Robert T. Green. 1986. "Determinants of Bilateral Trade Flows." *Journal of Business* 59:623–40.

Staar, Richard F. et al., eds. 1991. *Yearbook on International Communist Affairs*. Stanford: Hoover Institution Press.

Stein, Arthur A. 1983. "Coordination and Collaboration: Regimes in an Anarchic World." In Stephen D. Krasner, ed., *International Regimes*. Ithaca: Cornell University Press.

Steiner, George. 1994. "The Magus." *The New Yorker*, June 20:92–94.

Streissler, Erich W. 1992. "Good Money Driving Out Bad: A Model of the Hayek Process in Action." In Ernst Baltensperger and Hans-Werner Sinn, eds., *Exchange-Rate Regimes and Currency Unions*. New York: St. Martin's Press.

Summary, Rebecca M. 1989. "A Political-Economic Model of U.S. Bilateral Trade." *Review of Economics and Statistics* 71:179–82.

Summers, Robert and Alan Heston. 1991. "The Penn World Table (Mark 5): An Expanded Set of International Comparisons." *Quarterly Journal of Economics* 106:327–68.

Taguchi, Hiroo. 1994. "On the Internationalization of the Japanese Yen." In Takatoshi Ito and

Anne O. Krueger, eds., *Macroeconomic Linkage: Savings, Exchange Rates, and Capital Flows.* Chicago: University of Chicago Press.

Talbott, Strobe. 1995. "Why NATO Should Grow." *The New York Review of Books*, August 10: 27–30.

Tapkin, David. 1994. "Leadership and Cooperative Institutions in the Asia-Pacific." In Andrew Mack and John Ravenhill, eds., *Pacific Cooperation: Building Economic and Security Regimes in the Asia-Pacific Region.* St. Leonards, Australia: Allen and Unwin.

"Tariff Accord Hits a Snag." 1994. *New York Times*, January 17, Nexus.

Tavlas, George S. 1991. *On the International Use of Currencies: The Case of the Deutsche Mark.* Essays in International Finance no. 181. Princeton: International Finance Section.

Tavlas, George S. 1993. "The 'New' Theory of Optimum Currency Areas." *The World Economy* 16:663–85.

Tavlas, George S. 1994. "The Theory of Monetary Integration." *Open Economies Review* 5:211–30.

Taylor, Paul. 1983. *The Limits of European Integration.* New York: Columbia University Press.

Telser, Lester A. 1980. "A Theory of Self-Enforcing Agreements." *Journal of Business* 27:27–44.

Thompson, Aileen. 1994. "Trade Liberalization, Comparative Advantage, and Scale Economies: Stock Market Evidence from Canada." *Journal of International Economics* 37:1–27.

Thompson, William R. 1973. "The Regional Subsystem: A Conceptual Explication of a Propositional Inventory." *International Studies Quarterly* 17:89–117.

Thygesen, Niels et al. 1995. *International Currency Competition and the Future Role of the Single European Currency.* Final Report of a Working Group on European Monetary Union—International Monetary System. London: Kluwer Law International.

Tinbergen, Jan. 1962. *Shaping the World Economy: Suggestions for an International Economic Policy.* New York: Twentieth Century Fund.

"Trade Integration Faces Setbacks: Talks with Mercosur are Slow and Arduous." 1995. *Latin America Regional Reports: Andean Group Report*, April 13, Nexus.

Trefler, Daniel. 1993. "Trade Liberalization and the Theory of Endogenous Protection." *Journal of Political Economy* 101:138–60.

USITC (U.S. International Trade Commission). 1992a. *U.S. Market Access in Latin America: Recent Liberalization Measures and Remaining Barriers.* Washington D.C.: USITC pub. no. 2521.

USITC. 1992b. *The Year in Trade 1992.* Washington, D.C.: GPO.

"U.S. Promises: But Mercosur Still a Magnet." 1994. *Latin America Regional Reports: Mexico and Central America*, February 24, Nexus.

"U.S. Seeks Japan's OK to Upgrade APEC as Summit Forum." 1993. *Japan Economic Newswire*, May 16, Nexus.

Ullman-Margalit, Edna. 1977. *The Emergence of Norms.* Oxford: Clarendon Press.

Vaitsos, Constantine V. 1978. "Crisis in Regional Economic Cooperation (Integration) Among Developing Countries." *World Development* 6:719–70.

Vargas-Hildago, Rafael. 1979. "The Crisis of the Andean Pact: Lessons for Integration Among Developing Countries." *Journal of Common Market Studies* 17:213–26.

Vatikiotis, Michale. 1993. "Market or Mirage." *Far Eastern Economic Review*, April 15: 48–50.

Vaubel, Roland. 1977. "Free Currency Competition." *Weltwirtschaftliches Archiv* 113:435–61.

Venables, Anthony. 1985."Trade and Trade Policy with Imperfect Competition." *Journal of International Economics* 19:1–20.

Venables, Anthony. 1987. "Customs Union and Tariff Reform Under Imperfect Competition." *European Economic Review* 31:103–10.

"Venezuela Wants Free Trade Zone Agreement with Mercosur." 1995. *BBC Summary of World Broadcasts*, May 20, Nexus.

Viner, Jacob. 1950. *The Customs Union Issue*. New York: Carnegie Endowment for International Peace.

Vousden, Neil. 1990. *The Economics of Trade Protection*. Cambridge: Cambridge University Press.

Vydrin, Dmitri. 1994. "Ukraine and Russia." In Robert Blackwill and Sergei Karaganov, eds., *Damage Limitation or Crisis? Russia and the Outside World*. Washington, D.C.: Brassey.

Walt, Stephen. 1987. *The Origins of Alliances*. Ithaca: Cornell University Press.

Walter, Andrew. 1991. *World Power and World Money: The Role of Hegemony and International Monetary Order*. New York: St. Martin's Press.

Waltz, Kenneth N. 1979. *Theory of International Politics*. Reading: Addison-Wesley.

Ward, Vicky. 1991. "Understanding Cooperative Agreements: the Impact of Differing Objectives on Club Formation Behavior." Paper presented at the annual meeting of the American Political Science Association, Washington, D.C., August 29–31.

Weintraub, Sidney. 1991. "The New U.S. Economic Initiative Toward Latin America." *Journal of Interamerican Studies and World Affairs* 33:1–18.

Wendt, Alexander. 1992. "Anarchy Is What the State Makes of It: The Social Construction of Power Politics." *International Organization* 46:391–425.

Westhoff, Frank H., Robert M. Yarbrough, and Beth V. Yarbrough. 1994. "Preferential Trade Agreements and the GATT: Can Bilateralism and Multilateralism Coexist?" *Kyklos* 47:179–95.

Westhoff, Frank H., Robert M. Yarbrough, and Beth V. Yarbrough. 1995. "Harassment Versus Lobbying for Trade Protection." *International Trade Journal* 9:203–24.

Westhoff, Frank H., Robert M. Yarbrough, and Beth V. Yarbrough. 1996. "Complexity, Organization, and Stuart Kauffman's *The Origins of Order*." *Journal of Economic Behavior and Organization* 29:1–25.

Whalley, John. 1992. "CUSTA and NAFTA: Can WHFTA Be Far Behind?" *Journal of Common Market Studies* 30:125–41.

White, Halbert. 1980. "A Heteroskedasticity-Consistent Covariance Matrix Estimator and a Direct Test for Heteroskedasticity." *Econometrica* 48:817–38.

Widgren, Michel. 1994 "The Relation Between Voting Power and Policy Impact in the European Union." Center for Economic Policy Research Discussion Paper no. 1033.

Williams, John H. 1947. *Postwar Monetary Plans and Other Essays*. New York: Knopf.

Williamson, Oliver E. 1985. *Economic Institutions of Capitalism*. New York: Free Press.

Winham, Gilbert. 1988. "Why Canada Acted." In William Diebold, Jr., ed., *Bilateralism, Multilateralism and Canada in U.S. Trade Policy*. Cambridge: Ballinger.

Winters, L. Alan. 1993. "Expanding EC Membership and Association Accords: Recent Experience and Future Prospects." In Kym Anderson and Richard Blackhurst, eds., *Regional Integration and the Global Trading System*. London: Harvester Wheatsheaf.

Witt, Ulrich. 1989. "The Evolution of Economic Institutions as a Propagation Process." *Public Choice* 36:234–45.

Wolfers, Arnold. 1962. "Collective Defense versus Collective Security." In Arnold Wolfers, ed., *Discord and Collaboration*. Baltimore: Johns Hopkins University Press.

Wonnacott, Paul and Mark Lutz. 1989. "Is There a Case for Free Trade Areas?" In Jeffrey Schott, ed., *Free Trade Areas and U.S. Trade Policy*. Washington D.C.: Institute for International Economics.

Wonnacott, Ronald J. 1991. *The Economics of Overlapping Free Trade Areas and the Mexican Challenge*. Toronto: C.D. Howe Institute.

World Bank. 1993a. *Latin America and the Caribbean: A Decade After the Debt Crisis.* Washington D.C.: The World Bank.

World Bank. 1993b. *Sustaining Rapid Development in East Asia and the Pacific.* Washington, D.C.: The World Bank.

Yamazawa, Ippei. 1992. "On Pacific Economic Integration." *The Economic Journal* 102:1519–29.

Yamazawa, Ippei. 1994. "A Japanese View." Paper prepared for the Institute of the Americas conference on the Regionalization of the Global Economy, Washington D.C., October 4–5.

Yarbrough, Beth V. 1994. "Preferential Trade Arrangements and the GATT: EC 1992 as Rogue or Role Model?" In Berhanu Abegaz et al., eds., *The Challenge of European Integration.* Boulder: Westview.

Yarbrough, Beth V. and Robert M. Yarbrough. 1986. "Reciprocity, Bilateralism, and Economic 'Hostages': Self-Enforcing Agreements in International Trade." *International Studies Quarterly* 30:7–21.

Yarbrough, Beth V. and Robert M. Yarbrough. 1987a. "Cooperation in the Liberalization of International Trade: After Hegemony, What?" *International Organization* 41:1–26.

Yarbrough, Beth V. and Robert M. Yarbrough. 1987b. "Institutions for the Governance of Opportunism in International Trade." *Journal of Law, Economics, and Organization* 3:129–39.

Yarbrough, Beth V. and Robert M. Yarbrough. 1990a. "Economic Integration and Governance: The Role of Preferential Trade Agreements." *Journal of International Economic Integration* 5:1–20.

Yarbrough, Beth V. and Robert M. Yarbrough. 1990b. "International Institutions and the New Economics of Organization." *International Organization* 44:235–59.

Yarbrough, Beth V. and Robert M. Yarbrough. 1992. *Cooperation and Governance in International Trade: The Strategic Organizational Approach.* Princeton: Princeton University Press.

Yarbrough, Beth V. and Robert M. Yarbrough. 1994a. "International Contracting and Territorial Control: The Boundary Question." *Journal of Institutional and Theoretical Economics* 150:239–64.

Yarbrough, Beth V. and Robert M. Yarbrough. 1994b. "Regionalism and Layered Governance: The Choice of Trade Institutions." *Journal of International Affairs* 48:95–17.

Yarbrough, Beth V. and Robert M. Yarbrough. 1995a. "Coordination Games and Group Size: Unification and Secession as Escape from Lock-In." Amherst College Department of Economics Working Paper.

Yarbrough, Beth V. and Robert M. Yarbrough. 1995b. "Governance Structures, Boundaries, and 'International' Organization." Amherst College Department of Economics Working Paper.

Yarbrough, Beth V. and Robert M. Yarbrough. 1996. "The 'Globalization' of Trade: What's Changed and Why?" In S. Gupta and N. K. Choudry, eds., *Studies in Globalization and Development*, vol. 3. Boston: Kluwer.

Yeutter, Clayton. 1988. Testimony before the U.S. Congress, House Committee on Foreign Affairs, Subcommittee on International Economic Policy and Trade, February 25 and March 16, 1988. *United States–Canada Free Trade Agreement*, House Hearing, 100-65. Washington, D.C.: GPO.

Yoffie, David. 1983. *Power and Protectionism.* New York: Columbia University Press.

Index

Africa, 58
AFTA (Asia Free Trade Agreement); *see* AFTA; ASEAN
Aggarwal, Vinod, 22, 35, 45, 185n1
Agglomeration effects, 109, 127
"Aggressor states," defined, 217, deterring them, 225
Agriculture, 77, 103*app*.; in Europe, 113, 114, 116; wheat, 49n10; sugar, 37
Aglietta, Michel, 75n10
Aho, C. Michael, 20, 22
Aitken, Norman D., 190, 192, 207n14
Akerlof, George, 162n24
Alesina, Alberto, 109, 110, 126
Alfonsin, Raul, 38
Alliances, 10, 64, 93; effects on deterrence, 220; effects on trade, 11, 18, 93, 188, 190–92, 194, 205, vs. PTAs, 189–90, 205; types of, 198, and effects of type on trade, 198–99; stability of and effects on trade, 204; *see also* Security externalities; Security institutions
Americas (Western Hemisphere), 8, 13, 16, 33, 43, 45, 58; hegemonic leadership in, 174; regionalism in, 95–101, 165–85; *see also* Canada; Central America; Latin America; Mercosur; Mexico; NAFTA; North America; South America; U.S.
Anarchy (international), 9, 17, 147, 160n4, 162n20, 190, 217; *see also* Neorealism; Self-help
Andean Pact, 30, 48n2, 166–67, 184
Anderson, Kym, 189, 192
Andrews, A. Piatt, 61
Andrews, David, 73
APEC (Asia-Pacific Economic Cooperation): 1, 2, 8, 9, 13, 14, 20–26 *passim*, 30, 43–47 *passim*, 168–79 *passim*, 184; distribution of wealth within, 177; "Eminent Persons Group," 44; level of institutional authority, 169; scope of, 168–169; trade encapsulation within, 172; summits, in Bogor, 168, Jakarta, 43, 44, Osaka, 44, 45, 168, and Seattle, 43, 44, 169
Argentina, 33, 38, 40, 41, 166
ASEAN (Association of South East Asian Nations), 9, 30, 43, 46, 48n2, 77, 167–69, 174–79 *passim*, 189; AFTA, 167, 170, 184; distribution of wealth within, 177; trade encapsulation in, 177
Asia (East), 1, 8, 9, 10, 13, 15, 16, 20–28 *passim*; hegemonic leadership in, 174; imports to America, 27; regionalism in 32–36, 43–47, 165–85 *passim*; *see also* APEC; ASEAN
Asmus, Ronald, 237n17, 238n29

demise of, 210, 214; former republics of, 222, 229; trade with allies, 189, 200; trade with nonallies, 203; *see also* East Europe; Russia

Spain, 113, 114, 116, 120, 131*n*7, 165, 230; *see also* EC; Europe; NATO; West Europe

Spillover, 6; *see also* Integration, theory of; Neofunctionalism

"Spoke to Spoke" negotiations, 41, 19*n*13

Srivastava, Rajendra K., 192

Staar, Richard F., 207*n*13

Steel (industry), 37, in Europe, 114

Stein, Arthur A., 6, 186*n*15

Streissler, Erich W., 75*n*6

Structural adjustment, 37

Structural funds: in Europe, 113, 115, 116, 120

Structural realism, 217; *see also* Neorealism

Suasion games, 31–32; *see also* Games

Subsidies, 34, 37, 149

Summary, Rebecca, 191, 192, 207*n*14

Summers, Robert, 206*n*7

Super 301, 25, 35, 39, 48*n*8

Sweden, 113, 165

Switzerland, 131, 165

Taguchi, Hiroo, 75*n*9

Taiwan, 30, 44, 46, 167, 168, 170

Talbott, Strobe, 237*n*17

Tariffs, 26, 27, 28, 37, 41, 95, 120, 166, 168, 206*nn*2, 3; optimal, 4, 11, 26, 91, 191; revenues, 88, 95, 106*nn*20, 21; *see also* NTBs; Protectionism

Tavlas, George S., 52, 55, 58, 72, 74*n*1, 74*nn*2, 3

Taylor, Paul, 147

Telecommunications (industry), 35, 37, 78, 92, 97*tab.*, 103*app.*, 169

Tesler, Lester A., 136

Textiles and apparel (industry) 28, 78, 97, 102*app.*, 112; in Europe, 114

Thailand, 167

Third party: adjudication, 141, binding, 143–46; information dissemination, 136, 139, 140 (*see also* Monitoring); enforcement, 136, 139, 147–48; tariffs toward, 30

Thompson, Aileen, 105*n*16, 106*n*29

Thygesen, Niels, 55, 62, 75*nn*4, 10, 11

Tinbergen, Jan, 190, 192

Tobacco (industry), 48*n*7

Trade, 9, 11, 18, 33, 34; bilateralism, 23, 33, 35, 39, "bad bilateralism," 26, 27, 29; encapsulation, defined, 171, 175, in Europe, Asia, and Americas, 172, 186*n*16; free-trade lobbying, 30; integration, 108–9, 130; interindustry, 93, 108–9, in Europe, 113; intraindustry, 93, 108–9, in Europe, 112–13, in NAFTA, 95; liberalization, 45, 77–78, 138; multilateral, 20, 22, 23, 25, 27, 45, 79, 84, 86, 89, regional, 82, 86, 90, 97, 105*n*12, unilateral, 90–91; "war," 120; *see also* Major powers; Trade

Trade theory, 2, 22, 135; "new," 80, 108, 109; strategic, 5, 12, 18; traditional (neoclassical), 108, 160*n*2, 176

Transaction costs, 8, 20, 22, 24, 54, 62, 110, 127, 154, 213, 219

Transnational actors, 9, 19*n*3, 43; *see also* Industries

Transparency, 212, 213, 217, 219

Transport (industry), 37, 97*tab.*, 103*app.*

Treaty of Mutual Cooperation and Security (U.S. and Japan), 207*n*9

Trefler, Daniel, 86, 97, 99*tab.*

Ukraine, 7, 219, 226; as "pivot-state," 210, 229–32

Ulman-Magalit, Edne, 151

Uruguay, 41, 166

Uruguay Round; *see* GATT, Uruguay Round

U.S. (United States): Congress, 34–35, 161*n*15, 184, 237*n*20; Federal Reserve, 69; firms, 85, 86, 100–101, 156; and GATT, 24, 143; as hegemon, 64, 173, 174, 180; ratio of GDP to NAFTA GDP, 177*tab.*; ratio of GDP to APEC GDP, 177*tab.*; relations with Asia, *see* APEC; relations with Canada and Mexico, 15, 21, 33, 36, 77, 94, 95, 166 (*see also* NAFTA; U.S.-Canada FTA); security policy in Europe, *see* NATO; trade policy, 21, 28, 29–46 *passim*, 42, 167; trade with allies, 189, 200; trade with nonallies, 203; trade with other democracies, 208*n*18; *see also* Americas; North America